KT-131-287

Greens Annotated Rules of the Court of Session 2022/2023

Greens Annotated Rules of the Court of Session 2022/2023

REPRINTED FROM DIVISION C (COURT OF SESSION PRACTICE) OF THE PARLIAMENT HOUSE BOOK

GREENS ANNOTATED RULES OF THE COURT OF SESSION

by

NIGEL MORRISON, QC
formerly Sheriff of Lothian and Borders at Edinburgh formerly First Counsel to the Lord President of the Court of Session

DAVID BARTOS, LLB
Advocate
formerly Legal Assistant to the Lord President of the Court of Session

NEIL CRICHTON, WS
Auditor of the Court of Session

THOMAS HIGGINS
Depute Clerk of Session and Justiciary and formerly Clerk to the First Division of the Court of Session

IAIN MACLEAN, LLB, LLM, MSc
Advocate
formerly Legal Assistant to the Lord President of the Court of Session

J. HALDANE TAIT, SSC
formerly Auditor of the Court of Session

MATTHEW WEIR
Depute Clerk of Session and Justiciary and Clerk to the First Division of the Court of Session

SARAH WOLFFE, BA, LLB
Advocate

W. GREEN

THOMSON REUTERS

Published in 2022 by Thomson Reuters, trading as W. Green.
Thomson Reuters is registered in England & Wales, Company No.1679046
Registered Office and address for service:
5 Canada Square, Canary Wharf, London, E14 5AQ
For further information on our products and services, visit *http://www.sweetandmaxwell.co.uk/wgreen*

ISBN (print) 9780414105140

ISBN (e-book) 9780414105171

ISBN (print and e-book) 9780414105157

Printed and bound by CPI Group (UK) Ltd, Croydon, CR0 4YY
A CIP catalogue record for this book is available from the British Library.
For orders, go to: *http://www.tr.com/uki-legal-contact*; Tel: 0345 600 9355.

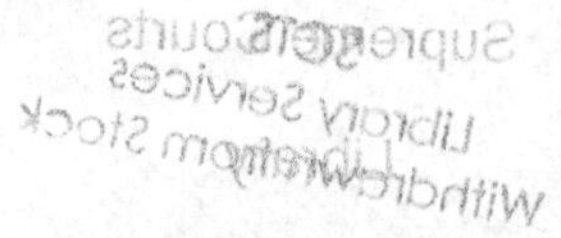

Reprinted from the *Parliament House Book*, published in looseleaf form and updated five times a year by W. Green, the Scottish Law Publisher

The following paperback titles are also available in the series:

Sheriff Court and Sheriff Appeal Court Rules 2022/2023

Solicitors Professional Handbook 2022/2023

Parliament House Book consists of the following Divisions:

A Fees and Stamps

B Courts, Upper

C Court of Session Practice

D Courts, Lower

E Licensing

F Solicitors

G Legal Aid

H Bankruptcy and other Mercantile

I Companies

J Conveyancing, Land Tenure and Registration

K Family Law

L Landlord and Tenant

M Succession, Trusts, Liferents and Judicial Factors

S Sheriff Appeal Court Practice

MAIN TABLE OF CONTENTS

Volume 1

ACT OF SEDERUNT (SI 1994 NO.1443)

Volume 2

OTHER ACTS OF SEDERUNT

COURT FEES

DIRECTIONS

PRACTICE NOTES

TABLE OF CASES

TABLE OF STATUTES

***(References in* bold type are to a rule in the R.C.S. 1994; references in ordinary type are to annotations)**

TABLE OF STATUTORY INSTRUMENTS

(References in bold type are to a rule in the R.C.S. 1994; references in ordinary type are to annotations)

TABLE OF DERIVATIONS

R.C.S. 1994 rule		Derivation (r. = rule in R.C.S. 1965)
Chapter 1,	r. 1.3(2)	r. 168(3)
	r. 1.3(3)	r. 68G
Chapter 2,	r. 2.1	A.S. (Rules of Court, consolidation and amendment) 1965, para. (4)
Chapter 3,	r. 3.1	r. 12(a) (part) and (b) (part)
	r. 3.2(1)	r. 12(b) (part)
	r. 3.2(2)	r. 13(a) as amended by S.I. 1982/1679
	r. 3.2(3)	r. 15
	r. 3.3(1)	r. 12(b) (part)
	r. 3.3(2)	r. 13(b)
	r. 3.4(2)	r. 14
	r. 3.5(1)	r. 12(b) (part)
	r. 3.5(4)	A.S. (Edictal Citations, Commissary Petitions and Petitions of Service) 1971 [S.I. 1971/1165]
	r. 3.6(1)	r. 12(b) (part)
	r. 3.6(2)	r. 13(c)
Chapter 4,	r. 4.1	r. 19
	r. 4.2(1) and (7)	r. 73(a) as amended by S.I. 1991/2483
	r. 4.2(2)	r. 73(b)
	r. 4.2(3), (4) and (8)	r. 28(1) as amended by S.I. 1991/2483
	r. 4.2(3) and (4)	r. 193 as amended by S.I. 1986/514 and 1991/2483
	r. 4.2(9)	r. 28(2) inserted by S.I. 1991/2483
	r. 4.3	P.N. No. 3 of 1976, para. 3(i)
	r. 4.4(1) and (2)	r. 20
	r. 4.4(3)	r. 78(d) as amended by S.I. 1990/705, and r. 194
	r. 4.5	r. 25
	r. 4.6	r. 21
	r. 4.6(1)(b)	r. 83(d)
	r. 4.7	r. 26(b)
	r. 4.8	r. 26(a)
	r. 4.9	r. 27
	r. 4.10	r. 29
	r. 4.11(1) and (2)	r. 31(a)
	r. 4.12(1) to (4)	r. 32(a)
	r. 4.12(5)	r. 32(b)
	r. 4.14	r. 23
	r. 4.15(2) and (5)	r. 30(1) substituted by S.I. 1984/472
	r. 4.15(3)	r. 93A inserted by S.I. 1978/799 and as amended by S.I. 1984/472
	r. 4.15(4)	r. 30(3) substituted by S.I. 1984/472

R.C.S. 1994 rule		Derivation (r. = rule in R.C.S. 1965)
	r. 4.15(6)	r. 30(2) substituted by S.I. 1984/472
	r. 4.16(2), (3) and (5)	r. 295
	r. 4.16(4)	r. 30(3) inserted by S.I. 1986/1937
	r. 4.16(6)	r. 30(1) substituted by S.I. 1984/472
	r. 4.16(7)	r. 30(2) substituted by S.I. 1984/472
Chapter 5,	r. 5.1	r. 68H inserted by S.I. 1990/2118
	r. 5.1(d)	r. 218A(1)
	r. 5.2	r. 681 inserted by S.I. 1990/2118
Chapter 6,	r. 6.1	r. 18
	r. 6.2(2)	r. 17
	r. 6.2(3)	r. 94(a)
	r. 6.2(4)	P.N. 5th May 1972
	r. 6.2(7) (part)	P.N. No. 2 of 1987, para. 5
	r. 6.2(13) and (14)	P.N. 29th May 1975
	r. 6.3(5) and (6)	r. 294C(7) and (8) inserted by S.I. 1987/1206
	r. 6.3(8)	P.N. No. 2 of 1987, para. 5
	r. 6.4	r. 16
Chapter 7,	r. 7.1	P.N. 9th July 1980, regs. 1 and 3
	r. 7.2(1)	r. 168(11) substituted by S.I. 1978/106
	r. 7.2(2)	r. 170K inserted by S.I. 1982/1679
	r. 7.2(3)	P.N. 9th July 1980, regs. 6, 7 and 8
	r. 7.3	P.N. 9th July 1980, reg. 1
	r. 7.4	P.N. 9th July 1980, reg. 2
	r. 7.5	P.N. 9th July 1980, reg. 5A
	r. 7.6	P.N. 9th July 1980, reg. 5
	r. 7.7	r. 66 as amended by S.I. 1969/1819, 1974/2090, 1983/398, 1985/1178 and 1993/770
	r. 7.8	r. 63A inserted by S.I. 1986/1937
	r. 7.9(2) and (3)	r. 63 substituted by S.I. 1986/1937
	r. 7.10	r. 64
	r. 7.11(2)	r. 170D(6) inserted by S.I. 1976/1994
Chapter 8,	r. 8.1	r. 36
Chapter 9,	r. 9.1	r. 32A inserted by S.I. 1976/745 and as amended by S.I. 1982/1825
	r. 9.2	r. 34
Chapter 10,	r. 10.1(2) and (3)	r. 68B inserted by S.I. 1987/2160
	r. 10.2	r. 68C inserted by S.I. 1987/2160
	r. 10.3	r. 68D inserted by S.I. 1987/2160
	r. 10.5	r. 68E inserted by S.I. 1987/2160
	r. 10.6	r. 68F inserted by S.I. 1987/2160
Chapter 11,	r. 11.1	r. 1 as amended by S.I. 1987/1206
Chapter 12,	r. 12.1(1)	r. 37 as amended by S.I. 1978/955, and r. 38
	r. 12.1(2)	r. 40

R.C.S. 1994 rule		Derivation (r. = rule in R.C.S. 1965)
	r. 12.1(3)	Nautical Assessors (Scotland) Act 1894 (c. 40), s. 2; r. 41
	r. 12.2	r. 44(c)
	r. 12.3	r. 39(a)
	r. 12.4	r. 39(c)
	r. 12.5	Nautical Assessors (Scotland) Act 1894, s. 4; rr. 38 and 46(a)
	r. 12.6	r. 43
	r. 12.7(1)	r. 146
	r. 12.7(2) to (4)	r. 42
	r. 12.8	Nautical Assessors (Scotland) Act 1894, s. 3; r. 45
	r. 12.9	Nautical Assessors (Scotland) Act 1894, s. 5; r. 44(b)
Chapter 13,	r. 13.1	r. 69 (part)
	r. 13.2(1) to (3) and (5)	r. 70(1)(a) and (b) as amended by S.I. 1984/472
	r. 13.2(4)	r. 70(1)(c) inserted by S.I. 1986/1941 and as amended byS.I. 1987/1206
	r. 13.3	r. 71
	r. 13.4(1)(a) to (c) and (3)	r. 72(1) and (3) substituted by S.I. 1986/1941
	r. 13.4(1)(d)	r. 75(7) substituted by S.I. 1986/1941
	r. 13.5(1) and (2)	r. 74 (preamble (part))
	r. 13.5(2) to (5)	P.N. No. 3 of 1976
	r. 13.6	r.74 (preamble (part)) as amended by S.I. 1986/1941
	r. 13.6A	Debtors (Scotland) Act 1838 (c. 114), s. 16; r. 70(2)(b) inserted by S.I. 1984/472, and r. 74 (preamble (part)) as amended by S.I. 1986/1941
	r. 13.7(2)	A.S. 8th July 1831, para. III
	r. 13.8A(1)	r. 74(d)
	r. 13.11	r. 74(g) and (h), and r. 140(d) and (dd), as amended by S.I. 1990/705
	r. 13.12	r. 76 as amended by S.I. 1991/2483
	r. 13.13(1) and (2)	r. 78; P.N. No. 3 of 1976, para. 3(vi)
	r. 13.13(1) to (5)	r. 78(a) to (c) and (e)
	r. 13.13(6)	A.S. 8th July 1831, para. III
	r. 13.14	r. 80(a)
Chapter 14,	r. 14.2(a) to (h)	r. 69 and r. 189(a) (preamble) (as amended by S.I. 1970/134), (i), (ii), (iii) (substituted by S.I. 1987/1206), (iv) (as amended by S.I. 1987/1206) and (xxxvii) (inserted by S.I. 1990/705)
	r. 14.3(a)to(j)	r. 190 (preamble) (as amended by S.I. 1970/134), (i) (as amended by S.I. 1980/1144), (iv)

R.C.S. 1994 rule	Derivation (r. = rule in R.C.S. 1965)
	(as amended by S.I. 1992/1422), (v) and (vi) (as amended by S.I. 1976/283 and 1987/1206), (vii) (as amended by S.I. 1976/283 and 1977/1621), (viii)–(x) (substituted by S.I. 1987/1206) and (xi) (inserted by S.I. 1992/1422)
r. 14.4	r. 191 as amended by S.I. 1987/1206
r. 14.5	r. 195(a) (part)
r. 14.6(1)(a) to (c)	r. 192(1) substituted by S.I. 1986/1941
r. 14.6(2)	r. 192(3) substituted by S.I. 1986/1941
r. 14.7(1)	r. 195(a)(part)
r. 14.7(2)	r. 195(c) as amended by S.I. 1986/1941
r. 14.9(1)	r. 197 (preamble) as amended by S.I. 1986/1941
r. 14.9(2)	r. 197(a) substituted by S.I. 1986/1941
r. 14.9(3)	r. 197(b) substituted by S.I. 1986/1941
r. 14.9(4)	r. 197(c) substituted by S.I. 1986/1941
r. 14.9(5)	r. 197(d)
Chapter 16, r. 16.1(1)	r. 74A(1) inserted by S.I. 1984/472 and as amended by S.I. 1985/1600, 1986/1941 and 1990/705
r. 16.1(3)	r. 74A(3) inserted by S.I. 1984/472, and r. 77
r. 16.1(4)	r. 195(d)
r. 16.2(2)	r. 74B(1) inserted by S.I. 1986/1941
r. 16.2(3)	r. 74B(4) inserted by S.I. 1986/1941
r. 16.2(4)	r. 74B(5) inserted by S.I. 1986/1941
r. 16.2(5)	r. 74B(6) inserted by S.I. 1986/1941
r. 16.3(1), (2), (3) and (5)	r. 74A(4) inserted by S.I. 1984/472 and as amended by S.I. 1990/705 and 1991/1157
r. 16.3(4)	r. 74(i)
r. 16.4(2)	r. 68A inserted by S.I. 1968/1150, and r. 74A(5) (inserted by S.I. 1984/472) and (6) (inserted by S.I. 1984/472 and as amended by S.I. 1991/2483), and r. 74B(3)(a) (part) inserted by S.I. 1986/1941 and as amended by S.I. 1991/2483
r. 16.4(3)	r. 74B(7)(b) inserted by S.I. 1986/1941
r. 16.4(4)	r. 74(a) (part), r. 74A(7) inserted by S.I. 1984/472, and r.74B(3)(b) inserted by S.I. 1986/1941
r. 16.4(6)	r. 72(2), and r. 192(2), substituted by S.I. 1986/1941
r. 16.4(7)	r. 74A(8) substituted by S.I. 1984/472
r. 16.5(1)	r. 75(1) substituted by S.I. 1986/1941 and as amended by S.I. 1987/1206, and r. 75(2) substituted by S.I. 1986/1941
r. 16.5(3)	r. 75(4) substituted by S.I. 1986/1941
r. 16.5(5)	r. 75(3) substituted by S.I. 1986/1941 and as amended by S.I. 1991/2483

R.C.S. 1994 rule		Derivation (r. = rule in R.C.S. 1965)
	r. 16.5(6)	r. 75(5) substituted by S.I. 1986/1941
	r. 16.6(1)	r. 74B(7)(a) inserted by S.I. 1986/1941
	r. 16.6(3)	r. 74B(4)(b), (5)(b), (6)(b) and (7)(a), inserted by S.I. 1986/1941
	r. 16.6(4)	r. 74B(8) inserted by S.I. 1986/1941
	r. 16.10	r. 74(b) as amended by S.I. 1991/2483
	r. 16.11	r. 82
	r. 16.12(4)	Court of Session Act 1825 (c. 120), s. 53
	r. 16.13(1) (part), (3) and (4)	r. 140(a)
	r. 16.14	r. 140(b)
	r. 16.15(2)	r. 74(c) and r. 140(c)
Chapter 17,	r. 17.1(1)	r. 81(1) substituted by S.I. 1991/2483
	r. 17.1(2)	r. 81(1B) inserted by S.I. 1991/2483
	r. 17.1(3)	r. 86
	r. 17.2	r. 81(2) inserted by S.I. 1986/1941
Chapter 18,	r. 18.1(1)	r. 83(b)
	r. 18.1(2)	r. 83(a)
	r. 18.2	r. 83(e) inserted by S.I. 1986/1941
	r. 18.3(2)	r. 196(b)
	r. 18.3(3)	r. 196(a)
Chapter 19,	r. 19.1(1) and (2)	r. 89(a) (part) as amended by S.I. 1984/472
	r. 19.1(4)	r. 89(aa) inserted by S.I. 1984/472
	r. 19.1(5)	r. 89(b) substituted by S.I. 1986/1941
	r. 19.1(6)	r. 89(c) substituted by S.I. 1986/1941
	r. 19.1(7)	r. 89(i) inserted by S.I. 1984/472 and as amended by S.I. 1986/1941
	r. 19.2(1)	r. 89(ab) inserted by S.I. 1984/472
	r. 19.2(2), (3) and (4)	r. 89(e) and (f)
	r. 19.2(5)	r. 89(d) substituted by S.I. 1986/1941
Chapter 20,	r. 20.1(b), (3) and r. 94(d) as amended by S.I. 1991/2483	
Chapter 21,	r. 21.1	r. 89B(1) inserted by S.I. 1984/499 and as amended by S.I. 1990/705
	r. 21.2	r. 89B(2) to (6) inserted by S.I. 1984/499
	r. 21.3(1)	r. 89B(7) inserted by S.I. 1984/499
Chapter 22,	r. 22.1(3)	r. 90(2) as amended by S.I. 1980/1144
	r. 22.2(2)	r. 90(3) inserted by S.I. 1980/1144
	r. 22.2(3) and (4)	r. 90A(2)(a) and (3) inserted by S.I. 1980/1144
	r. 22.3(1)	r. 91(2) substituted by S.I. 1982/1825 and r. 91(5) substituted by S.I. 1982/1825
	r. 22.3(5)	r. 91(3) substituted by S.I. 1982/1825

R.C.S. 1994 rule		Derivation (r. = rule in R.C.S. 1965)
	r. 22.3(6)	r. 91(6) substituted by S.I. 1982/1825
Chapter 23,	r. 23.2(1)	r. 93(a)
	r. 23.2(2)	r. 93(b) and (c) (part), r. 198 (amended by S.I. 1978/799) and P.N. No. 8 of 1991, para. 10(3)
	r. 23.2(3)	P.N. No. 8 of 1991, para. 2
	r. 23.2(4)	P.N. No. 8 of 1991, para. 10(2)
	r. 23.2(7)	r. 93(d) (part)
	r. 23.3(1) and (3)	r. 93(c) as amended by S.I. 1980/1144
	r. 23.3(4)	r. 105
	r. 23.3(5)	r. 93(b) (part)
	r. 23.4(1), (5) and (6)	r. 93(3) (part)
	r. 23.4(4)	r. 93(e) (part) as amended by S.I. 1980/1144
	r. 23.6(1)	r. 93(d) (part)
	r. 23.7	P.N. 31st March 1970
	r. 23.9	r. 79(1) (part) and (2), and r. 236(b) amended by S.I. 1984/499
	r. 23.12	r. 93(f)
Chapter 24,	r. 24.1	r. 92(1) and (3)
	r. 24.2(3) and (4)	P.N. 27th March 1986 (procedure following minute of amendment)
	r. 24.2(5)	P.N. 26th March 1981
	r. 24.3(1)	r. 92(3)
	r. 24.4	r. 92(2)
	r. 24.5	r. 92(4)
Chapter 25,	r. 25.1(1)	r. 84(a) (part) and (j)
	r. 25.1(2)	r. 84(a) (part)
	r. 25.1(3)	r. 84(b)
	r. 25.2	r. 84(c)
	r. 25.3	r. 84(k)

R.C.S. 1994 rule		Derivation (r. = rule in R.C.S. 1965)
	r. 25.4(1)	r. 84(d)
	r. 25.4(2)	r. 84(f)
	r. 25.5	r. 84(g)
	r. 25.6	r. 84(h)
Chapter 26,	r. 26.1(1)	r. 85(1) (preamble (part)) as amended by S.I. 1980/1144
	r. 26.1(2)	r. 85(1)(g) and (2) as amended by S.I. 1980/ 1144
	r. 26.2	r. 85(1) (preamble (part)) as amended by S.I. 1980/1144
	r. 26.3	r. 85(1)(b)
	r. 26.4	r. 85(1)(a)
	r. 26.5	r. 85(1) (preamble (part)) as amended by S.I. 1980/1144
	r. 26.7(1)	r. 85(1)(c) (part) as amended by S.I. 1976/2197 and 1980/1144
	r. 26.7(3) and (4)	r. 85(1)(e)
Chapter 27,	r. 27.1	r. 134E inserted by S.I. 1990/705
Chapter 28,	r. 28.1(1) and (2)	r. 94(c) as amended by S.I. 1991/2483
	r. 28.1(4)	r. 94(e)
Chapter 29,	r. 29.1(1)(b), (2) and (3)	r. 91A inserted by S.I. 1984/472
	r. 29.2	r. 84(e)
Chapter 31,	r. 31.1	r. 106 (part)
	r. 31.2	r. 106 (part)
Chapter 32,	r. 32.1	r. 104B inserted by S.I. 1986/1955 and as amended by S.I. 1987/1206
	r. 32.2	r. 104A inserted by S.I. 1984/472
	r. 32.3	r. 274 substituted by S.I. 1980/1801
	r. 32.4(1)	r. 275(2) substituted by S.I. 1982/1825
	r. 32.4(2)	r. 275(3)
	r. 32.5	r. 275(5)(a) and (b)(i) substituted by S.I. 1982/ 1825
	r. 32.6	r. 275(5)(b)(ii) substituted by S.I. 1982/1825
	r. 32.7	r. 275(6) substituted by S.I. 1982/1825
Chapter 33,	r. 33.6	r. 238(a)
	r. 33.7(1)	238(c)
	r. 33.8	r. 240
	r. 33.9	r. 238(f)
	r. 33.12(1)	r. 13(d)
	r. 33.12(2)	P.N. 14th May 1970
Chapter 34,	r. 34.1	r. 91B(1) inserted by S.I. 1984/472 and as amended by S.I. 1986/1937 and r. 198A inserted by S.I. 1986/1937
Chapter 35,	r. 35.2(1), (2) and	r. 95(b) and r. 95A(b) (inserted by S.I. 1972/

R.C.S. 1994 rule		Derivation (r. = rule in R.C.S. 1965)
	(3)	2021)
	r. 35.2(1)(b)	r. 95A(d)(i) substituted by S.I. 1987/1206
	r. 35.2(4)	r. 95A(b) inserted by S.I. 1972/2021
	r. 35.2(5)	r. 95(a) (part) as amended by S.I. 1992/88, and r. 95A(a) (part) inserted by S.I. 1972/2021
	r. 35.2(6)	r. 95(a) (part), r. 95A(a) (part) inserted by S.I. 1972/2021
	r. 35.3	r. 96(a) to (f)
	r. 35.4	r. 97
	r. 35.8	r. 98
	r. 35.9	r. 103(a) to ()c)
	r. 35.10	r. 104
	r. 35.11	rr. 100 and 101
	r. 35.14	A.S. 16th February 1841, s. 17
	r. 35.15	r. 102 substituted by S.I. 1976/283
Chapter 36,	r. 36.1	r. 108
	r. 36.2(2)	r. 106A inserted by S.I. 1984/472
	r. 36.2(5)	r. 106B inserted by S.I. 1985/1955
	r. 36.3	r. 107 (part) as amended by S.I. 1972/2022
	r. 36.5	r. 107 (part)
	r. 36.7	r. 109
	r. 36.9	r. 111(a) to (d)
	r. 36.11	r. 122A(2) inserted by S.I. 1984/472
	r. 36.11(1), (4) and (5)	r. 113(a)
	r. 36.11(2)	r. 110; P.N. 2nd March 1972
	r. 36.11(3) and (8)	r. 113(b)
	r. 36.11(6)	r. 113(d)
	r. 36.11(7)	r. 113(c)
	r. 36.12	r. 264(f)
	r. 36.13(1) to (4)	r. 112 as amended by S.I. 1976/137
Chapter 37,	r. 37.1(1) to (5)	r. 114(1) to (5) substituted by S.I. 1982/1825
	r. 37.1(6) and (7)	r. 114(6) substituted by S.I. 1982/1825
	r. 37.1(9)	r. 114(7) substituted by S.I. 1982/1825
	r. 37.1(10)	P.N. 28th January 1955
	r. 37.2(1)	r. 117A(1) inserted by S.I. 1990/2118
	r. 37.2(4)	r. 117A(2) inserted by S.I. 1990/2118
	r. 37.2(5)	r. 119(b)
	r. 37.3	r. 119(a) and (c)
	r. 37.4 (part)	r. 121, r. 122, r. 122A(2) (inserted by S.I. 1984/472), and 123
	r. 37.5	r. 127
	r. 37.6	r. 122A(1) inserted by S.I. 1984/472
	r. 37.7	r. 124

R.C.S. 1994 rule		Derivation (r. = rule in R.C.S. 1965)
	r. 37.8	r. 116(b)
	r. 37.9	r. 125(a)
	r. 37.10	r. 125(b)
Chapter 38,	r. 38.1	r. 153C inserted by S.I. 1984/472, r. 261 and r. 262(a) (part)
	r. 38.2(1)	r. 264(a) (part) substituted by S.I. 1990/705
	r. 38.2(3)	r. 134D inserted by S.I. 1984/919
	r. 38.2(4) and (5)	r. 264(b) as amended by S.I. 1977/1621, 1980/1144 and 1985/1600
	r. 38.2(6)	r. 264(c) (part)
	r. 38.3(1)	r. 89B(8) inserted by S.I. 1984/499
	r. 38.3(2)	r. 88G(3) inserted by S.I. 1988/2060
	r. 38.3(3)	r. 269B(21) inserted by S.I. 1985/500
	r. 38.3(5)	r. 349(7) substituted by S.I. 1983/836
	r. 38.4(2), (6) and (7)	r. 264(c) (part)
	r. 38.5(1)	r. 262(a) and (b)
	r. 38.5(2)	r. 117
	r. 38.6(1) and (3)	r. 262(c)
	r. 38.6(5)	r. 264(a) (part) substituted by S.I. 1990/705
	r. 38.7	r. 63B inserted by S.I. 1986/1937
	r. 38.9	r. 264(e)
	r. 38.10(1)	r. 264(d)
	r. 38.12(1) to (3)	r. 263(b)
	r. 38.16(2)	r. 294B(5)(b)
	r. 38.17	P.N. 26th March 1981
	r. 38.18(1)	r. 294B(3) inserted by S.I. 1987/1206
	r. 38.18(2)	r. 294B(5)(a) inserted by S.I. 1987/1206
	r. 38.18(3)	r. 294B(6) inserted by S.I. 1987/1206
	r. 38.20	r. 262(d)
Chapter 39,	r. 39.1(1) to (3)	r. 126(a)
	r. 39.9(3)	r. 125(c) inserted by S.I. 1984/472
Chapter 40,	r. 40.1	r. 267
	r. 40.2(5) and (6)	P.N. 6th November 1986
	r. 40.4	r. 268(1) substituted by S.I. 1990/2118 and as amended by S.I. 1991/2483
	r. 40.5	r. 268(2) substituted by S.I. 1990/2118
	r. 40.6	r. 268(3) and (4) as amended by S.I. 1990/2118
	r. 40.7(1)	r. 269(a) as amended by S.I. 1974/845 and 1991/2483; P.N. 13th November 1969, para. 2
	r. 40.7(2)	r. 269(b) (part) as amended by S.I. 1974/845
	r. 40.8	r. 269(b) (part) as amended by S.I. 1974/845
	r. 40.10(1) and (3)	r. 270
	r. 40.15(1)	r. 269(b) (part) as amended by S.I. 1974/845

R.C.S. 1994 rule	Derivation (r. = rule in R.C.S. 1965)
r. 40.15(2) to (6)	r. 272 as amended by S.I. 1985/1600
r. 40.16(1) and (2)	r. 271
r. 40.17	P.N. 26th March 1981
r. 40.18(1) to (3)	r. 294B(3), (4) and (6) inserted by S.I. 1987/1206
r. 40.20	r. 262(d) Chapter 41,
r. 41.1	r. 276 as amended by S.I. 1972/2021, and r. 290(a) (part) as amended by S.I. 1973/540 and 1986/1955
r. 41.2(4) and (5)	P.N. 6th November 1986
r. 41.4	r. 276 as amended by S.I. 1972/2021
r. 41.5(1) and (2)	r. 277(a) as amended by S.I. 1982/1825
r. 41.6	r. 277(b)
r. 41.7	r. 277(c) and (d)
r. 41.8	r. 278
r. 41.9(1) (part) and (2)	r. 279
r. 41.9(1) (part) and (3)	r. 277(e)
r. 41.9(4) and (5)	r. 277(1)
r. 41.9(6)	r. 277(g)
r. 41.10(1)	r. 277(h)(i)
r. 41.10(2) and (3)	r. 277(j)
r. 41.11	r. 277(h)(ii) (part) and (k)(i) (part) (as amended by S.I. 1984/499)
r. 41.12(1)	r. 277(k)(i) (part)
r. 41.12(2)	r. 277(k)(ii)
r. 41.13	r. 277(k)(i) (part)
r. 41.14	r. 277(k)(iii)
r. 41.15	r. 280(a)
r. 41.16	r. 280(b) (part)
r. 41.17(1)	r. 280(b) (part)
r. 41.18	r. 290(a) (part) as amended by S.I. 1973/540
r. 41.19(1) (part)	r. 290(a) (part) and (d)
r. 41.19(2)	r. 290(a) (part), (b) and (c)
r. 41.20(1) (part)	r. 290(a) (part) as amended by S.I. 1984/499
r. 41.20(1)(b)(iii)	r. 290(i) inserted by S.I. 1982/1825
r. 41.21(1)	r. 290(e)
r. 41.21(2)	r. 293(a) as amended by S.I. 1972/1835
r. 41.21(3)	r. 293B(5) inserted by S.I. 1980/1754 and as amended by S.I. 1992/2289
r. 41.21(4)	r. 292(a) as amended by S.I. 1972/1835
r. 41.21(5)	r. 293A(a) and (b) inserted by S.I. 1976/847
r. 41.23(1)	r. 281(1) (part) substituted by S.I. 1976/1849

R.C.S. 1994 rule		Derivation (r. = rule in R.C.S. 1965)
		and as amended by S.I. 1984/499
	r. 41.25	r. 282(1) substituted by S.I. 1976/1849 and as amended by S.I. 1990/705
	r. 41.26(1)	r. 283(1) substituted by S.I. 1976/1849 and as amended by S.I. 1990/705
	r. 41.26(2)	r. 283(7) substituted by S.I. 1976/1849 and as amended by S.I. 1990/705
	r. 41.26(6)	r. 283(13) inserted by S.I. 1990/705
	r. 41.26(7)	r. 283(12) substituted by S.I. 1976/1849
	r. 41.27	r. 286(1)
	r. 41.30	r. 289A(2) and (4) (part) inserted by S.I. 1971/203
	r. 41.31	r. 289A(6) and (8) inserted by S.I. 1971/203
	r. 41.32	r. 289A(7) inserted by S.I. 1971/203
	r. 41.33	r. 289A(9) inserted by S.I. 1971/203
	r. 41.34	r. 284 (preamble) as amended by S.I. 1980/1144
	r. 41.35	r. 284 (preamble) as amended by S.I. 1980/1144
	r. 41.36	r. 284(a)
	r. 41.37	r. 284(b)
	r. 41.38	r. 284(c)
	r. 41.39	r. 291(2) (preamble)
	r. 41.40	r. 291(2)(a), (b), (c) and (d) (as amended by S.I. 1985/1600)
	r. 41.41	r. 288(1) substituted by S.I. 1992/2289
	r. 41.42	r. 288(3) and (4) substituted by S.I. 1992/2289
Chapter 42,	r. 42.1	r. 348(1) and (2) substituted by S.I. 1983/826
	r. 42.2	r. 348(3) and (4) substituted by S.I. 1983/826
	r. 42.3(1)(a)	r. 349(1) substituted by S.I. 1983/826
	r. 42.4(1)	r. 349(2) substituted by S.I. 1992/1433
	r. 42.4(2)	r. 349(3) substituted by S.I. 1983/826 and as amended by S.I. 1991/1157
	r. 42.4(3) to (5)	r. 349(4) to (6) substituted by S.I. 1983/826
	r. 42.5(1)	r. 347(c)
	r. 42.6	r. 349(8) substituted by S.I. 1983/826; P.N. 16th January 1970
	r. 42.7	r. 350 substituted by S.I. 1992/1433
	r. 42.8(1)	r. 347(aa) inserted by S.I. 1984/499
	r. 42.9	r. 347(a) (part) inserted by S.I. 1974/1686
	r. 42.10(1)	r. 347(a) (part) inserted by S.I. 1974/1686
	r. 42.10(2)	r. 347, Table of Fees, Chapter I, note 5
	r. 42.10(3)	r. 347(e) (part) substituted by S.I. 1970/1746 and as amended by S.I. 1981/497
	r. 42.10(4)	r. 347(e) (part) substituted by S.I. 1970/1746 and as amended by S.I. 1981/497

R.C.S. 1994 rule		Derivation (r. = rule in R.C.S. 1965)
	r. 42.10(5)	r. 347(f) substituted by S.I. 1970/1746
	r. 42.11(1) and (2)	r. 347(g) substituted by S.I. 1974/1686
	r. 42.12	r. 347(h) inserted by S.I. 1973/360
	r. 42.13(1)	r. 347, Table of Fees, Chapter II, para. 8
	r. 42.13(2) and (3)	r. 347, Table of Fees, Chapter II, para. 9
	r. 42.14	r. 347(d) substituted by S.I. 1970/1746 and as amended by S.I. 1991/272
	r. 42.15	r. 347(b) substituted by S.I. 1970/1746
	r. 42.16	r. 347(a) (part) substituted by S.I. 1970/1746 and as amended by S.I. 1992/1433, and Table of Fees amended by S.I. 1971/1161, 1989/445, 1993/900 and 1357, 1994/1139 and 1140
	r. 42.17	r. 350A inserted by S.I. 1992/1898
Chapter 43,	r. 43.1(2)(part)	r. 75A(2) (part) substituted by S.I. 1984/920 and as amended by S.I. 1986/1941
	r. 43.2(2)	r. 134B inserted by S.I. 1984/919
	r. 43.11(1) to (8)	r. 89A(1)(a) to (g) inserted by S.I. 1974/845
	r. 43.11(9) (part)	r. 89A(1)(h) inserted by S.I. 1974/845
	r. 43.12	r. 89A(2) inserted by S.I. 1974/845
	r. 43.13	r. 134C inserted by S.I. 1984/919
	r. 43.14(1)	r. 75A(1) and (2) substituted by S.I. 1984/920 and as amended by S.I. 1986/1941
	r. 43.14(2)	r. 75A(3) substituted by S.I. 1984/920 and as amended by S.I. 1986/1941
	r. 43.15	r. 75A(6) substituted by S.I. 1984/920 and as amended by S.I. 1986/1941
	r. 43.16(1)	r. 75A(4) substituted by S.I. 1984/920 and as amended by S.I. 1986/1941
	r. 43.16(2) and (3)	r. 75A(5) substituted by S.I. 1984/920 and as amended by S.I. 1986/1941
	r. 43.17	r. 75A(7) (part) substituted by S.I. 1984/920 and as amended by S.I. 1986/1941
	r. 43.18(1)	r. 75A(9) and (10) substituted by S.I. 1984/920 and as amended by S.I. 1986/1941
	r 43.19(1)	r. 75A(11) substituted by S.I. 1984/920 and as amended by S.I. 1986/1941
Chapter 44,	r. 44.1(2)	r. 88A inserted by S.I. 1988/2060
	r. 44.2	r. 88B inserted by S.I. 1988/2060
	r. 44.3	r. 88C inserted by S.I. 1988/2060
	r. 44.4	r. 88D inserted by S.I. 1988/2060
	r. 44.5	r. 88E inserted by S.I. 1988/2060
	r. 44.6	r. 88F inserted by S.I. 1988/2060
	r. 44.7	r. 88H inserted by S.I. 1988/2060
Chapter 46,	r. 46.1	r. 135
	r. 46.2	r. 136

R.C.S. 1994 rule		Derivation (r. = rule in R.C.S. 1965)
	r. 46.3	r. 137(a) and (b)
	r. 46.4(1) to (3)	r. 138
	r. 46.4(4) and (5)	r. 142
	r. 46.5	r. 143
	r. 46.6	r. 144
	r. 46.7	r. 145
	r. 46.8	r. 147
	r. 46.9	r. 147A inserted by S.I. 1979/670
Chapter 47,	r. 47.2	r. 149 substituted by S.I. 1988/1521
	r. 47.3(1)	r. 148(3) substituted by S.I. 1988/1521
Chapter 48,	r. 48.1(1)	r. 153A(2) inserted by S.I. 1984/472
	r. 48.1(2)	r. 153B inserted by S.I. 1984/472
	r. 48.2	r. 153A(1) inserted by S.I. 1984/472
	r. 48.3	r. 153E inserted by S.I. 1984/472
Chapter 49,	r. 49.1(1), (2) and (3)	r. 154(1) and (2) substituted by S.I. 1976/1994 and as amended by S.I. 1986/1231
	r. 49.2	r. 157(3) substituted by S.I. 1976/1994
	r. 49.3(1)	r. 170B(11) inserted by S.I. 1988/615, and r. 260EA inserted by S.I. 1988/615; the Family Law Act 1986 (c.55), s. 39
	r. 49.4	r. 157(1) substituted by S.I. 1976/1994
	r. 49.7(1)	r. 155A(1) inserted by S.I. 1991/1157
	r. 49.8(1)(a)	r. 155(3)(a) and (4) substituted by S.I. 1976/1994
	r. 49.8(1)(b)	r. 155(1) and (2) substituted by S.I. 1976/1994
	r. 49.8(1)(c)	r. 155(3)(b) and (4) substituted by S.I. 1976/1994
	r. 49.8(1)(d)	r. 155(5) substituted by S.I. 1976/1994
	r. 49.8(1)(e)	r. 155(6) substituted by S.I. 1976/1994, and r. 170B(6)(a) inserted by S.I. 1976/1994 and as amended by S.I. 1986/1955 and 1990/705
	r. 49.8(1)(f)	Children Act 1975 (c. 72), s. 48 as amended by the Law Reform (Parent and Child) (Scotland) Act 1986 (c. 9), Sched. 2
	r. 49.8(1)(g)	Children Act 1975, s. 49(1)(a) as amended by the Law Reform (Parent and Child) (Scotland) Act 1986, Sched.1, para. 14
	r. 49.8(1)(i)	r. 170D(9) inserted by S.I. 1986/1231
	r. 49.8(1)(j)	r. 155(7) inserted by S.I. 1982/1825, and r. 170D(4)(c) substituted by S.I. 1977/1621 and as amended by S.I. 1986/1231
	r. 49.8(1)(k)	r. 188D(7) and (10) inserted by S.I. 1982/1381
	r. 49.8(4)	Children Act 1975, s. 49(1)(b) as amended by the Law Reform (Parent and Child) (Scotland) Act 1986, Sched.1, para. 14

R.C.S. 1994 rule	Derivation (r. = rule in R.C.S. 1965)
r. 49.9	r. 162 substituted by S.I. 1976/1994
r. 49.11	Children Act 1975, s. 49 as amended by the Law Reform (Parent and Child) (Scotland) Act 1986, Sched. 1, para.14
r. 49.12	r. 159(2) substituted by S.I. 1986/1941 and as amended by S.I. 1987/1206
r. 49.13	r. 159(5) and (6) substituted by S.I. 1976/1994
r. 49.14	r. 161 substituted by S.I. 1976/1994
r. 49.15(1)	r. 164 substituted by S.I. 1976/1994
r. 49.16	r. 165 substituted by S.I. 1976/1994
r. 49.17(1) to (7)	r. 167(1) substituted by S.I. 1976/1994
r. 49.17(9)	P.N. 10th February 1983
r. 49.18	r. 167(2) substituted by S.I. 1976/1994
r. 49.19	r. 166 substituted by S.I. 1976/1994
r. 49.22(1), (4) and (5)	r. 170B(14)(c), (d), (f) and (g) inserted by S.I. 1990/705, and r. 260D(4), (5), (7) and (8) inserted by S.I. 1986/515
r. 49.22(2)(b)	P.N. 13th November 1969, para. 3
r. 49.23	r. 170B(15), and r. 260D(10), inserted by S.I. 1990/705
r. 49.24	r. 170B(12), and r. 260EB, inserted by S.I. 1988/615
r. 49.25(1) (part)	r. 170B(13), and r. 260EC, inserted by S.I. 1988/615
r. 49.25(1) (part)	r. 170C(2), and r. 260E(2) and (3), inserted by S.I. 1986/515
r. 49.26	P.N. No. 1 of 1988
r. 49.27	r. 170B(5) inserted by S.I. 1976/1994
r. 49.28(1) to (4)	r. 168(1), (2), (5) and (6) substituted by S.I. 1978/106 and as amended by S.I. 1980/1144
r. 49.29	r. 168(7) to (11) substituted by S.I. 1978/106
r. 49.30	r. 170A inserted by S.I. 1976/1994
r. 49.31	r. 170B(3) and (4) inserted by S.I. 1976/1994, r. 170D(2) inserted by S.I. 1976/1994 and as amended by S.I. 1986/1231, 1990/705 and 1991/1157, r. 170D(4)(a) substituted by S.I. 1977/1621 and as amended by S.I. 1986/1231, r.170D(5) substituted by S.I. 1986/1231, and r. 170D(7)(b) inserted by S.I. 1986/1231
r. 49.33(5) (part)	r. 168A inserted by S.I. 1980/1144 and as amended by S.I. 1982/1381
r. 49.34	r. 169 substituted by S.I. 1976/1994
r. 49.35(1)	r. 170B(1)(b) inserted by S.I. 1976/1994
r. 49.37	r. 170B(6)(b)(i) and (7)(a)(ii) inserted by S.I. 1976/1994
r. 49.38	r. 170B(6)(b)(ii) inserted by S.I. 1976/1994

R.C.S. 1994 rule	Derivation (r. = rule in R.C.S. 1965)
r. 49.40(1)(a) and (2)	P.N. 13th November 1969, para. 1
r. 49.42(1) to (4)	r. 170B(10) inserted by S.I. 1977/1621
r. 49.43	r. 170B(10) inserted by S.I. 1977/1621
r. 49.45(1)	r. 170D(11) inserted by S.I. 1986/1231
r. 49.46	r. 170D(1) and (2) (part) inserted by S.I. 1976/1994 and as amended by S.I. 1986/1231, r. 170D(4)(a) substituted by S.I. 1977/1621, and r. 188D(4) (part) and (5) (part) inserted by S.I. 1982/1381
r. 49.48(2)	P.N. 13th November 1969, para. 1
r. 49.49	r. 170D(3) substituted by S.I. 1977/1621 and as amended by S.I. 1987/1206, and r. 170D(7)(a) and (8) inserted by S.I. 1986/1231
r. 49.50	r. 170D(7)(c) inserted by S.I. 1986/1231
r. 49.51(1)	r. 170D(4)(a) substituted by S.I. 1977/1621 and as amended by S.I. 1986/1231
r. 49.51(2)	r. 170D(7)(c) inserted by S.I. 1986/1231
r. 49.53	r. 170M inserted by S.I. 1986/1231
r. 49.55	r. 170N inserted by S.I. 1986/1231
r. 49.56	r. 170P inserted by S.I. 1986/1231
r. 49.57	r. 170R inserted by S.I. 1986/1231
r. 49.58(1)	r. 260C(1) inserted by S.I. 1986/515
r. 49.61(2)	P.N. 13th November 1969, para. 1
r. 49.63(1)	r. 260E(1)(b) inserted by S.I. 1986/515
r. 49.64	r. 188D(1)(c) inserted by S.I. 1982/1381
r. 49.65	r. 188D(2), (4)(b) and (5) inserted by S.I. 1982/1381
r. 49.66	r. 188D(7)(a) and (b) inserted by S.I. 1982/1381
r. 49.67(1)	r. 188D(3) inserted by S.I. 1982/1381
r. 49.67(2)	r. 188D(7) and (9) inserted by S.I. 1982/1381
r. 49.68	r. 188D(6) inserted by S.I. 1982/1381
r. 49.69	r. 188D(11) inserted by S.I. 1982/1381
r. 49.70(1)	r. 188D(12) inserted by S.I. 1982/1381 and as amended by S.I. 1991/2483
r. 49.70(2)	r. 188D(13) inserted by S.I. 1982/1381
r. 49.71(1)	r. 188D(15) inserted by S.I. 1982/1381
r. 49.72(1) to (3)	r. 170E inserted by S.I. 1982/1679
r. 49.72(4)	r. 170H(1) inserted by S.I. 1982/1679
r. 49.73	r. 170F inserted by S.I. 1982/1679
r. 49.74(1)	r. 170G inserted by S.I. 1982/1679
r. 49.74(2)	r. 170H(2) inserted by S.I. 1982/1679
r. 49.75(1)	r. 1701(1) inserted by S.I. 1982/1679
r. 49.75(2)	r. 1701(3) inserted by S.I. 1982/1679 and as amended by S.I. 1987/1206

R.C.S. 1994 rule		Derivation (r. = rule in R.C.S. 1965)
	r. 49.77	r. 170J inserted by S.I. 1982/1679
	r. 49.80	r. 170L inserted by S.I. 1982/1679
Chapter 50,	r. 50.1	r. 188B(1) inserted by S.I. 1978/161
	r. 50.2(4)	r. 188B(3) and (4) (part) inserted by S.I. 1978/161
	r. 50.2(5)	r. 188B(4) (part) and (5) inserted by S.I. 1978/161
	r. 50.2(6)	r. 188B(6) inserted by S.I. 1978/161
	r. 50.5(1) and (2)	r. 188B(2), (3), (5) and (6) inserted by S.I. 1978/161
	r. 50.6	r. 188B(8) and (9) inserted by S.I. 1978/161
Chapter 51,	r. 51.2	r. 175 substituted by S.I. 1986/1941
	r. 51.3	r. 176(a) and (b) (part) as amended by S.I. 1986/1941
	r. 51.4(1) (part), (2) and (4)	r. 176(b) (part) as amended by S.I. 1986/1941
	r. 51.4(1) (part)	r. 177(a) as amended by S.I. 1986/1941
	r. 51.4(3)	r. 177(b) as amended by S.I. 1986/1941
	r. 51.5(1) and (2)(a)	r. 182(a)
	r. 51.6	r. 180
	r. 51.7(1)	r. 182(c)
	r. 51.7(3)	r. 179 (part) as amended by S.I. 1986/1941
	r. 51.8	r. 178 (part) as amended by S.I. 1986/1941
	r. 51.9	r. 178 (part) as amended by S.I. 1986/1941
	r. 51.11	r. 181
	r. 51.12(1)	r. 183 (part)
	r. 51.12(2)	r. 185
	r. 51.13	r. 183 (part)
	r. 51.14	r. 184
Chapter 52,	r. 52.1	r. 186
	r. 52.2	r. 187
	r. 52.3	r. 188
Chapter 53,	r. 53.3(1)	r. 171
	r. 53.3(4)	r. 173 (part)
	r. 53.4(1)	r. 172
	r. 53.4(2)	r. 173 (part)
	r. 53.7	r. 173 (part)
	r. 53.8	r. 174
Chapter 54,	r. 54.1	r. 188A(a) (part) inserted by S.I. 1966/868
	r. 54.2	r. 188A(a) (part) and (b) inserted by S.I. 1966/868
Chapter 55,	r. 55.1	r. 250 substituted by S.I. 1991/1621
	r. 55.2	r. 251 substituted by S.I. 1991/1621
	r. 55.3	r. 252 substituted by S.I. 1991/1621

R.C.S. 1994 rule	Derivation (r. = rule in R.C.S. 1965)
r. 55.4	r. 253 substituted by S.I. 1991/1621
r. 55.5	r. 254 substituted by S.I. 1991/1621
r. 55.6	r. 255 substituted by S.I. 1991/1621
r. 55.7	r. 256 substituted by S.I. 1991/1621
r. 55.8	r. 257 substituted by S.I. 1991/1621
r. 55.9	r. 257A substituted by S.I. 1991/1621
r. 55.10	r. 257B substituted by S.I. 1991/1621
r. 55.11	r. 257C substituted by S.I. 1991/1621
r. 55.12	r. 257D substituted by S.I. 1991/1621
r. 55.13	r. 257E substituted by S.I. 1991/1621
r. 55.14	r. 257F substituted by S.I. 1991/1621
r. 55.15	r. 257G substituted by S.I. 1991/1621
r. 55.16	r. 257H substituted by S.I. 1991/1621
r. 55.17	r. 2571 substituted by S.I. 1991/1621
r. 55.18	r. 257.1 substituted by S.I. 1991/1621
Chapter 57, r. 57.3(2)	r. 351 substituted by S.I. 1968/1016
Chapter 58, r. 58.3	r. 260B(1), (2) and (3) inserted by S.I. 1985/500
r. 58.4	r. 260B(4) inserted by S.I. 1985/500
r. 58.5	r. 260B(6) inserted by S.I. 1985/500
r. 58.6(1)	r. 260B(5) inserted by S.I. 1985/500 and as amended by S.I. 1990/705
r. 58.6(2) to (4)	r. 260B(8) to (10) inserted by S.I. 1985/500
r. 58.7	r. 260B(11) inserted by S.I. 1985/500
r. 58.8	r. 260B(13) and (14) inserted by S.I. 1985/500
r. 58.9	r. 260B(15) and (16) inserted by S.I. 1985/500
r. 58.10	r. 260B(17) to (20) inserted by S.I. 1985/500
Chapter 59, r. 59.1(2)	r. 68J(1) inserted by S.I. 1991/2483
r. 59.1(4)	r. 68J(2) inserted by S.I. 1991/2483
r. 59.1(5)	r. 68J(3) inserted by S.I. 1991/2483
Chapter 60, r. 60.2	r. 234 (part)
r. 60.3	r. 236(d) (part)
r. 60.4	r. 243
r. 60.5	r. 247
r. 60.6	r. 242(a)
r. 60.7	r. 242(b)
Chapter 61, r. 61.1(2)	r. 199
r. 61.6(1)	r. 200(a)
r. 61.6(2)	r. 200(b)
r. 61.8	r. 200(e) (preamble (part))
r. 61.9(2)	r. 200(c) (part)
r. 61.9(3)	r. 200(e)(i) (part)
r. 61.9(4)	r. 200(e)(ii) (part)
r. 61.9(5)	r. 200(d)

R.C.S. 1994 rule	Derivation (r. = rule in R.C.S. 1965)
r. 61.9(6)	r. 200(e)(i) (part)
r. 61.9(7)	r. 200(e)(iii) as amended by S.I. 1985/1600
r. 61.10	r. 200(e)(i) (part) as amended by S.I. 1967/487
r. 61.12	r. 200(g)
r. 61.13	r. 200B inserted by S.I. 1990/705
r. 61.14	r. 200A inserted by S.I. 1980/1803
r. 61.16	r. 201 (preamble) substituted by S.I. 1986/514
r. 61.17	r. 201(a) as amended by S.I. 1986/514
r. 61.18	r. 201(b) (part)
r. 61.19	r. 201(c) (part)
r. 61.20	r. 201(d) as amended by S.I. 1967/487
r. 61.21	r. 201(e)
r. 61.22	r. 201(f) (part) as amended by S.I. 1967/487
r. 61.23	r. 201(n)
r. 61.24	r. 201(g) (part)
r. 61.25(1)	r. 201(h)
r. 61.25(2)	r. 2010) (part)
r. 61.26(1)	r. 201(f) (part)
r. 61.26(2) and (3)	r. 201(k)
r. 61.27	r. 201(1)
r. 61.28	r. 201(m)
r. 61.29	r. 201(g) (part)
r. 61.30	r. 201(o)
r. 61.31(1)	r. 201Z inserted by S.I. 1991/1915
r. 61.31(2)	r. 201AA inserted by S.I. 1991/1915
r. 61.31(3)	r. 201BB(1) inserted by S.I. 1991/1915
r. 61.31(4)	r. 201CC inserted by S.I. 1991/1915
r. 61.31(5)	r. 201DD inserted by S.I. 1991/1915
r. 61.31(6) and (7)	r. 201EE inserted by S.I. 1991/1915
r. 61.32	r. 201FF inserted by S.I. 1991/1915
r. 61.33	r. 201(p)
Chapter 62, r. 62.2	P.N. No. 7 of 1988
r. 62.3	r. 249E(2)(a)(v) inserted by S.I. 1986/1941
r. 62.5(1)	r. 248(a) (part)
r. 62.5(2)	r. 249.1
r. 62.6	r. 248(a) (part), and r. 249.2 as amended by S.I. 1980/891
r. 62.7(1)	r. 248(b) as amended by S.I. 1980/891, and r. 249.5(1)
r. 62.7(2) and (3)	r. 248(c) and 249.5(2) and (3)
r. 62.8(1)	r. 249.6
r. 62.8(2) and (3)	r. 248(d) as amended by S.I. 1986/1941, and r. 249.7 as amended by S.I. 1986/1941
r. 62.9	r. 248(e) as amended by S.I. 1986/1941, and r.

R.C.S. 1994 rule	Derivation (r. = rule in R.C.S. 1965)
	249.8
r. 62.10(1) and (2)	r. 249.9
r. 62.10(3)	r. 248(f) (part) and r. 249.11
r. 62.10(4)	r. 248(g)
r. 62.11	r. 248(h) and r. 249.13
r. 62.12(2)	r. 249A.1 inserted by S.I. 1971/1809
r. 62.13	r. 249A.2 and 3 inserted by S.I. 1971/1809
r. 62.14	r. 249A.5 inserted by S.I. 1971/1809
r. 62.15(1)	r. 249A.6 inserted by S.I. 1971/1809
r. 62.15(3)	r. 249A.7(3) (part) inserted by S.I. 1971/1809
r. 62.16	r. 249A.7(1) and (2) inserted by S.I. 1971/1809
r. 62.17	r. 249A.8 and 9 inserted by S.I. 1971/1809
r. 62.18	r. 296F inserted by S.I. 1972/1982
r. 62.19	r. 296G inserted by S.I. 1972/1982
r. 62.20(1)	r. 296H(i) (part) inserted by S.I. 1972/1982
r. 62.20(2)	r. 296H(iii)(a) and (b) inserted by S.I. 1972/1982
r. 62.20(3)	r. 296H(ii) (part) inserted by S.I. 1972/1982
r. 62.21(1)	r. 296H(i) (part) inserted by S.I. 1972/1982
r. 62.23	r. 296H(iv) (part) inserted by S.I. 1972/1982
r. 62.24	r. 296J inserted by S.I. 1972/1982
r. 62.25	r. 296K inserted by S.I. 1972/1982
r. 62.26(2)	r. 249D(1) (part) inserted by S.I. 1986/1941
r. 62.28(1)	r. 249E(1)(a) inserted by S.I. 1986/1941
r. 62.28(2) and (3)	r. 249E(2) and (3) inserted by S.I. 1986/1941
r. 62.29(1)	r. 249G(3) inserted by S.I. 1986/1941
r. 62.30	r. 249G(1) and (2) inserted by S.I. 1986/1941
r. 62.31	r. 249H inserted by S.I. 1986/1941
r. 62.32	r. 2491 inserted by S.I. 1986/1941
r. 62.33	r. 249J(1) inserted by S.I. 1986/1941
r. 62.34	r. 249K inserted by S.I. 1986/1941
r. 62.35	r. 249L inserted by S.I. 1986/1941
r. 62.36	r. 249M inserted by S.I. 1986/1941
r. 62.37	r. 249P(2), (3) and (4) inserted by S.I. 1986/1941
r. 62.38	r. 249Q(4) to (9) inserted by S.I. 1986/1941
r. 62.39	r. 249R inserted by S.I. 1986/1941
r. 62.40	r. 249N inserted by S.I. 1986/1941
r. 62.41	r. 249P(1) and (2) inserted by S.I. 1986/1941
r. 62.42	r. 249Q(1) to (3) inserted by S.I. 1986/1941
r. 62.44	r. 249B(1) to (4) inserted by S.I. 1986/799
r. 62.45	r. 249C(1) inserted by S.I. 1986/799
r. 62.46	r. 249C(2) and (3) inserted by S.I. 1986/799

R.C.S. 1994 rule		Derivation (r. = rule in R.C.S. 1965)
	r. 62.47	r. 249S(1) inserted by S.I. 1987/12 and as amended by S.I. 1990/705 and 1991/1183
	r. 62.48	r. 249T(1) substituted by S.I. 1991/1157, r. 249T(1A) inserted by S.I. 1991/1157 and as amended by S.I. 1991/1183, and r. 249T(2) inserted by S.I. 1987/12
	r. 62.49	r. 249U(1) inserted by S.I. 1987/12 and as amended by S.I. 1990/705 and 1991/1183
	r. 62.50	r. 249U(2) inserted by S.I. 1987/12 and as amended by S.I. 1990/705 and 1991/1183, and r. 249U(3) inserted by S.I. 1987/12
	r. 62.51	r. 249V inserted by S.I. 1987/12 and as amended by S.I. 1991/1183
	r. 62.52	r. 249W inserted by S.I. 1987/12 and as amended by S.I. 1990/705
	r. 62.53	r. 249X inserted by S.I. 1987/12 and as amended by S.I. 1991/1157
	r. 62.54	r. 249Y inserted by S.I. 1987/12 and as amended by S.I. 1990/705 and 1991/1183
	r. 62.55	r. 249AA inserted by S.I. 1990/705
	r. 62.57	r. 249AB inserted by S.I. 1991/2213
	r. 62.58	r. 249AC inserted by S.I. 1991/2213
Chapter 63,	r. 63.2	r. 260(d)
	r. 63.3	r. 260(c) and (e)
	r. 63.4	r. 232
	r. 63.5(1) and (2)	r. 233(a)
	r. 63.5(3)	r. 233(b)
	r. 63.6	r. 233(c)
	r. 63.7(2)	r. 233A inserted by S.I. 1992/1533
	r. 63.8	r. 233C inserted by S.I. 1992/1533
	r. 63.10(1)	r. 233B(1) inserted by S.I. 1992/1533
	r. 63.10(2)	r. 233B(2) inserted by S.I. 1992/1533
	r. 63.10(4)	r. 233H(1) inserted by S.I. 1992/1533
	r. 63.11	r. 233D inserted by S.I. 1992/1533
	r. 63.12	r. 233E inserted by S.I. 1992/1533
	r. 63.13	r. 233F inserted by S.I. 1992/1533
	r. 63.14	r. 233G inserted by S.I. 1992/1533
	r. 63.15	r. 2331 inserted by S.I. 1992/1533
Chapter 64,	r. 64.2	r. 95A(c) (part) inserted by S.I. 1972/2021, and 95A(d)(ii) substituted by S.I. 1987/1206
	r. 64.4	r. 95A(c) (part) inserted by S.I. 1972/2021
Chapter 65,	r. 65.1	r. 296A inserted by S.I. 1972/1981
	r. 65.2	r. 296B inserted by S.I. 1972/1981
	r. 65.4	r. 296C inserted by S.I. 1972/1981
	r. 65.5	r. 296D inserted by S.I. 1972/1981

R.C.S. 1994 rule		Derivation (r. = rule in R.C.S. 1965)
Chapter 66,	r. 66.3(1)	r. 102A(2) (part) inserted by S.I. 1976/283 and amended by S.I. 1982/1825
	r. 66.5	r. 102A(5) inserted by S.I. 1990/705
	r. 66.6	r. 102A(3) inserted by S.I. 1976/283
	r. 66.7	r. 102A(4) inserted by S.I. 1978/955
Chapter 67	inserted by SSI 2009/283	
Chapter 67 (old),	r. 67.1(2)	r. 219(1) substituted by S.I. 1984/997
	r. 67.2	rr. 220(2), 221(2), 222(2) and 226(2), substituted by S.I. 1984/997
	r. 67.3	r. 230(6) substituted by S.I. 1984/997
	r. 67.4	r. 230(8) substituted by S.I. 1984/997
	r. 67.5(1)(a) and (b)	r. 222(9)(a) substituted by S.I. 1984/997
	r. 67.5(1)(c)	r. 220(8)(a) substituted by S.I. 1984/997
	r. 67.5(2)(a)	r. 222(9)(b) substituted by S.I. 1984/997
	r. 67.5(2)(b)	r. 220(4) substituted by S.I. 1984/997
	r. 67.5(2)(c)	r. 220(8)(b) substituted by S.I. 1984/997
	r. 67.5(3)	r. 230(1) substituted by S.I. 1984/997
	r. 67.6(1)	r. 230(5) substituted by S.I. 1984/997
	r. 67.7	r. 230(7) substituted by S.I. 1984/997
	r. 67.9(1)	r. 220(1) substituted by S.I. 1984/997
	r. 67.9(2)	r. 220(3) substituted by S.I. 1984/997
	r. 67.9(3)	r. 220(5) substituted by S.I. 1984/997
	r. 67.10(1) and (2)	r. 220(6) and (7) substituted by S.I. 1984/997
	r. 67.10(3) to (7)	r. 225 substituted by S.I. 1984/997
	r. 67.11(1)	r. 224(1) substituted by S.I. 1984/997
	r. 67.11(2)	r. 224(4) substituted by S.I. 1984/997
	r. 67.11(3)	r. 220(8) substituted by S.I. 1984/997
	r. 67.11(4)	r. 220(9) substituted by S.I. 1984/997
	r. 67.12(1)	r. 220(8)(c) substituted by S.I. 1984/997
	r. 67.12(3)	r. 220(14) substituted by S.I. 1984/997
	r. 67.12(4)	r. 230(2) substituted by S.I. 1984/997
	r. 67.13	r. 220(10) to (13) substituted by S.I. 1984/997
	r. 67.14(1) to (4) and (6)	r. 221(1) to (5) substituted by S.I. 1984/997
	r. 67.14(5)	r. 224(5) substituted by S.I. 1984/997
	r. 67.15(2) to (5)	r. 221(6) to (9) substituted by S.I. 1984/997
	r. 67.16	r. 221(10) substituted by S.I. 1984/997
	r. 67.17	r. 226(1) substituted by S.I. 1984/997
	r. 67.18	r. 227(1)(b) and (2)(b) substituted by S.I. 1984/997
	r. 67.20	r. 222(3) substituted by S.I. 1984/997
	r. 67.21	r. 222(7) and (8) substituted by S.I. 1984/997

R.C.S. 1994 rule		Derivation (r. = rule in R.C.S. 1965)
	r. 67.22(1)	r. 222(1) substituted by S.I. 1984/997
	r. 67.22(2)	r. 222(4) substituted by S.I. 1984/997
	r. 67.23(1) and (2)	r. 222(5) and (6) substituted by S.I. 1984/997
	r. 67.23(3) to (7)	r. 225 substituted by S.I. 1984/997
	r. 67.24(1)	r. 224(2) and (3) substituted by S.I. 1984/997
	r. 67.24(2)	r. 224(6) substituted by S.I. 1984/997
	r. 67.24(3) and (4)	r. 222(9) and (10) substituted by S.I. 1984/997
	r. 67.25	r. 222(11) to (14) substituted by S.I. 1984/997
	r. 67.26	r. 222(16) substituted by S.I. 1984/997
	r. 67.27(1) and (2)	r. 223 substituted by S.I. 1984/997
	r. 67.28(1)	r. 227(1)(a) and (c) substituted by S.I. 1984/997
	r. 67.28(2)	r. 227(2)(a) and (c) substituted by S.I. 1984/997
	r. 67.28(3) and (4)	r. 227(3) substituted by S.I. 1984/997
	r. 67.29	r. 228 substituted by S.I. 1984/997
	r. 67.30	r. 229 substituted by S.I. 1984/997
	r. 67.31	r. 230(3) substituted by S.I. 1984/997
	r. 67.32	r. 230(4) substituted by S.I. 1984/997
	r. 67.33	r. 230A inserted by S.I. 1978/1373 and as amended by S.I. 1984/997
	r. 67.34	r. 230B inserted by S.I. 1978/1373 and as amended by S.I. 1984/997
	r. 67.35	r. 230C(1), (2) and (4) inserted by S.I. 1978/ 1373
	r. 67.36	r. 230C(3) inserted by S.I. 1978/1373
	r. 67.40	r. 230J inserted by S.I. 1978/1373 and as amended by S.I. 1984/997
	r. 67.41	r. 2301 inserted by S.I. 1978/1373 and as amended by S.I. 1984/997
Chapter 68,	r. 68.2	r. 2 substituted by S.I. 1992/1422
	r. 68.3	r. 3 substituted by S.I. 1992/1422
	r. 68.4	r. 4 substituted by S.I. 1992/1422
	r. 68.5	r. 5 substituted by S.I. 1992/1422
	r. 68.6	r. 6 substituted by S.I. 1992/1422
	r. 68.7	r. 8 substituted by S.I. 1992/1422
Chapter 69,	r. 69.2	r. 298 as amended by S.I. 1979/516 and 1985/ 1426
	r. 69.3	r. 297(a) as amended by S.I. 1979/516, and r. 299(a) as amended by S.I. 1991/2483
	r. 69.4(1)	r. 299A inserted by S.I. 1985/1426
	r. 69.4(3)	r. 300 as amended by S.I. 1985/1426
	r. 69.5	r. 303 as amended by S.I. 1985/1426
	r. 69.6(1)(a) and (b)	r. 304(6)
	r. 69.6(1)(c)	r. 304(e)
	r. 69.6(2)	r. 305

R.C.S. 1994 rule		Derivation (r. = rule in R.C.S. 1965)
	r. 69.6(3)	r. 306(c) (part)
	r. 69.8	r. 307 as amended by S.I. 1979/516 and 1985/1426
	r. 69.9	r. 308 as amended by S.I. 1979/516 and 1985/1426
	r. 69.10	r. 312
	r. 69.11	r. 310 as amended by S.I. 1985/1426
	r. 69.12	r. 311 as amended by S.I. 1985/1426
	r. 69.13	r. 313 as amended by S.I. 1985/1426
	r. 69.14	r. 314
	r. 69.15	r. 315
	r. 69.16	r. 317 as amended by S.I. 1979/516
	r. 69.17	r. 316
	r. 69.18	r. 318(1) as amended by S.I. 1985/1426
	r. 69.19(1), (2) and (3)	r. 320 as amended by S.I. 1985/1426
	r. 69.19(4)	r. 321
	r. 69.20	r. 322
	r. 69.21	r. 324
	r. 69.22	r. 323
	r. 69.23	r. 325 as amended by S.I. 1985/1426
	r. 69.24	r. 326
	r. 69.25	r. 327 as amended by S.I. 1985/1426
	r. 69.26	r. 328 as amended by S.I. 1979/516 and 1985/1426
	r. 69.27	r. 329 as amended by S.I. 1985/1426
	r. 69.28	r. 330
	r. 69.29(1)	r. 309
Chapter 70,	r. 70.1	r. 260H(2) inserted by S.I. 1986/1955
	r. 70.2	r. 260J(6), and 260K(9), inserted by S.I. 1986/1955
	r. 70.3	r. 260L(1) inserted by S.I. 1986/1955
	r. 70.4	r. 260L(2) inserted by S.I. 1986/1955
	r. 70.5(1)	r. 260.1(1) inserted by S.I. 1986/1955 and as amended by S.I. 1991/1157
	r. 70.5(2) and (3)	r. 260J(2) and (3) inserted by S.I. 1986/1955
	r. 70.6(1) and (2)	r. 260J(4) inserted by S.I. 1986/1955, and r. 260J(5) inserted by S.I. 1986/1955 and as amended by S.I. 1991/1157
	r. 70.7	r. 260.1(7) and (8) inserted by S.I. 1986/1955
	r. 70.8	r. 260J(9) to (12) inserted by S.I. 1986/1955
	r. 70.9	r. 260K(1) to (5) inserted by S.I. 1986/1955
	r. 70.10(1)	r. 260K(6) inserted by S.I. 1986/1955
	r. 70.10(2)	r. 260K(8) inserted by S.I. 1986/1955 and as

R.C.S. 1994 rule	Derivation (r. = rule in R.C.S. 1965)
	amended by S.I. 1991/1157
r. 70.11	r. 260K(10) inserted by S.I. 1986/1955
r. 70.12	r. 260(11) and (12) inserted by S.I. 1986/1955
r. 70.13	r. 260(13) to (16) inserted by S.I. 1986/1955
r. 70.14	r. 260(17) and (18) inserted by S.I. 1986/1955
Chapter 71, r. 71.1	r. 260P(1) inserted by S.I. 1988/615
r. 71.2(1) and (2)	r. 260Q inserted by S.I. 1988/615 and as amended by S.I. 1991/2483
r. 71.2(3)	r. 260X(3) inserted by S.I. 1988/615
r. 71.3	r. 260R inserted by S.I. 1988/615 and as amended by S.I. 1990/2118 and 1991/2483
r. 71.4	r. 260S inserted by S.I. 1988/615
r. 71.5	r. 260T inserted by S.I. 1988/615 and as amended by S.I. 1990/2118
r. 71.6	r. 260U inserted by S.I. 1988/615 and as amended by S.I. 1990/2118
r. 71.7	r. 260V inserted by S.I. 1988/615
r. 71.8	r. 260W inserted by S.I. 1988/615
r. 71.9	r. 260X(1) inserted by S.I. 1988/615
r. 71.10	r. 260X(2) inserted by S.I. 1988/615
Chapter 72, r. 72.2	P.N. No. 1 of 1987, para. 1 (part)
r. 72.5	r. 201B inserted by S.I. 1986/514
r. 72.6(1), (3), (4) and (5)	r. 201A inserted by S.I. 1986/514 and as amended by S.I. 1993/899
Chapter 73, r. 73.2	r. 189(6) inserted by S.I. 1986/1955 and as amended by S.I. 1991/2483
Chapter 74, r. 74.1(2) and (3)	r. 202(1) (part) and (2) substituted by S.I. 1986/2298
r. 74.2	r. 202(1) (part) substituted by S.I. 1986/2298, and r. 218Q (part) inserted by S.I. 1986/2298
r. 74.3	r. 218S inserted by S.I. 1986/2298
r. 74.4	r. 203(1) to (5) substituted by S.I. 1986/2298
r. 74.5	r. 204(1) to (5) substituted by S.I. 1986/2298
r. 74.6	r. 203(6), and r. 204(6), substituted by S.I. 1986/2298
r. 74.7	r. 206 substituted by S.I. 1986/2298
r. 74.8	r. 207 substituted by S.I. 1986/2298
r. 74.9	r. 205, and r. 208, substituted by S.I. 1986/2298
r. 74.10	r. 209(1), (3) and (4) substituted by S.I. 1986/2298
r. 74.11	r. 210 substituted by S.I. 1986/2298
r. 74.12	r. 212 substituted by S.I. 1986/2298
r. 74.13	r. 213 substituted by S.I. 1986/2298
r. 74.14	r. 211(2) substituted by S.I. 1986/2298
r. 74.15(1) and (2)	r. 211(1) substituted by S.I. 1986/2298

R.C.S. 1994 rule		Derivation (r. = rule in R.C.S. 1965)
	r. 74.15(3) and (4)	r. 211(3) and (4) inserted by S.I. 1991/1157
	r. 74.17	r. 214(3) substituted by S.I. 1986/2298
	r. 74.18	r. 215(1), (2), (6), (7) and (8) substituted by S.I. 1986/2298
	r. 74.19	r. 216 substituted by S.I. 1986/2298
	r. 74.21	r. 217(3) substituted by S.I. 1986/2298
	r. 74.22	r. 218(2), (6), (7) and (8) substituted by S.I. 1986/2298
	r. 74.23	r. 218B inserted by S.I. 1986/2298
	r. 74.24	r. 218C inserted by S.I. 1986/2298
	r. 74.25	r. 218E inserted by S.I. 1986/2298
	r. 74.26	r. 218D, and r. 218H, inserted by S.I. 1986/2298
	r. 74.27	r. 218F inserted by S.I. 1986/2298
	r. 74.28	r. 218G inserted by S.I. 1986/2298
	r. 74.29	r. 218J inserted by S.I. 1986/2298
	r. 74.30	r. 218K inserted by S.I. 1986/2298
	r. 74.31	r. 218L(1), (3), (4) and (5) inserted by S.I. 1986/2298
	r. 74.32	r. 218M inserted by S.I. 1986/2298 and as amended by S.I. 1991/1157
	r. 74.33	r. 218N(1) inserted by S.I. 1986/2298
	r. 74.34	r. 218N(3) substituted by S.I. 1990/705
Chapter 75,	r. 75.1(2)	r. 260M inserted by S.I. 1987/2160
	r. 75.2	r. 260N(1) and (2) inserted by S.I. 1987/2160
	r. 75.3	r. 260N(3) inserted by S.I. 1987/2160
	r. 75.4	r. 260N(4) inserted by S.I. 1987/2160
Chapter 76,	r. 76.1	r. 201C inserted by S.I. 1990/705
	r. 76.3(1)	r. 201E(1) inserted by S.I. 1990/705
	r. 76.3(2)	r. 201F(2) inserted by S.I. 1990/705
	r. 76.4(1)	r. 201G(1) inserted by S.I. 1990/705
	r. 76.4(2)	r. 201F(1) inserted by S.I. 1990/705
	r. 76.4(3)	r. 201G(4) inserted by S.I. 1990/705
	r. 76.4(4)	r. 201G(5) inserted by S.I. 1990/705
	r. 76.4(6)	r. 201G(6) inserted by S.I. 1990/705
	r. 76.5	r. 201G(7) inserted by S.I. 1990/705
	r. 76.6	r. 201G(8) inserted by S.I. 1990/705
	r. 76.7	r. 201H inserted by S.I. 1990/705
	r. 76.8	r. 201J inserted by S.I. 1990/705
	r. 76.9	r. 201K(2) inserted by S.I. 1990/705
	r. 76.10	r. 201L inserted by S.I. 1990/705
	r. 76.11(2)	r. 201M inserted by S.I. 1990/705
	r. 76.13	r. 201N inserted by S.I. 1990/705
	r. 76.14	r. 201P inserted by S.I. 1990/705
	r. 76.15	r. 201Q inserted by S.I. 1990/705

R.C.S. 1994 rule		Derivation (r. = rule in R.C.S. 1965)
	r. 76.17	r. 201R inserted by S.I. 1990/705
	r. 76.19	r. 201S inserted by S.I. 1991/1183
	r. 76.21(1)	r. 201T(1) inserted by S.I. 1991/1183
	r. 76.21(2)	r. 201U(1) inserted by S.I. 1991/1183
	r. 76.22	r. 201V(1) to (4) inserted by S.I. 1991/1183
	r. 76.23	r. 201V(5) inserted by S.I. 1991/1183
	r. 76.24	r. 201W inserted by S.I. 1991/1183
	r. 76.25	r. 201X inserted by S.I. 1991/1183
	r. 76.26	r. 201Y inserted by S.I. 1991/1183
Chapter 77,	r. 77.3	r. 231(a) (part) and (b)
	r. 77.4(1) and (2)	r. 231(d) substituted by S.I. 1976/387
	r. 77.4(3)	r. 231(e) substituted by S.I. 1976/387
	r. 77.4(4)	r. 231(f)
	r. 77.5	r. 231(j)
	r. 77.6	r. 231(g)
	r. 77.7	r. 231(h)
	r. 77.8	r. 231(k) (part)
	r. 77.9	r. 231(1)
	r. 77.10	r. 231(m)
	r. 77.11	r. 231(n)
Chapter 78,	r. 78.2(1)	r. 265(a)
	r. 78.2(2)	r. 265(b)
	r. 78.3(1)	r. 265(c) inserted by S.I. 1984/472
	r. 78.4	r. 266
Chapter 79,	r. 79.1	r. 260Y(1) and (2) inserted by S.I. 1991/2652
	r. 79.2(1) and (3)	r. 260Y(3) and (5) inserted by S.I. 2652
	r. 79.3	r. 260Y(4) inserted by S.I. 1991/2652
Chapter 80,	r. 80.2	r. 9 substituted by S.I. 1992/1422
	r. 80.3	r. 10 substituted by S.I. 1992/1422
	r. 80.4	r. 11 substituted by S.I. 1992/1422
	r. 80.5(1)	r. 11B substituted by S.I. 1992/1422

TABLE OF DESTINATIONS

Section, rule or paragraph	Destination in R.C.S. 1994
Court of Session Act 1825 (6 Geo.4, c.120)	
s.53	r.16.12(4)
National Assessors (Scotland) Act 1894 (57 & 58 Vict. C.40)	
s.2	r.12.1(2)
s.3	r.12.8
s.4	r.12.5
s.5	r.12.9
A.S. (Rules of Court, consolidation and amendment) 1965 (S.I. 1965/321)	
para.(4)	r.2.1
r.1	r.11.1
r.2	r.68.2
r.3	r.68.3
r.4	r.68.4
r.5	r.68.5
r.6	r.68.6
r.8	r.68.7
r.9	r.80.2
r.10	r.80.3
r.11	r.80.4
r.11B	r.80.5(1)
r.12(a)	r.3.1
r.12(b)	r.3.1, r.3.2(1), r.3.3(1), r.3.5(1) and r.3.6(1)
r.13(a)	r.3.2(2)
r.13(b)	r.3.3(2)
r.13(c)	r.3.6(2)
r.13(d)	r.33.12(1)
r.14	r.3(4)(2)
r.15	r.3.2(3)
r.16	r.6.4
r.17	r.6.2(2)
r.18	r.6.1
r.19	r.4.1
r.20	r.4.4(1) and (2)
r.21	r.4.6
r.23	r.4.14
r.25	r.4.5
r.26(a)	r.4.8
r.26(b)	r.4.7
r.27	r.4.9

Section, rule or paragraph	Destination in R.C.S. 1994
r.28(1)	r.4.2(3), (4) and (8)
r.28(2)	r.4.2(9)
r.29	r.4.10
r.30(1)	r.4.15(2) and (5), and r.4.16(7)
r.30(2)	r.4.15(6) and r.4.16(6)
r.30(3)	r.4.15(4) and r.4.16(4)
r.31(a)	r.4.11(1) and (2)
r.32(a)	r.4.12(1) to (4)
r.32(b)	r.4.12(5)
r.32A	r.9.1
r.34	r.9.2
r.36	r.8.1
r.37	r.12.1(1)
r.38	r.12.1(1) and r.12.5(1)
r.39(a)	r.12.3
r.39(c)	r.12.4
r.40	r.12.1(2)
r.41	r.12.1(3)
r.42	r.12.7(2) to (4)
r.43	r.12.6
r.44(b)	r.12.9
r.44(c)	r.12.2
r.45	r.12.8
r.46(a)	r.12.5(2) and (3)
r.63	r.7.9(2) and (3)
r.63A	r.7.8
r.63B	r.38.7
r.64	r.7.10
r.66	r.7.7
r.67	r.16.12(2)(part)
r.68A	r.16.4(2)
r.68B	r.10.1(2)and (3)
r.68C	r.10.2
r.68D	r.10.3
r.68E	r.10.5
r.68F	r.10.6
r.68G	r.1.3(3)
r.68H	r.5.1
r.68I	r.5.2
r.68J(1)	r.59.1(2)
r.68J(2)	r.59.1(4)
r.68J(3)	r.59.1(5)
r.69	r.13.1 and r.14.2(h)

Section, rule or paragraph	Destination in R.C.S. 1994
r.70(1)(a) and (b)	r.13.2(1) to (3) and (5)
r.70(1)(c)	r.13.2(4)
r.70(2)(b)	r.13.6(c)(ii)(part)
r.71	r.13.3
r.72(1)	r.13.4(1)(a) to (c)
r.72(2)	r.16.4(6)(part)
r.72(3)	r.13.4(3)
r.73(a)	r.4.2(1) and (7)
r.73(b)	r.4.2(2)
r.74(preamble)(part)	r.13.5(1) and (2)
r.74(preamble)(part)	r.13.6(part)
r.74(preamble)(part)	r.13.6A
r.74(a)(part)	r.16.4(4)(b)
r.74(b)	r.16.10
r.74(c)	r.16.15(2)(part)
r.74(d)	r.13.8A(1)
r.74(f)	r.13.8(2) and (3), and r.13.9(part)
r.74(g) and (h)	r.13.10 and r.13.11(part)
r.74(i)	r.16.3(4)
r.74A(1)	r.16.1(1)
r.74A(3)	r.16.1(3)
r.74A(4)	r.16.3(1), (2), (3) and (5)
r.74A(5)	r.16.4(2)(part)
r.74A(6)	r.16.4(2)(part)
r.74A(7)	r.16.4(4) and r43.5
r.74A(8)	r.16.4(2)(7)
r.74B(1)	r.16.2(2)
r.74B(3)(a)(part)	r.16.4(2)(part)
r.74B(3)(b)	r.16.4(4)
r.74B(4)	r.16.2(3)
r.74B(4)(b), (5)(b), (6)(b) and (7)(a)(part)	r.16.6(3)
r.74B(5)	r.16.2(4)
r.74B(6)	r.16.2(5)
r.74B(7)(a)(part)	r.16.6(1)
r.74B(7)(b)	r.16.4(3)
r.74B(8)	r.16.6(4)
r.75(1) and (2)	r.16.5(1)
r.75(3)	r.16.5(5)
r.75(4)	r.16.5(3)
r.75(5)	r.16.5(4)
r.75(7)	r.13.4(1)(d)
r.75A(1)	r.43.1(1)

Section, rule or paragraph	Destination in R.C.S. 1994
r.75A(2)	r.43.1(2)(part)
r.75A(3)	r.43.14(2)
r.75A(4)	r.43.16(1)
r.75A(5)	r.43.16(2) and (3)
r.75A(6)	r.43.15
r.75A(7)(part)	r.43.17
r.75A(9) and (10)	r.43.18(1)
r.75A(11)	r.43.19(1)
r.76	r.13.12
r.78(a) to (c) (e)	r.13.13(1) to (5)
r.78(d)	r.4.4(3)
r.79(1)(part) and (2)	r.23.9(part)
r.80(a)	r.13.14
r.81(1)	r.17.1(1)
r.81(1B)	r.17.1(2)
r.81(2)	r.17.2
r.82	r.16.11
r.83(a)	r.18.1(2)
r.83(b)	r.18.1(1)
r.83(d)	r.4.6(1)(b)
r.83(e)	r.18.2
r.84(a)	r.25.1(1)(part) and (2)
r.84(b)	r.25.1(3)
r.84(c)	r.25.2
r.84(d)	r.25.4(1)
r.84(e)	r.29.2
r.84(f)	r.25.4(2)
r.84(g)	r.25.5
r.84(h)	r.25.6
r.84(j)	r.25.1(preamble)(part)
r.84(k)	r.25.3
r.85(1)(preamble)	r.26.1(1), r.26.2 and r.26.5
r.85(1)(a)	r.26.4
r.85(1)(b)	r.26.3
r.85(1)(c)	r.26.7(1)
r.85(1)(e)	r.26.7(3) and (4)
r.85(1)(g)	r.26.1(2)
r.85(2)	r.26.1(2)
r.86	r.17.1(3)
r.88A	r.44.1(2)
r.88B	r.44.2
r.88C	r.44.3
r.88D	r.44.4

Section, rule or paragraph	Destination in R.C.S. 1994
r.88E	r.44.5
r.88F	r.44.6
r.88G(3)	r.38.3(2)
r.88H	r.44.7
r.89(a)	r.19.1(1) and (2)
r.89(aa)	r.19.1(4)
r.89(ab)	r.19.2(1)
r.89(b)	r.19.1(5)
r.89(c)	r.19.1(6)
r.89(d)	r.19.2(5)
r.89(e) and (f)	r.19.2(2), (3) and (4)
r.89(i)	r.19.1(7)
r.89(j)	r.19.2(7)
r.89A(1)(a) to (g)	r.43.1(1) to (8)
r.89A(1)(h)	r.43.11(9)(part)
r.89A(2)	r.43.12
r.89B(1)	r.21.1
r.89B(2) to (6)	r.21.2
r.89B(7)	r.21.3(1)
r.89B(8)	r.38.3(1)
r.90(1)	r.22.1(1)
r.90(2)	r.22.1(3)
r.90(3)	r.22.2(3)
r.90(4)	r.22.2(1)
r.90(5)	r.22.2(2)
r.90A(2)(a) and (3)	r.22.2(4) and (5)
r.91(1)	r.22.3(1)
r.91(2)	r.22.3(2)
r.91(3)	r.22.3(5)
r.91(5)	r.22.3(3)
r.91(6)	r.22.3(6)
r.91A	r.29.1
r.91B	r.34.1(part)
r.91C	r.6.2(5) to (11)
r.92(1) and (3)	r.24.1
r.92(2)	r.24.4
r.92(3)	r.24.3(1)
r.92(4)	r.24.5
r.93(a)	r.23.2(1)
r.93(b)(part) and (c)(part)	r.23.2(2)
r.93(b) (part)	r.23.3(5)
r.93(c)	r.23.3(1) and (3)
r.93(d)(part)	r.23.2(7) and r.23.6(1)

Section, rule or paragraph	Destination in R.C.S. 1994
r.93(e)	r.23.4(1), (4), (5) and (6)
r.93(f)	r.23.12
r.93A	r.4.15(3)
r.94(a)	r.6.2(3)
r.94(c)	r.28.1(1) and (2)
r.94(d)	r.20.1(b), (3) and (4)
r.94(e)	r.28.1(4)
r.95(a)(part)	r.35.2(5) and (6)
r.95(b)	r.35.2(1), (2) and (3)
r.95A(a)(part)	r.35.2(5) and (6)
r.95A(b)	r.35.2(1), (2) and (3), and r.35.2(4)
r.95A(c)(part)	r.64.7
r.95A(c)(part) and (d)(ii)	r.64.2(1)
r.95A(d)	r.35.2(1)(b)
r.96(a) to (f)	r.35.3
r.97	r.35.4
r.98	r.35.8
r.100	r.35.11
r.101	r.35.11
r.102	r.35.15
r.102A(2)	r.66.3(1) and (2)
r.102A(3)	r.66.6
r.102A(4)	r.66.7
r.102A(5)	r.66.5r.66.5
r.103(a) to (c)	r.35.9
r.104	r.35.10
r.104A	r.32.2
r.104B	r.32.1
r.105	r.23.3(4)
r.106	r.31.1 and r.31.2
r.106A	r.36.2(2)
r.106B	r.36.2(5)
r.107	r.36.3 and r.36.5
r.108	r.36.1
r.109	r.36.7
r.110	r.36.11(2)
r.111((a) to (d)	r.36.9
r.112	r.36.13(1) to (4)
r.113(a)	r.36.11(1), (4) and (5)
r.113(b)	r.36.11(3) and (8)
r.113(c)	r.36.11(9)
r.113(d)	r.36.11(6)
r.114(1) to (5)	r.37.1(1) to (5)

Section, rule or paragraph	Destination in R.C.S. 1994
r.114(6)	r.37.1(6) and (7)
r.114(7)	r.37.1(9)
r.116(b)	r.37.8
r.117	r.38.5(2)
r.117A(1)	r.37.2(1)
r.117A(2)	r.37.2(4)
r.119(a) and (c)	r.37.3
r.119(b)	r.37.2(5)
r.121	r.37.4(part)
r.122	r.37.4(part)
r.122A(1)	r.37.6
r.122A(2)	r.36.10 and r.37.4(part)
r.123	r.37.4(part)
r.124	r.37.7
r.125(a)	r.37.9
r.125(b)	r.37.10
r.125(c)	r.39.6(3)
r.126(a)	r.93.1(1) to (3)
r.127	r.37.4(part) and r.37.5
r.134B	r.43.2(2)
r.134C	r.43.13
r.134D	r.38.3
r.134E	r.27.1
r.135	r.46.1
r.136	r.46.2
r.137(a) and (b)	r.46.3
r.138	r.46.4
r.140(a)	r.16.13(1)(part), (3) and (4)
r.140(b)	r.16.14
r.140(c)	r.16.15(2)(part)
r.140(d)	r.13.11
r.140(dd)	r.13.11
r.142	r.46.4(4) and (5)
r.143	r.46.5
r.144	r.46.6
r.145	r.46.7
r.146	r.12.7(1)
r.147	r.46.8
r.147A	r.46.9
r.148(3)	r.47.3(1)
r.149	r.47.2
r.153A(1)	r.48.2
r.153A(2)	r.48.1(1)

Section, rule or paragraph	Destination in R.C.S. 1994
r.153B	r.48.1(2)
r.153C	r.38.1
r.154(1)	r.48.3
r.154(1)	r.49.1(1)
r.154(2)	r.49.1(2)
r.155(1) and (2)	r.49.8(1)(b)
r.155(3)(a) and (4)	r.49.8(1)(a)
r.155(3)(b) and (4)	r.49.8(1)(c)
r.155(5)	r.49.8(1)(d)
r.155(6)	r.49.8(1)(e)
r.155(7)	r.49.8(1)(j)
r.155A(1)	r.49.7(1)
r.157(1)	r.49.4
r.157(3)	r.49.2
r.159(2)	r.49.12
r.159(5) and (6)	r.49.13
r.161	r.49.14
r.162	r.49.9
r.164	r.49.15(1)
r.165	r.49.16
r.166	r.49.19
r.167(1)	r.49.17(1) to (7)
r.167(2)	r.49.18
r.168(1), (2), (5) and (6)	r.49.28(1) to (4)
r.168(3)	r.1.3(2)
r.168(7) to (11)(part)	r.49.29
r.168(11)(part)	r.7.2(1)
r.168A	r.49.33(5)(part)
r.169	r.49.34
r.170A	r.49.30
r.170B(1)(b)	r.49.35(1)
r.170B(3) and (4)	r.49.31(part)
r.170B(5)	r.49.27
r.170B(6)(a)	r.49.8(1)(e)
r.170B(6)(b)(i) and (7)(a)(ii)	r.49.37
r.170B(6)(b)(ii)	r.49.38
r.170B(10)	r.49.42(1) to (4) and r.49.43
r.170B(11)	r.49.3(1)
r.170B(12)	r.49.24
r.170B(13)	r.49.25(1)(part)
r.170B(14)(c), (d), (f) and (g)(part)	r.49.20(1), (4) and (5)(part)
r.170B(14)(e) and (g)(part)	r.49.21(1) and (2)(part)
r.170B(15)	r.49.23(part)

Section, rule or paragraph	Destination in R.C.S. 1994
r.170C(2)	r.49.25(1)(part)
r.170D(1), (2)(part) and (4)(a)	r.49.46(part)
r.170D(2), (4)(1), (5) and (7)(b)	r.49.31
r.170D(3), (7)(a) and (8)	r.49.49
r.170D(4)(a)	r.49.51(1)
r.170D(4)(c)	r.49.80(1)(j)
r.170D(6)	r.7.11(2)
r.170D(7)(c)	r.49.50 and 49.51(2)
r.170D(9)	r.49.8(1)(i)
r.170D(11)	r.49.45(1)
r.170E	r.49.72(1) to (3)
r.170F	r.49.73
r.170G	r.49.74(1)
r.170H(1)	r.48.72(4)
r.170H(2)	r.49.74(2)
r.170I(1)	r.49.75(1)
r.170E(3)	r.49.75(2)
r.170J	r.49.77
r.170K.	r.7.2(2)
r.170L	r.49.80
r.170M	r.49.53
r.170N	r.49.55
r.170P	r.49.56
r.170R	r.49.57
r.171	r.53.3(1)
r.172	r.53.4(1)
r.173(part)	r.53.3(4), r.53.4(2) and r.53.7
r.174	r.53.8
r.175	r.51.2
r.176(a) and (b)(part)	r.51.3(part)
r.176(b)(part)	r.51.4(1)(part), (2) and (4)
r.177(a)	r.51.4(1)(part)
r.177(b)	r.51.4(3)
r.178	r.51.8 and r.51.9
r.179	r.51.7(3)
r.180	r.51.6
r.181	r.51.11
r.182(a)(part)	r.51.5(1) and (2)(a)
r.182(c)	r.51.7(1)
r.183	r.51.12(1) and 51.13
r.184	r.51.14
r.185	r.51.12(2)
r.186	r.52.1

Section, rule or paragraph	Destination in R.C.S. 1994
r.187	r.52.2
r.188	r.52.3
r.188A(a)(part)	r.54.1
r.188A(a)(part) and (b)	r.54.2
r.188B(1)	r.50.1
r.188B(2), (3), (5) and (6)	r.50.5(1) and (2)
r.188B(3) and (4)(part)	r.50.2(4)
r.188B(4)(part) and (5)	r.50.2(5)
r.188B(6)(part)	r.50.2(6)
r.188B(8) and (9)	r.50.6
r.188D(1)(c)	r.49.64
r.188D(2), (4)(b) and (5)	r.49.65
r.188D(3)	r.49.67(1)
r.188D(4)(part) and (5)(part)	r.49.46(part)
r.188D(6)	r.49.68
r.188D(7)(a) and (b)	r.49.66
r.188D(7) and (9)	r.49.67(2)
r.188D(7) and (10)	r.49.8(1)(k)
r.188D(11)	r.49.69
r.188D(12)	r.49.70(1)
r.188D(13)	r.49.70(2)
r.188D(15)	r.49.71(1)
r.189(a)(preamble), (i), (ii), (iii), (iv) and (xxxvii)	r.14.2
r.189(b)	r.73.2
r.190(preamble), (i) and (iv) to (xi)	r.14.3(a) to (j)
r.191	r.14.4
r.192(1)	r.14.6(1)(a) to (c)
r.192(2)	r.16.4(6)
r.192(3)	r.14.6(2)
r.193	r.4.2(3) and (4)
r.194	r.4.4(3)
r.195(a)	r.14.5 and r.14.7(1)
r.195(c)	r.14.7(2)
r.195(d)	r.16.1(4)
r.196(a)	r.18.3(3)
r.196(b)	r.18.3(2)
r.197(preamble)	r.14.9(1)
r.197(a)	r.14.9(2)
r.197(b)	r.14.9(3)
r.197(c)	r.14.9(4)
r.197(d)	r.14.9(5)
r.198	r.23.2(2)

Section, rule or paragraph	Destination in R.C.S. 1994
r.198A	r.34.1(part)
r.199	r.61.1(2)
r.200(a)	r.61.6(1)
r.200(b)	r.61.6(2)
r.200(c)(part)	r.61.9(2)
r.200(d)	r.61.9(5)
r.200(e)(part)	r.61.8, r.61.9(3), (4), (6) and (7), and r.61.10
r.200(g)	r.61.12
r.200A	r.61.14
r.200B	r.61.13
r.201(preamble)	r.61.16
r.201(a)	r.61.17
r.201(b)(part)	r.61.18
r.201(c)(part)	r.61.19
r.201(d)	r.61.20
r.201(e)	r.61.21
r.201(f)	r.61.22 and r.61.26(1)
r.201(g)	r.61.24 and r.61.29
r.201(h)	r.61.25(1)
r.201(j)(part)	r.61.25(2)
r.201(k)	r.61.26(2) and (3)
r.201(l)	r.61.27
r.201(m)	r.61.28
r.201(n)	r.61.23
r.201(o)	r.61.30
r.201(p)	r.61.33
r.201A	r.72.6(1), (3), (4) and (5)
r.201B	r.72.5
r.201C	r.76.1
r.201E(1)	r.76.3(1)
r.201F(1)	r.76.4(2)
r.201F(2)	r.76.3(2)
r.201G(1)	r.76.4(1)
r.201G(4)	r.76.4(3)
r.201G(5)	r.76.4(4)
r.201G(6)	r.76.4(6)
r.201G(7)	r.76.5
r.201G(8)	r.76.6
r.201H	r.76.7
r.201J	r.76.8
r.201K(2)	r.76.9
r.201L	r.76.10

Section, rule or paragraph	Destination in R.C.S. 1994
r.201M	r.76.11(2)
r.201N	r.76.13
r.201P	r.76.14
r.201Q	r.76.15
r.201R	r.76.17
r.201S	r.76.19
r.201T(1)	r.76.21(1)
r.201U(1)	r.76.21(2)
r.201V(1) to (4)	r.76.22
r.201V(5)	r.76.23
r.201W	r.76.24
r.201X	r.76.25
r.201Y	r.76.26
r.201Z	r.61.31(1)
r.201AA	r.61.31(2)
r.201BB(1)	r.61.31(3)
r.201CC	r.61.31(4)
r.201DD	r.61.31(5)
r.201EE	r.61.31(6) and (7)
r.201FF	r.61.32
r.202(1)(part) and (2)	r.74.1(2) and (3)
r.202(1)(part)	r.74.2
r.203(1) to (5)	r.74.4
r.203(6)	r.74.6(part)
r.204(1) to (5)	r.74.5
r.204(6)	r.74.6(part)
r.205	r.74.9(part)
r.206	r.74.7
r.207	r.74.8
r.208	r.74.9(part)
r.209(1), (3) and (4)	r.74.10
r.210	r.74.11
r.211(1)	r.74.15(1)and (2)
r.211(2)	r.74.14
r.211(3) and (4)	r.74.15(3) and (4)
r.212	r.74.12
r.213	r.74.13
r.214(3)	r.74.17
r.215(1), (2), (6), (7) and (8)	r.74.18
r.216	r.74.19
r.217(3)	r.74.21
r.218(2), (6), (7) and (8)	r.74.22
r.218A(1)	r.5.1(d)

Section, rule or paragraph	Destination in R.C.S. 1994
r.218B	r.74.23
r.218C	r.74.24
r.218D	r.74.26(part)
r.218E	r.74.25
r.218F	r.74.27
r.218G	r.74.28
r.218H	r.74.26(part)
r.218J	r.74.29
r.218K	r.74.30
r.218L(1), (3), (4) and (5)	r.74.31
r.218M	r.74.32
r.218N(1)	r.74.33
r.218N(3)	r.74.34
r.218Q(2)	r.74.2
r.218S	r.74.3
r.219(1)	r.67.1(2)
r.220(1)	r.67.9(1)
r.220(2)	r.67.2(part)
r.220(3)	r.67.9(2)
r.220(4)	r.67.5(2)(b)
r.220(5)	r.67.9(3)
r.220(6) and (7)	r.67.10(1) and (2)
r.220(8)	r.67.11(3)
r.220(8)(a)	r.67.5(1)(c)
r.220(8)(b)	r.67.5(2)(c)
r.220(8)(c)	r.67.12(1)
r.220(9)	r.67.11(4)
r.220(10) to (13)	r.67.13
r.220(14)	r.67.12(3)
r.221(1) to (5)	r.67.14(1) to (4) and (6)
r.221(2)	r.67.2
r.221(6) to (9)	r.67.15(2) to (5)
r.221(10)	r.67.16
r.222(1)	r.67.22(1)
r.222(2)	r.67.2
r.222(3)	r.67.20
r.222(4)	r.67.22(2)
r.222(5) and (6)	r.67.23(1) and (2)
r.222(7) and (8)	r.67.21
r.222(9) and (10)	r.67.24(3) and (4)
r.222(11) to (14)	r.67.25
r.222(16)	r.67.26
r.223	r.67.27(1) and (2)

Section, rule or paragraph	Destination in R.C.S. 1994
r.224(1)	r.67.11(1)
r.224(2) and (3)	r.67.24(1)
r.224(4)	r.67.11(2)
r.224(5)	r.67.14(5)
r.224(6)	r.67.24(2)
r.225	r.67.10(3) to (7), and r.67.23(3) to (7)
r.226(1)	r.67.17
r.226(2)	r.67.2(part)
r.227(1)(a) and (c)	r.67.28(1)
r.227(1)(b) and (2)(b)	r.67.18
r.227(2)(a) and (c)	r.67.28(2)
r.227(3)	r.67.28(3) and (4)
r.228	r.67.29
r.229	r.67.30
r.230(1)	r.67.5(3)
r.230(2)	r.67.12(4)
r.230(3)	r.67.31
r.230(4)	r.67.32
r.230(5)	r.67.6(1)
r.230(6)	r.67.3
r.230(7)	r.67.7
r.230(8)	r.67.4
r.230A	r.67.33
r.230B	r.67.34
r.230C(1), (2) and (4)	r.67.35
r.230C(3)	r.67.36
r.230E	r.67.37
r.230F	r.67.38(1) to (4), (6) and (7)
r.230G	r.67.38(5)
r.230H	r.67.39
r.230I	r.67.41
r.230J	r.67.40
r.231(a)(part) and (b)	r.77.3
r.231(d)	r.77.4(1) and (2)
r.231(e)	r.77.4(3)
r.231(f)	r.77.4(4)
r.231(g)	r.77.6
r.231(h)	r.77.7
r.231(j)	r.77.5
r.231(k)(part)	r.77.8
r.231(l)	r.77.9
r.231(m)	r.77.10
r.231(n)	r.77.11

Section, rule or paragraph	Destination in R.C.S. 1994
r.232	r.63.4
r.233(a)	r.63.5(1) and (2)
r.233(b)	r.63.5(3)
r.233(c)	r.63.6
r.233A	r.63.7(2)
r.233B(1)	r.63.10(1)
r.233B(2)	r.63.10(2)
r.233C	r.63.8
r.233D	r.63.11
r.233E	r.63.12
r.233F	r.63.13
r.233G	r.63.14
r.233H	r.63.10(4)
r.233I	r.63.15
r.234(part)	r.60.2
r.236(b)	r.23.9(part)
r.236(d)(part)	r.60.3
r.238(a)	r.33.6
r.238(c)	r.33.7(1)
r.238(f)	r.33.9
r.240	r.33.8
r.242(a)	r.60.6
r.242(b)	r.60.7
r.243	r.60.4
r.247	r.60.5
r.248(a)	r.62.5(1) and r.62.6(part)
r.248(b)	r.62.7(1)(part)
r.248(c)	r.62.7(2) and (3)(part)
r.248(d)	r.62.8(2) and (3)(part)
r.248(e)	r.62.9(part)
r.248(f)(part)	r.62.10(3)(part)
r.248(g)	r.62.10(4)
r.248(h)	r.62.11(part)
r.249.1	r.62.5(2)
r.249.2	r.62.6(part)
r.249.5(1)	r.62.7(1)(part)
r.249.5(2) and (3)	r.62.7(2) and (3)(part)
r.249.6	r.62.8(1)
r.249.7	r.62.8(2) and (3)(part)
r.249.8	r.62.9(part)
r.249.9	r.62.10(1) and (2)
r.249.11	r.62.10(3)(part)
r.249.13	r.62.11(part)

Section, rule or paragraph	Destination in R.C.S. 1994
r.249A.1	r.62.12(2)
r.249A.2 and 3	r.62.13
r.249A.5	r.62.14
r.249A.6	r.62.15(1)
r.249A.7(1) and (2)	r.62.16
r.249A.7(3)(part)	r.62.15(3)
r.249A.8 and 9	r.62.17
r.249AA	r.62.55
r.249AB	r.62.57
r.249AC	r.62.58
r.249B(1) to (4)	r.62.44
r.249C(1)	r.62.45
r.249C(2) and (3)	r.62.46
r.249D(1)(part)	r.62.26(2)
r.249D(2)	r.62.26(3)
r.249E(1)(a)	r.62.28(1)
r.249E(2) and (3)	r.62.28(2) and (3)
r.249E(2)(a)(v)	r.62.3
r.249G(1) and (2)	r.62.30
r.249G(3)	r.62.29(1)
r.249H	r.62.31
r.249I	r.62.32
r.249J(1)	r.62.33
r.249K	r.62.34
r.249L	r.62.35
r.249M	r.62.36
r.249N	r.62.40
r.249P(1) and (2)	r.62.41
r.249P(2), (3) and (4)	r.62.37
r.249Q(1) to (3)	r.62.42
r.249Q(4) to (9)	r.62.38
r.249R	r.62.39
r.249S(1)	r.62.47
r.249T(1), (1A) and (2)	r.62.48
r.249U(1)	r.62.49
r.249U(2) and (3)	r.62.50
r.249V	r.62.51
r.249W	r.62.52
r.249X	r.62.53
r.249Y	r.62.54
r.250	r.55.1
r.251	r.55.2
r.252	r.55.3

Section, rule or paragraph	Destination in R.C.S. 1994
r.253	r.55.4
r.254	r.55.5
r.255	r.55.6
r.256	r.55.7
r.257	r.55.8
r.257A	r.55.9
r.257B	r.55.10
r.257C	r.55.11
r.257D	r.55.12
r.257E	r.55.13
r.257F	r.55.14
r.257G	r.55.15
r.257H	r.55.16
r.257I	r.55.17
r.257J	r.55.18
r.260(c) and (e)	r.63.3
r.260(d)	r.63.2
r.260B(1), (2) and (3)	r.58.3
r.260B(4)	r.58.4
r.260B(5)	r.58.6(1)
r.260B(6)	r.58.5
r.260B(8) to (10)	r.58.6(2) to (4)
r.260B(11)	r.58.7
r.260B(13) and (14)	r.58.8
r.260B(15) and (16)	r.58.9
r.260B(17) to (20)	r.58.10
r.260B(21)	r.38.4(4)
r.260C(1)	r.49.58(1)
r.260D(4), (5), (7) and (8)(part)	r.49.22(1), (4) and (5)(part)
r.260D(10)	r.49.23(part)
r.260E(1)(b)	r.49.63(1)
r.260E(2) and (3)	r.49.25(1)(part)
r.260EA	r.49.3(1)(part)
r.260EB	r.49.24(part)
r.260EC	r.49.25(1)(part)
r.260H(2)	r.70.1
r.260J(1)	r.70.5(1)
r.260J(2) and (3)	r.70.5(2) and (3)
r.260J(4) and (5)	r.70.6(1) and (2)
r.260J(6)	r.70.2(part)
r.260J(7) and (8)	r.70.7
r.260J(9) to (12)	r.70.8
r.260K(1) to (5)	r.70.9

Section, rule or paragraph	Destination in R.C.S. 1994
r.260K(6)	r.70.10(1)
r.260K(7)	r.70.10(2)
r.260K(9)	r.70.2(part)
r.260K(10)	r.70.11
r.260K(11) and (12)	r.70.12
r.260K(13) to (16)	r.70.13
r.260K(17) and (18)	r.70.14
r.260L(1)	r.70.3
r.260L(2)	r.70.4
r.260M	r.75.1(2)
r.260N(1) and (2)	r.75.2
r.260N(3)	r.75.3
r.260N(4)	r.75.4
r.260P(1)	r.71.1
r.260Q	r.71.2(1) and (2)
r.260R	r.71.3
r.260S	r.71.4
r.260T	r.71.5
r.260U	r.71.6
r.260V	r.71.7
r.260W	r.71.8
r.260X(1)	r.71.9
r.260X(2)	r.71.10
r.260X(3)	r.71.2(3)
r.260Y(1) and (2)	r.79.1
r.260Y(3) and (5)	r.79.2(1) and (3)
r.260Y(4)	r.79.3
r.261	r.38.1
r.262(a)(part)	r.38.1(part)
r.262(a) and (b)	r.38.5(1)
r.262(c)	r.38.6(1) and (3)
r.262(d)	r.38.20 and r.40.20
r.263(b)	r.38.14(1) to (3)
r.264(a)(part)	r.38.2(1) and r.38.6(5)
r.264(b)	r.38.2(4) and (5)
r.264(c)(part)	r.38.2(6) and r.38.4(2), (6) and (7)
r.264(d)	r.38.10(1)
r.264(e)	r.38.9
r.264(f)	r.36.12
r.265(a)	r.78.2(1)
r.265(b)	r.78.2(2)
r.265(c)	r.78.3(1)
r.266	r.78.4

Section, rule or paragraph	Destination in R.C.S. 1994
r.267	r.40.1
r.268(1)	r.40.4
r.268(2)	r.40.5
r.268(3) and (4)	r.40.6
r.269(a)	r.40.7(1)(part)
r.269(b)(part)	r.40.7(2), r.40.8 and r.40.15(1)
r.270	r.40.10(1) and (3)
r.271	r.40.16(1) and (2)
r.272	r.40.15(2) to (6)
r.274	r.32.3
r.275(2)	r.32.4(1)
r.275(3)	r.32.4(2)
r.275(5)	r.32.5 and r.32.6
r.275(6)	r.32.7
r.276	r.41.1 and r.41.4
r.277(a)	r.41.5(1) and (2)
r.277(b)	r.41.6
r.277(c) and (d)	r.41.7
r.277(e)	r.41.9(1)(part) and (3)
r.277(f)	r.41.9(4) and (5)
r.277(g)	r.41.9(6)
r.277(h)(i)	r.41.10(1)
r.277(h)(ii)(part)	r.41.11 (part)
r.277(j)	r.41.10(2) and (3)
r.277(k)(i)	r.41.11 (part), r.41.12(1) and r.41.13
r.277(k)(ii)	r.41.12(2)
r.277(k)(iii)	r.41.14
r.278	r.41.8
r.279	r.41.9(1) and (2)
r.280(a)	r.41.15
r.280(b)	r.41.16 and r.41.17(1)
r.281(1)(part)	r.41.23(1)
r.282(1)	r.41.25(1)
r.283(1)	r.41.26(1)
r.283(7)	r.41.26(2)
r.283(12)	r.41.26(7)
r.283(13)	r.41.26(6)
r.284(preamble)	r.41.34 and r.41.35
r.284(a)	r.41.36
r.284(b)	r.41.37
r.284(c)	r.41.38
r.286(1)	r.41.27
r.288(1)	r.41.41

Section, rule or paragraph	Destination in R.C.S. 1994
r.288(3) and (4)	r.41.42
r.289A(2)	r.41.30
r.289A(4)(part)	r.41.30
r.289A(6) and (8)	r.41.31
r.289A(7)	r.41.32
r.289A(9)	r.41.33
r.290(a)(part)	r.41.1, r.41.18 and r.41.20(1)
r.290(a)(part), (b) and (c)	r.41.19(2)
r.290(a)(part) and (d)	r.41.19(1)
r.290(e)	r.41.20(1)(b)(ii)
r.290(i)	r.41.21(1)
r.291(2)(preamble)	r.41.39
r.291(2)(a) to (d)	r.41.40
r.292(a)	r.41.21(4)
r.293	r.41.21(2)
r.293A(a) and (b)	r.41.21(5)
r.293B(5)	r.41.21(3)
r.294B(3)	r.38.18(1) and r.40.18(1)
r.294B(5)(a)	r.38.18(2) and r.40.18(2)
r.294B(5)(b)	r.38.16(2)
r.294B(6)	r.38.16(4) and r.40.14(4)
r.294C(7) and (8)	r.6.3(5) and (6)
r.295	r.4.16(2), (3) and (5)
r.296A	r.65.1
r.296B	r.65.2
r.296C	r.65.4
r.296D	r.65.5
r.296F	r.62.18
r.296G	r.62.19
r.296H(i)	r.62.20(1) and r.62.21(1)
r.296H(ii)(part)	r.62.20(3)
r.296H(iii)(a) and (b)	r.62.20(2)
r.296H(iv)(part)	r.62.23
r.296J	r.62.24
r.296K	r.62.25
r.297(a)	r.69.3(part)
r.298	r.69.2
r.299(a)	r.69.3(part)
r.299A	r.69.4(1)(part)
r.300	r.69.4(3)
r.303	r.69.5
r.304(b)	r.69.6(1)(a) and (b)
r.304(c)	r.69.6(1)(c)

Section, rule or paragraph	Destination in R.C.S. 1994
r.305	r.69.6(2)
r.306(c)	r.69.6(3)
r.307	r.69.8
r.308	r.69.9
r.309	r.69.29(1)
r.310	r.69.11
r.311	r.69.12
r.312	r.69.10
r.313	r.69.13
r.314	r.69.14
r.315	r.69.15
r.316	r.69.17
r.317	r.69.16
r.318(1)	r.69.18
r.320	r.69.19(1), (2) and (3)
r.321	r.69.19(4)
r.322	r.69.20
r.323	r.69.22
r.324	r.69.21
r.325	r.69.23
r.326	r.69.24
r.327	r.69.25
r.328	r.69.26
r.329	r.69.27
r.330	r.69.28
r.347(a)	r.42.9, r.42.10(1) and r.42.16
r.347(aa)	r.42.8(1)
r.347(b)	r.42.15
r.347(c)	r.42.5(1)
r.347(d)	r.42.14
r.347(e)	r.42.10(3) and (4)
r.347(f)	r.42.10(5)
r.347(g)	r.42.11(1) and (2)
r.347(h)	r.42.12
r.347, Table of Fees, Chapter I, note 5	r.42.10(2)
r.347, Table of Fees, Chapter II, para.8	r.42.13(1)
r.347, Table of Fees, Chapter II, para.9	r.42.13(2) and (3)
r.348(1) and (2)	r.42.1
r.348(3) and (4)	r.42.2
r.349(1)	r.42.3(1)(a)
r.349(2)	r.42.4(1)
r.349(3)	r.42.4(2)
r.349(4) to (6)	r.42.4(3) to (5)

Section, rule or paragraph	Destination in R.C.S. 1994
r.349(7)	r.38.3(5)
r.349(8)	r.42.6
r.350	r.42.7
r.350A	r.42.17
r.351	r.57.3(2)

OTHER ACTS OF SEDERUNT

RE-ALLOCATION OF DEFICIENCY OF STIPEND CAUSED BY SURRENDERS

(SR&O 1925/1060) **C2.1**

15 July 1925.

Whereas it is provided by the Church of Scotland (Property and Endowments) Act 1925, section 41, that section 106 of the Court of Session (Scotland) Act 1868, (which relates to Acts of Sederunt), shall, for the purposes of Acts of Sederunt relating to the Court of Teinds, have effect as if references to that Act in the section included reference to the Church of Scotland (Property and Endowments) Act 1925, and whereas it is, inter alia, enacted by the said Court of Session (Scotland) Act 1868, section 106, that the Court of Session may from time to time make such regulations by Act of Sederunt for altering the course of proceeding thereinbefore prescribed in respect to the matters to which that Act relates, and whereas it is provided in paragraph 8 of the Sixth Schedule of the said Church of Scotland (Property and Endowments) Act 1925, that in certain cases the deficiency of stipend caused by a surrender shall be re-allocated among the heritors in the parish (if any) who have unexhausted teinds not yet allocated for stipend, the Lords of Council and Session hereby enact and declare that:—

1. Any claim under said paragraph 8 of the Sixth Schedule to have a deficiency of stipend re-allocated among those heritors in the parish (if any) who have unexhausted teinds not yet allocated for stipend shall be disposed of either in a depending process of locality relative to the said parish or in the proceedings for adjustment of the teind roll thereof.

2. The notification which the Clerk of Teinds is required by said paragraph 8 to make to the common agent of the heritors shall be given in such depending process or in the proceedings for adjustment of the teind roll, as the case may be.

3. In the application of paragraph 8 to the case of a depending process of locality it shall not be necessary for the Clerk of Teinds to issue any certificate specifying the amounts of stipend payable by the heritors whose teinds are affected by the re-allocation. Said re-allocation shall be made in the interim or final locality, as the case may be.

REALLOCATION OF DEFICIENCY OF STIPEND CAUSED BY SURRENDERS

(S.R.& O. 1925/1060)

July 1925

Whereas it is provided by the Church of Scotland (Property and Endowments) Act 1925, section 41 that section 106 of the Court of Session (Scotland) Act 1868 (which relates to Acts of Sederunt) shall, for the purpose of Acts of Sederunt relating to the Court of Teinds, have effect as if references to that Act in the section included reference to the Church of Scotland (Property and Endowments) Act 1925 and whereas it is further enacted by the said Court of Session (Scotland) Act 1868, section 106, that the Court of Session may from time to time make such regulations by Act of Sederunt for regulating the course of procedure and the intention and operation in respect of the matters to which that Act relates; and whereas it is provided in paragraph 8 of the Sixth Schedule of the said Church of Scotland (Property and Endowments) Act 1925, that in certain cases the deficiency of stipend caused by a surrender shall be reallocated among the heritors in the parish (if any) who have unexhausted teinds not yet allocated for stipend, the Lords of Council and Session hereby enact and declare:

1. Any claim under said paragraph 8 of the Sixth Schedule to have a deficiency of stipend reallocated among those heritors in the parish (if any) who have unexhausted teinds not yet allocated for stipend shall be disposed of either in a depending process of locality relative to the said parish or in the process for adjustment of the rental thereof.

2. The notification which the Clerk of Teinds is required by said paragraph 8 to make to the designated agent of the heritors shall be given in such depending process of locality or for adjustment of rental as the case may be.

3. In the application of paragraph 8 to the case of a depending process of locality, it shall not be necessary for the Clerk of Teinds to issue any statement specifying the amount of stipend payable by the heritors whose teinds are affected by the reallocation, but such reallocation shall be made in the interim or final locality, as the case may be.

PROCEDURE UNDER SECTION 10 OF THE CHURCH OF SCOTLAND (PROPERTY AND ENDOWMENTS) ACT 1925, AND THE FOURTH SCHEDULE TO THE SAID ACT, AND FOR OTHER PURPOSES

(SR&O 1925/1062) C2.2

17 July 1925.

The Lords of Council and Session, in pursuance of the powers vested in them by the Church of Scotland (Property and Endowments) Act 1925, do hereby repeal Book H, Chapter ii, of the codifying Act of Sederunt without prejudice to any application for augmentation competently made before the passing of the said Act, or to anything following on such application or done therein, and enact and declare as follows:—

Sittings of Teind Court.—1. That the Court of the Commissioners for Teinds shall meet once a fortnight on Friday during the sitting of the Court of Session at such hours as shall be convenient.

Augmentation, Modification, and Locality

Applications under section 10, the Church of Scotland (Property and Endowments) Act 1925

1. Applications under section 10 may be made by way of summons to the Court of Teinds. The pursuer shall state in the summons as accurately as he can the date when the last application for an augmentation was made, the number of chalders modified in stipend by the court, the value of same (including any allowance for furnishing communion elements), calculated in accordance with the provisions of the Fourth Schedule of the statute, and the surplus teinds which the pursuer believes to be available to allow of augmentation in terms of the statute, and may be in the form of Schedule A hereto annexed.

Citation and Notice

2.—

(a) As soon as a summons of modification and locality is raised and signeted, it shall be competent to the pursuer to cite the titulars and tacksmen of the teinds, heritors, and liferenters, and all others having, or pretending to have, interest in the teinds of the parish, by a notice in writing affixed to the most patent door of the church, by the clerk of the kirk session or a police constable stating that the minister of the parish has raised a summons of modification and locality of his stipend which will be called in court on , being the day of next to come, not being less than six weeks after the date of the notice; and such clerk or constable shall return a certificate, subscribed by himself and two witnesses, that such notice has been affixed by him.

(b) The pursuer shall also cause notice to be inserted two several days in the *Scotsman* newspaper, and in a newspaper circulating in the county in which the parish referred to in such notice is situated, that he has raised a summons of modification and locality which will be called in court on being the day of, not being less than six weeks from the date of the first advertisement.

(c) The mode of citation and the induciae above mentioned shall be deemed sufficient although one or more of the defenders shall be a pupil or minor out of the kingdom at the time such citation shall be given.

Citation of Crown

3. When it is necessary to call the Lord Advocate on behalf of His Majesty or of the Crown, or any public department, he shall be cited upon the induciae of six weeks.

Certificates and Executions of Citation

4. Such certificate by the clerk or constable, with the notices in the newspapers above mentioned or certificate by the pursuer's agents of the due appearance in the requisite newspapers of such notices, and execution of citation to the Lord Advocate, shall be held as sufficient citation to all parties.

Death of a Defender

5. When any of the defenders die during the dependence of the process, his heir may be called by a diligence in the manner and upon the induciae hitherto used; but such diligence may be executed either by a messenger-at-arms or a constable or under the provision of the Citation Amendment (Scotland) Act 1882.

Wakening of Process

6. When it is necessary to waken a process, it must be done by a summons or by a minute of wakening, in which all parties having interest must be called in the same manner, and on the same induciae as in the original process.

Note of Stipend and Rental to be Lodged

7. The pursuer of every process of modification and locality shall, as soon as the summons is signeted, lodge with the clerk of court a note, stating the amount of the stipend, distinguishing how much is paid in money, and how much in victual, and in what species of victual, and the measure by which it is paid; and also stating the amount of the communion elements. The pursuer must also, at the same time, produce a rental of the parish, distinguishing the rent of each heritor.

First Enrolment

8. As soon as the summons is called in court the pursuer may enrol it in the Teind Motion Roll of the Lord Ordinary; and all concerned will be allowed to see the summons and writings therewith produced in the clerk's hands for fourteen days.

Second Enrolment

9. After the elapse of the time for seeing, the pursuer may enrol the cause for a remit to the clerk to report whether there are any surplus teinds in the parish.

Third Enrolment

10. When the clerk's report is prepared, the pursuer may enrol the cause to consider same and thereupon—

(a) If the clerk has reported that there appear to be no surplus teinds in the parish the Lord Ordinary may either pronounce a decree accordingly, or ordain the pursuer to lodge a condescendence giving detailed particulars of the surplus teinds in the parish alleged in the summons to be available for an augmentation in terms of the statute.

(b) If it shall appear that there are surplus teinds in the parish the Lord Ordinary shall find in general terms accordingly, and, at the same time, shall ordain the heritors or their agents to meet for the purpose of naming a person to be suggested to the Lord Ordinary as common agent for conducting the locality, and a short notice of this interlocutor shall be inserted in the *Scotsman* newspaper, and in a newspaper circulating in the county in which the parish referred to in said notice is situated, the expense thereof to be paid by the common agent out of the general fund (unless in any case the appointment of a common agent shall be dispensed with by the Lord Ordinary); and shall further ordain the heritors to produce their rights to their teinds, if they any have, in the hands of the clerk within a time to be specified in the interlocutor, not being less than three months from the date thereof; with certification that after the elapse of that time, a remit shall be made to the clerk to prepare a scheme of locality either according to the rental lodged by the pursuer in case no rights are produced, or according to the State of Teinds lodged by the common agent (or by the heritors, as the case may be) as to the rights and interests which are produced by the heritors.

(c) The Lord Ordinary may pronounce such other or further order as shall seem to him to be necessary or expedient.

Agent for Party may not be Common Agent

11. No person who is agent for the minister or titular, or for any heritor in the parish, shall be appointed common agent.

Common Agent to prepare State of Teinds

12. The common agent, after his nomination has been confirmed by the court (or the heritors, as the case may be), on the expiry of the time specified within which the heritors shall produce their rights to their teinds, shall prepare and lodge a State of Teinds.

Preparation of Locality before the Lord Ordinary

13. After the elapse of the time for the heritors producing their rights to their teinds, a remit shall be made to the clerk to prepare a scheme of locality, either according to the rental lodged by the pursuer, in case no rights are produced, or according to the State of Teinds lodged by the common agent (or by the heritors, as the case may be), in terms of section 10 of the statute; and this scheme so prepared shall immediately be approved by the Lord Ordinary as an interim scheme, according to which the minister's stipend shall be paid, until a final locality shall be settled, and the minister furnished by the common agent (or by the heritors, as the case may be) with an extracted decree, at the expense of the heritors, and for which he is entitled to take credit in his account.

Preparation and Approval of Rectified Locality

14. If it shall appear, at any period or periods, that, under an interim locality, prepared and approved of in terms of the foresaid provisions, the minister is unable through surrender of teinds or other causes affecting its efficacy to operate payment to any considerable extent of the stipend awarded to him, then and in that case it shall be competent to the Lord Ordinary, on the motion of the minister or other party interested, to appoint a new interim scheme of locality to be prepared, and also a state of arrears remaining due from the causes before specified, to be made up; and when the said rectified locality and state of arrears shall be approved of, the Lord Ordinary shall give decreet for the arrears, and the rectified locality shall subsist as a new interim rule of payment of the stipend then current, and until it be set aside by any other rule which may afterwards be granted, on cause shewn.

Heritors' Motion for Rectified Locality

15. Under the reservation after provided as to expenses, it shall be competent to any heritor or heritors, the state of whose teinds has been materially altered by decreets of valuation, or by other circumstances, which may have occurred subsequent to the approval of an interim scheme, to apply for a rectification of the locality, giving effect to the new or corrected State of Teinds; and when the rectified locality shall be approved of by the Lord Ordinary as a new rule of payment, he shall, at the same time, appoint a state of arrears to be prepared, if the state of the process and the interests of the parties render this necessary, with power to give him decreet for the same.

New Interim Scheme on Account of Surrenders

16. Where any new interim scheme or schemes shall be rendered necessary by surrenders, or by production of rights made by heritors, or by any other unexpected emergency occurring subsequent to the previous interim scheme or schemes, it shall be competent to the Lord Ordinary to lay the expense of the new interim scheme and state of arrears, or such part thereof as may appear proper, on the party whose surrender, or productions or proceedings as aforesaid, shall make such new interim scheme necessary, unless such heritor or heritors shall be able to instruct a reasonable cause to the contrary to the satisfaction of the Lord Ordinary; in which last case the expense shall be defrayed by the common agent (if any).

Preparation of Final Locality

17. That as soon as proceedings with regard to the interim locality are concluded, a scheme of a final locality shall be forthwith prepared, and the common agent shall distribute copies of this state and scheme among the agents for the heritors, as soon as may be after such state and scheme are prepared; and no new scheme shall thereafter be received, except upon payment of such expenses as may be occasioned by such new production, to be modified by the Lord Ordinary.

Disposal of Objections to Final Locality

18. After the foresaid state and scheme shall have been distributed among the heritors, the Lord Ordinary shall ordain objections thereto to be given in by any of the heritors who think themselves aggrieved by the proposed mode of allocation; and the Lord Ordinary may either hear parties viva voce upon such objections, and the answers that may be made thereto at the bar; or he may, if he shall see cause, allow all concerned to give in written answers to such objections within such time as he shall think & proper to appoint, and shall thereafter proceed, in so far as regards any application for prorogating the time for giving in papers, in the manner directed by section 12 of the Court of Session Act 1825[1].

[1] Now repealed: see the Court of Session Act 1988 (c. 36), Sched. 2, Pts. I and III.

Review of Lord Ordinary's Judgment

19. When the Lord Ordinary has pronounced a judgment, other than a finding or decree as to surplus teinds, it may be reviewed by the Division to which the cause belongs by giving in a note, which must be lodged within twenty-one days after the date of the judgment complained of, and the procedure on that note shall be the same as in reviewing judgments of a Lord Ordinary in the Court of Session.

Form of Extract of Decreets of Locality and Warrants of Charge

20. Decreets of locality and warrants of charge shall be issued, in the form and to the effect of the schedules B and C respectively hereto annexed, as nearly as the circumstances of each case may admit of: Reserving always right to parties so advised, to take full extracts, according to the ancient form, when they require the same, in terms of the statute; Provided also, that the dues of extract in whatever form the same may be given out, shall be charged in precise conformity with the statute.

SCHEDULES REFERRED TO

SCHEDULE A

SUMMONS OF MODIFICATION AND LOCALITY[1]

GEORGE THE FIFTH, ETC.—Whereas it is humbly meant and shewn to us by our lovite(s), The Reverend (*name*), the present Minister of the Parish of..........in the Presbytery of..........and County of..........,—*Pursuer*; That the last application for an augmentation of the stipend of this parish was made on (*being the date of the signeting of the summons*): That the augmentation then granted was..........chalders in addition to the then old stipend and allowance for furnishing the communion elements, making the amount of the present stipend, as last modified by the Court of Teinds,..........chalders, with £..........for furnishing the communion elements (*or as the case may be*), which modified stipend was found, in the Decree of Locality following upon said modification to be equivalent to (B F P L) of meal, (B F P L) of barley and £..........of money sterling, inclusive of the allowance for communion elements (*state precisely the totals of the different kinds of victual and of the money*): That the value thereof, converted into money according to the provisions of the Fourth Schedule of the [Church of Scotland (Property and Endowments) Act 1925][2] is £..........: That after deducting the said sum of £..........there are, according to the State of Teinds in the last locality process (*or otherwise as the pursuer may specifically condescend*), surplus teinds in the parish amounting to £..........or thereby available for an augmentation of the pursuer's stipend: That the following are the whole parties whom it is necessary to call as defenders in the present action, *videlicet*:—(*Here insert the names and designations of the defenders, specifying the characters in which they are called*): THEREFORE the Lords of our Council and Session, Commissioners appointed for Plantation of Kirks and Valuation of Teinds, per the Lord Ordinary in Teind causes, OUGHT and SHOULD find that there are surplus teinds in the parish available for an augmentation of the pursuer's stipend in accordance with the provisions of section 10 of the lastmentioned Act, and OUGHT and SHOULD modify, settle and appoint a constant local stipend, with the allow-

[1] N.B. When the Church of Scotland General Trustees are the Pursuers or the Pursuer's stipend has been standardised, this form may be applied mutatis mutandis.
[2] Substituted by S.I. 1925 No. 1063.

ance for furnishing communion elements, to the pursuer and his successors in right of the emoluments of the cure of said parish, and establish and proportion a locality of the same; and DECERN for payment thereof to the pursuer and his successors in right of the emoluments of the cure of said parish against the heritors, titulars, tacksmen, and others, intromitters with the rents and teinds of the said parish, and that at the terms following, *videlicet*:— the money stipend and allowance for furnishing the communion elements at Whitsunday and Martinmas yearly, by equal portions, and the value of the victual money according to the highest fiars' prices of the same in the county of..........between Yule and Candlemas yearly, after the separation of the crop from the ground, or as soon thereafter as the said fiars' prices shall have been struck, beginning the first payment thereof at Whitsunday (*next*) for one-half of the said money, and the other half at Martinmas thereafter, and the value of the victual betwixt Yule and Candlemas (*next*) or as soon thereafter as the said fiars' prices shall have been struck for crop and year..........; and so forth, yearly and termly thereafter, in all time coming; and for the greater expedition the pursuer is willing to refer the verity of the rental of the parish herewith produced to the heritors' oaths *simpliciter*, instead of all further probation; and in case of any of the said defenders appearing and occasioning unnecessary expense to the pursuer in the process to follow hereon, such defender or defenders OUGHT and SHOULD be DECERNED and ORDAINED, by decree foresaid, to make payment to the pursuer of the sum of £100 sterling, or of such other sum as our said Lords shall modify, as the expenses of the process to follow hereon, besides the dues of extract, conform to the [1][Acts of Parliament thereanent] of Parliament, writs libelled, laws, and daily practice of Scotland, used and observed in the like cases, as is alleged.—OUR WILL IS HEREFORE, and we charge you that on sight hereof ye pass, and in our name and authority lawfully SUMMON, WARN, AND CHARGE the defenders, personally or at their respective dwelling-places, if within Scotland upon six days' warning, and if in Orkney or Shetland upon forty days' warning, and if furth of Scotland by delivering a copy hereof at the office of the Keeper of the Record of Edictal Citations at Edinburgh, in terms of the statute and Act of Sederunt thereanent, and that upon sixty days' warning; and the tutors and curators or other guardians of such of the defenders as are minors, if they any have, for their interest, also at the said office of the Keeper of the Record of Edictal Citations at Edinburgh, on the same *inducite* as the minors themselves, or by the notices and in the forms prescribed by the Statute 15 & 16 Geo. 5, c. 33, and relative Acts of Sederunt, and that upon six weeks' warning; and all others having or pretending to have interest in the said matter, to compear before our said Lords Commissioners for Plantation of Kirks and Valuation of Teinds, at Edinburgh, or where they may then happen to be for the time, the..........day of..........Nineteen hundred and in the hour of cause, with continuation of days, to answer at the instance of the pursuer in the matter libelled: That is to say, the defenders to hear and see the premises verified and proven, and decree and sentence pronounced, conform to the conclusions above written, in all points, or else to allege a reasonable cause in the contrary, with certification as effeirs.—According to Justice, as ye shall answer to us thereupon: Which to do we commit to you and each of you full power by these our letters, delivering them by you duly executed and endorsed again to the bearer.—Given under our signet at Edinburgh, the..........day of..........in the..........year of our reign, 19..........

(*To be signed by the Clerk of Teinds.*)

[1] Substituted by S.I. 1925 No. 1063.

SCHEDULE B

Form of Extract Decreet of Modification and Locality[1]

At Edinburgh, the..........day of..........Sitting in judgment, the Lords of Council and Session, Commissioners appointed for Plantation of Kirks and Valuation of Teinds, in the process of Modification and Locality raised and pursued at the instance of the Reverend.......... Minister of the Gospel, of the Parish of..........against the Officers of State, as representing His Majesty, for the interest of the Crown, and also against the whole Heritors, Titulars, Tacksmen, Liferenters, and others, intromitters with the Rents and Teinds of the said Parish, modified, decerned, and ordained, and hereby modify, decern, and ordain the constant Stipend and Provision of the Kirk and Parish of..........to have been for crop, and year Nineteen hundred and..........yearly, since and in time coming, such a quantity of Victual, half Meal, half Barley, in Imperialy Weight and Measure, as shall be equal to..........Chalders of the late Standard Weight and Measure of Scotland, payable in Money, according to the highest fiars' prices of the County annually, with..........chalders of augmentation payable in money according to the Standard Value in terms of the Church of Scotland (Property and Endowments) Act 1925 (or with the sum of £..........sterling of augmentation in terms of the Church of Scotland (Property and Endowments) Act 1925, being the amount of the surplus teinds in the parish available to meet *pro tanto* the statutory augmentation of..........chalders), and that for Stipend, with..........Sterling for furnishing the Communion Elements, payable the money stipend and allowance for communion elements at Whitsunday and Martinmas yealy by equal portions, and the victual betwixt Yule and Candlemas yearly after the separation of the crop from the ground or as soon thereafter as the Fiars' Prices of the County of..........shall be struck. Which Modified Stipend, and Modification for furnishing the Communion Elements, the said Lords decern and ordain to be yearly paid to the said Kirk and Parish, by the Titulars and Tacksmen of the Teinds, Heritors, and Possessors of the Lands and others, intromitters with the Rents and Teinds of the said Parish, out of the first and readiest of the Teinds, parsonage and vicarage, of the same, conform to the Division and Locality following, viz. (*the Locality to be taken in here in figures and then say*), beginning the first term's payment thereof, for the said crop and year Nineteen hundred and.........., as at the term of Whitsunday, Nineteen hundred and..........as regards the money stipend and communion elements, and as regards the victual stipend betwixt Yule and Candlemas, after the separation of the crop from the ground, or as soon thereafter as the fiars' prices of the County are struck; and so forth yearly and termly in all time coming. The said Lords, as Commissioners foresaid, also decerned and ordained, and hereby decern and ordain, the whole Heritors of the said Parish, to make payment to..........Common Agent in the process of their respective shares of the sum of £..........sterling, being the amount of the account of the taxed expenses incurred by him in obtaining the Decreet of Locality; As also of their respective shares of the sum of £ sterling, being the expense of Extracting this Decreet and proportioning the Expenses among the Heritors, including therein Two pounds sterling, of fee-fund dues; making in whole £ sterling, and that in proportion to their several Teind Rentals in Process, and Scheme of Division made up and certified by the Clerk as relative hereto. And the said Lords of Council and Session, Commissioners foresaid, Grant Warrant to Messengers-at-Arms, in His Majesty's Name and Authority, to charge the Titulars and Tacksmen of the Teinds,

[1] N.B. When the Church of Scotland General Trustees are the Pursuers or the Pursuer's stipend has been standardised, this form may be applied mutatis mutandis.

Heritors, Feuars, Farmorers, Wadsetters, Liferenters, Factors, Chamberlains, Tenants, Occupiers, and Possessors of the Lands and others, intromitters with the Rents and Teinds of the said Parish of..........Defenders, personally, or at their respective dwelling-places, if within Scotland, and if furth thereof, by delivery of a Copy of Charge at the Office of the Keeper of Edictal Citations at Edinburgh, to make payment of the foresaid Stipend and Communion Element Money, each of them for his or her own part and portion thereof, conform to the Division and Locality above set down, and that at the terms of payment above expressed,—in terms and to the effect contained in the Decreet of Locality and Extract above written, and here held as repeated *brevitatis causa*: as also of their respective proportions of the foresaid sums of Expenses and Dues of Extract, conform to the Scheme of Division above referred to; and that to the Reverend.........., Pursuer, and his successors in right of the emoluments of the cure of said parish, and to the said Common Agent, respectively, within ten days if within Scotland, and if furth thereof, within sixty days after they are respectively charged to that effect, under the pain of Poinding, the terms of payment of said Stipend being always first come and bygone; And also Grant Warrant to Arrest the foresaid Defenders' readiest Goods, Gear, Debts, and sums of Money, in payment and satisfaction of their respective portions of Stipend and Communion Element Money, and also of their respective proportions of the Expenses foresaid, and Dues of Extract; And if the said Defenders fail to obey the said Charge, then after the said Charge is elapsed, to Poind their readiest Goods, Gear, Debts, and other effects; and if needful for effecting the said Poinding Grant Warrant to Open all shut and lockfast places, in form as effeirs.

SCHEDULE C

FORM OF WARRANT OF CHARGE IN TERMS OF THE DEBTORS (SCOTLAND) ACT 1838, SS. 1 AND 8

And the said Lords, as Commissioners foresaid, Grant Warrant to Messengers-at-Arms, in His Majesty's name and authority, to charge the foresaid titulars and tacksmen of Teinds, Heritors, Feuars, Farmorers, Wadsetters, Liferenters, Factors, Chamberlains, Tenants, Occupiers, and Possessors of the Lands and other intromitters with the Rents and Teinds of the said Parish of..........personally, or at their respective dwelling-places, if within Scotland, or if furth thereof, by delivering a Copy of Charge at the Office of the Keeper of the Record of Edictal Citations at Edinburgh, to make payment of the foresaid Stipend and Communion Element Money, each of them for his or her own part and portion thereof, conform to the Division and Locality inserted in the great decerniture of the foregoing Decreet, and that at the terms of payment therein the victual betwixt Yule and Candlemas yearly after the separation of the crop above written, and here referred to, and held as repeated *brevitatis causa*; and that to the Reverend..........now Minister of the Parish of..........within ten days, if within Scotland, and if furth thereof, within sixty days after they are respectively charged to that effect, under pain of Poinding, the terms of payment being always first come and bygone; And also Grant Warrant to Arrest the foresaid Defender' readiest Goods, Gear, Debts, and sums of Money, in payment and satisfaction of their respective portions of the aforesaid Stipend and Communion Element Money; and if the said Defenders fail to obey the said Charge, then after the said Charge is elapsed, to Poind their readiest Goods, Gear, and other effects; and if needful for effecting the said Poinding, Grant Warrant to Open all shut and lockfast places, in form as effeirs.—Given at Edinburgh, the.........day of..........One thousand nine hundred and.........

PROCEDURE RELATING TO THE PREPARATION, ISSUING, ADJUSTMENT, AND CUSTODY OF TEIND ROLLS UNDER THE CHURCH OF SCOTLAND (PROPERTY AND ENDOWMENTS) ACT 1925

(SR&O 1925/1063) C2.3

28 October 1925.

The Lords of Council and Session, in pursuance of the powers vested in them by the Church of Scotland (Property and Endowments) Act 1925, enact and declare as follows, viz.:—

1. A teind roll of a parish shall be prepared on application to the Court of Teinds by Petition at the instance of the Church of Scotland General Trustees.

2. The Petition may be presented at any time after the date of standardisation of the stipend of the parish provided that:

(a) a final decree of locality following upon any application for an augmentation of stipend under section 10 of the foresaid Act has been pronounced; or

(b) the time within which proceedings under section 10(2) of the foresaid Act may be taken has expired; or

(c) the General Trustees state in the Petition that it is not intended to make any application under section 10 of the foresaid Act.

3. The Petition may be in the form of the Schedule hereto annexed.

4. All petitions shall be enrolled in the Teind Motion Roll of the Lord Ordinary for an order for intimation. It shall be sufficient intimation to all parties concerned that a copy of the Petition be affixed to the most patent door of the church of the parish to which the application applies on two successive Sundays before the diet of public worship on each of these days, and a notice intimating the Petition be inserted in the *Scotsman* newspaper, and in a newspaper circulating in the county in which the parish referred to in said notice is situated, once a week for two successive weeks in each of such newspapers, provided always that the Lord Ordinary may make such other or further order regarding intimation as he may consider to be necessary or expedient in the circumstances of the case.

5. After the period of intimation ordered by the Lord Ordinary has expired, the Petition may be enrolled for an order as follows, viz.:—

(a) *If a state of teinds has been lodged with the Clerk of Teinds by the titulars or heritors*, for a remit to the Clerk to prepare a teind roll.

(b) *If no state of teinds has been so lodged* (and unless an application under paragraph 6 hereof shall be granted), for an order on the heritors to meet and choose a common agent, and to lodge a state of teinds within a time to be specified in such order, and upon such state of teinds being lodged for a remit to the Clerk to prepare a teind roll.

6. On enrolment under paragraph 5 hereof, the petitioners or any heritor or titular may apply by motion to dispense with the appointment of a common agent and also (if the circumstances justify that course) with the preparation and lodging by the heritors of a state of teinds.

7. In any case in which application is made to dispense with the appointment by the heritors of a common agent the Lord Ordinary may by interlocutor make such orders with regard to the conduct of the process as he may think just and expedient, and may require as a condition of granting the application that the party applying shall make such provision as to the court may appear just and sufficient for the payment of the fee fund dues, including the expense of preparing the teind roll.

8. In any case in which the preparation and lodging of a state of teinds by the heritors is dispensed with, the Lord Ordinary shall remit to the Clerk of Teinds to prepare and lodge a teind roll according to the state of the teinds as disclosed in the last locality process.

9. The procedure for the appointment of a common agent shall be the same mutatis mutandis as for the appointment of a common agent in a process of locality.

10. After the teind roll has been prepared the clerk shall print and report the same to the Lord Ordinary, who shall take the roll into consideration and shall make such order as he shall think fit with respect to intimation of the roll by advertisement or on the church door or otherwise (including where necessary an order on the heritors for the appointment of a common agent in the event of such appointment having been formerly dispensed with).

11. The teind roll shall be retained in the hands of the clerk subject to inspection by any party interested, and shall not be lent or given out to any person whatsoever. But after the Lord Ordinary has made an order for intimation printed copies may be supplied to the common agent for distribution among the heritors, and where there is no common agent to any heritor who applies.

12. The Lord Ordinary shall either hear parties viva voce upon such objections as may be lodged within eighteen months after the order for intimation of the teind roll, and upon any answers that may be made thereto at the Bar; or he may, if he shall see cause, allow all concerned to give in written answers to such objections within such time as he shall think proper to appoint, and shall thereafter proceed, in so far as regards any application for prorogating the time for giving in papers, in the manner directed by section 12 of the Court of Session Act 1825[1].

13. After (*a*) the objections (if any) to the teind roll have been disposed of by the Court, and (*b*) any extrajudicial surrenders of teind made before the passing of the said Church of Scotland (Property and Endowments) Act 1925, have been intimated, and evidence thereof produced, to the clerk (which shall be done before the expiry of six months after the date of the order for intimation of the teind roll), and (*c*) any surrenders of teind made in accordance with the provisions of the Sixth Schedule of the said Church of Scotland (Property and Endowments) Act 1925, have become effectual, and (*d*) intimation has been received by the clerk claiming that the deficiency of stipend caused by such surrenders shall be reallocated among the heritors in the parish who have unexhausted teinds not yet allocated for stipend, and (*e*) objections, if any, of any heritor to such reallocation have been disposed of by the Lord Ordinary, a remit shall be made to the clerk to amend the roll, and if, in virtue of the amendments, the Lord Ordinary shall deem it necessary, he may order the clerk to reprint the roll as amended before declaring the roll to be final.

14. After the Lord Ordinary has by interlocutor declared the roll to be final he shall, where a common agent has been appointed, direct that an account of the expenses incurred to the common agent be lodged in process, and when lodged remit the same to the auditor to tax and report; and after approving of such report, shall grant decree against the heritors in favour of the common agent for the taxed

---

[1] Now repealed: see the Court of Session Act 1988 (c. 36), Sched. 2, Pts. I and III.

amount of the expenses as approved, and for the expense of extracting the decree and proportioning the same in accordance with a scheme of apportionment thereof prepared by the clerk in terms of the provisions of section 11 (3) of the said Church of Scotland (Property and Endowments) Act 1925.

15. Except in the cases specified in the said Church of Scotland (Property and Endowments) Act 1925, in which the finding or judgment of the Lord Ordinary is declared to be final, any judgment of the Lord Ordinary may be submitted to review by the Division to which the cause belongs by giving in a Note, which must be lodged within twenty-one days after the date of the finding or judgment complained of, and the procedure on that Note shall be the same as in reviewing judgments of a Lord Ordinary in the Court of Session.

16. The clerk shall, on receiving notice of any change of ownership of the lands contained in one entry in the teind roll in respect of which lands a standard charge has been constituted in accordance with the provisions of section 12 of the said Church of Scotland (Property and Endowments) Act 1925, insert in the teind roll the name of the new proprietor as stated in said notice; such notice may be in the form of Schedule A annexed to the Conveyancing (Scotland) Act 1874, provided always that notice of change of ownership of part only of an entry in the teind roll shall be given effect to by the clerk only where the provisions of section 13 of the said Church of Scotland (Property and Endowments) Act 1925, are complied with in said notice.

17. Where a standard charge has been constituted on the lands of any heritor in terms of the provisions of section 12 of the said Church of Scotland (Property and Endowments) Act 1925, and the same has been redeemed in accordance with the provisions of that section, or where a stipend exigible from the teinds of any lands of a heritor has been redeemed in accordance with the provisions of section 14 of the last-mentioned Act, the clerk shall, on receiving notice in writing of such redemption signed on behalf of the General Trustees and the owner of the lands the standard charge on which has been redeemed, or of the lands the stipend in respect whereof has been redeemed, make an entry to that effect in the teind roll.

18. An excerpt from a teind roll of any entry or entries therein certified by the Clerk of Teinds shall be received in any Court of Law as sufficient evidence of such entry or entries.

SCHEDULE REFERRED TO

UNTO THE RIGHT HONOURABLE
THE LORDS OF COUNCIL AND SESSION,
COMMISSIONERS FOR THE PLANTATION OF KIRKS AND VALUATION
OF
TEINDS,
THE
PETITION
OF
THE CHURCH OF SCOTLAND GENERAL TRUSTEES, incorporated by the
Church of
Scotland (General Trustees) Order 1921;

Humbly sheweth,—

That by the Church of Scotland (Property and Endowments) Act 1925, section 11, it is provided, inter alia, that "There shall be prepared by the Clerk of Teinds for every parish in Scotland a Teind Roll specifying in sterling money *(a)* the total teind of that parish; and (*b*) the amount of that total applicable to the lands of each heritor; and (*c*) the value of the whole stipend payable to the minister, so far as payable out of teinds, including vicarage teinds payable as stipend and surrendered teinds so payable; and (*d*) the proportion of that value payable by each heritor in the parish."

That the stipend[s] of the Ministers] of the [United] Parishes] of [..........] in the Presbytery of [..........] and County [or Counties] of [..........], became standardised within the meaning of the foresaid Act as at the term of Martinmas 19[..........], in consequence of the [death, resignation or translation of the Minister, or intimation in terms of section 4 of the said Act by the Minister to the petitioners of his election, or notification in terms of section 5 of said Act by the petitioners to the Minister and other parties mentioned in the said section—*the particulars and dates should be shortly stated*].

That the final augmentation in terms of section 10 of said Act has been localted upon the heritors conform to Decree of Locality made final on [*give date*]: *or* That no proceedings are to be taken to obtain an augmentation under section 10 of said Act: *or* That the Lord Ordinary has pronounced a finding that there is no surplus teind in the parish available for an augmentation under section 10 of said Act: or That the time within which proceedings under section 10 (2) of the foresaid Act may be taken has expired.

That in these circumstances the preparation of a Teind Roll of the Parishfes] of [..........] should now be proceeded with in terms of section 11 of the said Act.

May it therefore please your Lordships to appoint this Petition to be intimated to all parties concerned by affixing a copy thereof to the most patent door of the church of the said parishfes) on two successive Sundays before the diet of public worship on each of these days, and by inserting a short notice thereof in the Scotsman newspaper and in [another newspaper circulating in the county in which the said parish[es] [are] situated] once a week for two successive weeks, or in such other or further form and manner as to your Lordships may seem proper; to appoint the heritors of the said parish[es] of..........to meet and choose a common agent; to appoint said heritors to lodge a State of Teinds; to remit to the Clerk of Teinds to prepare a Teind Roll in terms of said Act 15 & 16 Geo. 5, c. 33 , *and upon the Teind Roll being reported to your Lordships, and after considering the same with any Objections and any Answers thereto and along with any Surrenders of Teinds that may be duly made, to adjust and complete said Roll, and to declare the same to be a Final Teind Roll.*

According to Justice, etc.

INTIMATION OF DECREES REGISTERED IN THE BOOKS OF COUNCIL AND SESSION PURSUANT TO THE INDIAN AND COLONIAL DIVORCE JURISDICTION ACT 1926

(SR&O 1927/1054) **C2.4**

1 November 1927.

The Lords of Council and Session, considering that by section 1, subsection 3 of the Indian and Colonial Divorce Act, it is enacted that:—

> On production of a Certificate purporting to be signed by the proper officer of the High Court in India by which Decree of Divorce is made, the decree shall, if the parties to the marriage are domiciled in Scotland, be registered in the Books of Council and Session and upon such registration shall as from the date of registration, have the same force and effect, and proceedings may be taken thereunder as if it had been a decree made by the Court or Session on that date on which it was made by the High Court in India

do hereby enact and declare that it shall be the duty of the Keeper of the Register of Deeds in the Books of Council and Session on the registration of any such Decree to supply an Extract of same to the Registrar General and that without fee.

AMENDING THE FOUR ACTS OF SEDERUNT DATED 10TH JULY 1811, AND THE ACT OF SEDERUNT DATED 18TH FEBRUARY 1916, ANENT THE VARIOUS PUBLIC REGISTERS OF SCOTLAND, AND MAKING FURTHER REGULATIONS THEREANENT

(SR&O 1934/97) **C2.5**

2 February 1934.

The Lords of Council and Session considering that by four Acts of Sederunt of date 10th July 1811, it was inter alia provided that the various Minute Books and Registers therein referred to should be written in books issued and marked to the Keepers of the said Minute Books and Registers by the Lord Clerk Register or the Deputy Clerk Register, and that by the Lord Clerk Register (Scotland) Act 1879, s.6, it was provided that the Deputy Clerk Register should have the whole rights, authorities, privileges and duties in regard to the Public Registers, Records or Rolls of Scotland theretofore vested in the Lord Clerk Register. And considering that the foresaid Acts of Sederunt contained certain regulations and directions regarding the quality of paper, the number of lines and the numbers of words to be written on each page of the books to be issued and marked as aforesaid and that by an Act of Sederunt of date 18th February 1916 it was inter alia provided that the Deputy Clerk Register should have power to vary these regulations and directions from time to time as might be necessary, and that after the date of the passing of that Act the regulations and directions to be observed by the Keepers of the various Registers should be such as might from time to time be set forth on the title page of the volumes to be marked and issued to them as aforesaid. And considering that it was further declared that if at any time thereafter it should be necessary, in order to facilitate new methods of framing all or any of the various Registers, the books to be marked and issued as aforesaid might be so marked and issued in an unbound form or otherwise as the Deputy Clerk Register might direct. And further considering that by the Reorganisation of Offices (Scotland) Act 1928, s. 5 (1), it was provided that the whole powers and duties of the Deputy Clerk Register should be transferred to and vested in the Keeper of the Registers and Records of Scotland. And now seeing that it is expedient that a photographic process of copying writs should be substituted for typing in the Department of the Registers and Records of Scotland and that this process does not permit of the issuing of marked volumes in conformity with the practice enjoined by the foresaid Acts of Sederunt, the Lords hereby enact and enjoin that after the date of the passing of this Act a photographic process of copying writs may be introduced in substitution for typing under such conditions and subject to such regulations and at such time or times as the Keeper of the Registers and Records may deem expedient, and that thereafter it shall not be necessary to issue marked volumes in conformity with the said practice, except to the Town Clerks of those Burghs in which the Burgh Registers have not been discontinued, and to Sheriff Clerks for the Register of Deeds in the Sheriff Court Books.

And the Lords do further declare that if, after the introduction of a photographic process, any writ presented for registration be found unsuitable for the process, owing to its illegibility or inconvenient size or for any other reason, the Keeper of the Registers and Records may cause such writ to be typed in the manner heretofore in use, and the copy of the writ so typed shall form part of the Record in the same way as a copy of a writ reproduced by the photographic process.

And the Lords do further enact that the photographic record of the various Registers, along with the record of any writ or writs typed as aforesaid, shall be made up into bound volumes of such a size and form as may be found convenient, which volumes shall be authenticated on the first and last pages thereof by the signature of the Keeper of the Registers and Records, and shall be open to the lieges at such times and under such conditions as are at present applicable to the Public Records as hitherto framed and preserved in H.M. General Register House, or at such other times and under such other conditions as may be prescribed.

And the Lords further enact that if at any time difficulties emerge which, in the opinion of the Keeper of the Registers and Records, might constitute a danger to the safety or accessibility of the Public Registers, it shall be the duty of the said Keeper to report the same to the Lords of Council and Session.

EDICTAL CITATIONS, COMMISSARY PETITIONS AND PETITIONS OF SERVICE

(SI 1971/1165) **C2.6**

16 July 1971.

The Lords of Council and Session, by virtue of the powers conferred upon them by sections 16 and 34 of the Administration of Justice (Scotland) Act 1933 and section 22 of the Succession (Scotland) Act 1964 and of all other powers competent to them in that behalf, do hereby enact and declare as follows:—

1. *[Revoked by S.I. 1994 No. 1443.]*

2.—(1) The provisions of section 4 of the Confirmation and Probate Act 1858, in so far as they prescribe procedure in petitions for the appointment of an executor, shall no longer apply.

(2) Every petition for the appointment of an executor shall be intimated by the Sheriff Clerk affixing a full copy of the petition on the door of the Sheriff Court house or in some conspicuous place of the Court or of the office of the Sheriff Clerk, in such manner as the Sheriff shall direct.

3. *[Revoked by S.I. 1996 No. 2184.]*

4. This Act of Sederunt may be cited as the Act of Sederunt (Edictal Citations, Commissary Petitions and Petitions of Service) 1971, and shall come into operation on 16th August 1971.

EXPENSES OF PARTY LITIGANTS

(SI 1976/1606) **C2.7**

28 September 1976.

[*Revoked by the Act of Sederunt (Rules of the Court of Session, Sheriff Appeal Court Rules and Ordinary Cause Rules Amendment) (Taxation of Judicial Expenses) 2019 (S.S.I. 2019 No. 74) r. 6(a) (effective 29th April 2019).*]

SOLICITOR'S RIGHT OF AUDIENCE 1993

(SI 1993/1215) **C2.8**

29 April 1993.

The Lords of Council and Session, under and by virtue of the powers conferred on them by sections 5 and 48 of the Court of Session Act 1988 and of all other powers enabling them in that behalf, do hereby enact and declare:

Citation and commencement

1.—(1) This Act of Sederunt may be cited as the Act of Sederunt (Solicitor's Right of Audience) 1993 and shall come into force on 12th May 1993.

(2) This Act of Sederunt shall be inserted in the Books of Sederunt.

Interpretation

2. In this Act of Sederunt—

"the President" means the President of the Society for the time being, in his capacity as an office bearer of the Society;

"a right of audience by virtue of section 25A of the Solicitors (Scotland) Act 1980" means a right of audience in, on the one hand, the Court of Session, the House of Lords and the Judicial Committee of the Privy Council or, on the other hand, the High Court of Justiciary; and

"the Society" means the Law Society of Scotland established under the Solicitors (Scotland) Act 1980.

Right of audience

3. The President shall have a right of audience in the Outer House of the Court of Session for the purpose only of introducing to the court solicitors who have acquired a right of audience by virtue of section 25A of the Solicitors (Scotland) Act 1980 and inviting the Lord Ordinary to administer the appropriate declaration.

SOLICITORS' RIGHT OF AUDIENCE 1993

(SI 1993/[illegible])

[illegible] April 1993

The Lords of Council and Session, under and by virtue of the powers conferred on them by sections 5 and 48 of the Court of Session Act 1988 and of all other powers enabling them in that behalf, do hereby enact and declare:

Citation and commencement

1.—(1) This Act of Sederunt may be cited as the Act of Sederunt (Solicitors' Right of Audience) 1993 and shall come into force on 21st May 1993.

(2) This Act of Sederunt shall be inserted in the Books of Sederunt.

Interpretation

2. In this Act of Sederunt—

"the President" means the President of the Society for the time being or the person for the time being acting in that capacity as an office-bearer of the Society;

"a right of audience by virtue of section 25A of the Solicitors (Scotland) Act 1980" means a right of audience in the Court of Session, the House of Lords and the Judicial Committee of the Privy Council, or the High Court of Justiciary, or both;

"the Society" means the Law Society of Scotland constituted under the Solicitors (Scotland) Act 1980.

Right of audience

3. The President shall, as soon as practicable, make available to the Lord President of the Court of Session a list of solicitors who have acquired a right of audience by virtue of section 25A of the Solicitors (Scotland) Act 1980 and notify the Lord President of any change in that list.

TRANSFER OF JUDICIAL REVIEW APPLICATIONS FROM THE COURT OF SESSION 2008

(SI 2008/357) **C2.9**

10 November 2008.

The Lords of Council and Session, under and by virtue of the powers conferred by section 20(3) of the Tribunals, Courts and Enforcement Act 2007 and of all other powers enabling them in that behalf, and having obtained the consent of the Lord Chancellor in accordance with section 20(3) of the said Act of 2007, do hereby enact and declare:

Citation and commencement

1.—(1) This Act of Sederunt may be cited as the Act of Sederunt (Transfer of Judicial Review Applications from the Court of Session) 2008 and shall come into force on 10th November 2008.

(2) This Act of Sederunt shall be inserted in the Books of Sederunt.

Transfer of applications for judicial review from the Court of Session

2. Paragraph 3 specifies a class of application for the purposes of section 20(3) of the Tribunals, Courts and Enforcement Act 2007.

3. The class of application is an application which challenges a procedural decision or a procedural ruling of the First-tier Tribunal, established under section 3(1) of the Tribunals, Courts and Enforcement Act 2007.

TRANSFER OF JUDICIAL REVIEW APPLICATIONS FROM THE COURT OF SESSION 2008

(SSI 2008/357)

10 November 2008

The Lords of Council and Session, under and by virtue of the powers conferred by section 20(3) of the Tribunals, Courts and Enforcement Act 2007 and of all other powers enabling them in that behalf and having obtained the consent of the Lord Chancellor in accordance with section 20(3) of the said Act of 2007, do hereby enact and declare:

Citation and commencement

1.—(1) This Act of Sederunt may be cited as the Act of Sederunt (Transfer of Judicial Review Applications from the Court of Session) 2008 and shall come into force on 3rd November 2008.

(2) This Act of Sederunt shall be inserted in the Books of Sederunt.

Transfer of applications for judicial review from the Court of Session

2. Paragraph 3 specifies a class of application for the purposes of section 20(3) of the Tribunals, Courts and Enforcement Act 2007.

3. The class of application is an application which challenges a procedural decision or a procedural ruling of the First-tier Tribunal, established under section 3(1) of the Tribunals, Courts and Enforcement Act 2007.

COURT FEES

COURT OF SESSION ETC. FEES ORDER 1997

(SI 1997/688) C3.1

4 March 1997.

[*Repealed by S.S.I. 2015 No. 261 Sch.4 para.1 (effective 22 September 2015).*]

ACT OF SEDERUNT (RULES OF THE COURT OF SESSION AMENDMENT) (FEES OF SOLICITORS, SHORTHAND WRITERS AND WITNESSES) 2002

(SSI 2002/301) **C3.2**

18 June 2002.

The Lords of Council and Session, under and by virtue of the powers conferred upon them by section 5 of the Court of Session Act 1988 and of all other powers enabling them in that behalf, do hereby enact and declare:

Citation and commencement

1.—(1) This Act of Sederunt may be cited as the Act of Sederunt (Rules of the Court of Session Amendment) (Fees of Solicitors, Shorthand Writers and Witnesses) 2002 and shall come into force on 1st July 2002.

(2) This Act of Sederunt shall be inserted in the Books of Sederunt.

Increase in fees of solicitors and shorthand writers

2.—(1) The Table of Fees in rule 42.16(3) of the Rules of the Court of Session shall be amended in accordance with the following sub-paragraph.

(2) In the provisions mentioned in column 1 of Schedule 1 to this Act of Sederunt, for the amounts specified in column 2 of that Schedule, there shall be substituted the amounts specified in column 3.

Fees of witnesses

3. *[Revoked by S.S.I. 2007 No. 7 (effective 29th January 2007).]*

Saving and revocation

4.—(1) Paragraphs 2 and 3 shall not affect fees chargeable for work done, or outlays incurred before 1 July 2002.

(2) Chapter II of the Table of Fees set out in rule 42.16(3) of the Act of Sederunt (Rules of the Court of Session) 1994 is revoked, but shall continue to have effect in respect of fees chargeable and outlays incurred before the date on which this Act of Sederunt comes into force.

SCHEDULE 1

[Omitted.]

SCHEDULE 2

WITNESSES' FEES

[Revoked by S.S.I. 2007 No. 7 (effective 29th January 2007).]

THE COURT OF SESSION ETC. FEES ORDER 2015

(SSI 2015/261) **C3.3**

22 September 2015.

[*Revoked by S.S.I. 2018 No. 83 art.9 (effective 25 April 2018).*]

COURT OF SESSION ETC. FEES ORDER 2018

(SSI 2018/83)

25 April 2018.

The Scottish Ministers make the following Order in exercise of the powers conferred by section 107(1) and (2) of the Courts Reform (Scotland) Act 2014 and all other powers enabling them to do so.

Citation, commencement and effect

1.—(1) This Order may be cited as the Court of Session etc. Fees Order 2018 and, subject to paragraphs (2) and (3), comes into force on 25th April 2018. **C3.4**

(2) Article 3(2)(b) and schedule 2 come into force, and article 3(2)(a) and schedule 1 cease to have effect, on 1st April 2019.

(3) Article 3(2)(c) and schedule 3 come into force, and article 3(2)(b) and schedule 2 cease to have effect, on 1st April 2020.

Interpretation

2.—(1) In this Order— **C3.5**

"Office of Court" has the same meaning as in Rule 3.1 of the Rules of Court;

"partner" means a person to whom a person is married, or with whom the person is in a civil partnership;

"Rules of Court" mean the Rules of the Court of Session 1994;

"Table of Fees" means the Table of Fees in schedule 1, 2 or 3 of this Order.

(2) For the purposes of any reference in this Order to a party—

(a) except in relation to a special case, a set of persons with the same interest, for whom one and the same first paper is or has been lodged, is to be treated as a single party; and

(b) in relation to a special case, each person or set of persons who appear as one of the separate parties to the case is to be treated as a party.

Fees payable in the Court of Session etc.

3.—(1) This Order makes provision for the fees payable in the Office of Court, the office of the Accountant of Court and the office of the Auditor of the Court of Session. **C3.6**

(2) Subject to paragraph (4) and articles 4 to 8—

(a) the fees payable in respect of the matters specified in column 1 of the Table of Fees in schedule 1 (table of fees payable from 25th April 2018) are the fees specified in relation to those matters in column 2 of that Table;

(b) the fees payable in respect of the matters specified in column 1 of the Table of Fees in schedule 2 (table of fees payable from 1st April 2019) are the fees specified in relation to those matters in column 2 of that Table; and

(c) the fees payable in respect of the matters specified in column 1 of the Table of Fees in schedule 3 (table of fees payable from 1st April 2020) are the fees specified in relation to those matters in column 2 of that Table.

(3) The fees payable under this Order are to be paid—

(a) in relation to the Office of Court, to the Principal Clerk of Session or any officer acting for the Principal Clerk of Session;

(b) in relation to the office of the Accountant of Court, to the Accountant of Court or any officer acting for the Accountant of Court; and

(c) in relation to the office of the Auditor of the Court of Session, to the Auditor of the Court of Session, or any officer acting for the Auditor of the Court of Session.

(4) The fees provided for by this Order are not payable by the Crown in the enforcement of the criminal law or in the exercise of powers or the performance of duties arising out of or relating to that enforcement.

(5) No act is required of any officer or person specified in paragraph (3) in connection with a matter specified in relation to any fee prior to—

(a) the payment of that fee; or

(b) an arrangement being entered into for payment of that fee.

Exemption of certain persons from fees: legal aid

C3.7 **4.** A fee specified by this Order is not payable by a person if—

(a) the person is in receipt of civil legal aid within the meaning of section 13(2) of the Legal Aid (Scotland) Act 1986 in respect of the matter in the Table of Fees in schedule 1, 2 or 3 in connection with which the fee is payable;

(b) the fee is payable in connection with a simplified divorce or dissolution of a civil partnership application and the person is in receipt of advice and assistance from a solicitor under the Legal Aid (Scotland) Act 1986 in respect of that application; or

(c) the person's solicitor is undertaking work in relation to the matter in the Table of Fees in schedule 1, 2 or 3 in connection with which the fee is payable on the basis of any regulations made under section 36(1) of the Legal Aid (Scotland) Act 1986 providing for legal aid in a matter of special urgency.

Exemption of certain persons from fees: social security

C3.8 **5.** A fee specified by this Order is not payable by a person if—

(a) the person or the person's partner is in receipt of income support under the Social Security Contributions and Benefits Act 1992;

(b) the person is in receipt of an income-based jobseeker's allowance under the Jobseekers Act 1995;

(c) the person or the person's partner is in receipt of guarantee credit under the State Pension Credit Act 2002;

(d) the person or the person's partner is in receipt of working tax credit, provided that—

(i) child tax credit is being paid to the party, or otherwise following a claim for child tax credit made jointly by the members of a couple (as defined in section 3(5A) of the Tax Credits Act 2002) which includes the party; or

(ii) there is a disability element or severe disability element (or both) to the tax credit received by the party;

and that the gross annual income taken into account for the calculation of the working tax credit is £18,000 or less;

(e) the person or the person's partner is in receipt of income-related employment and support allowance under the Welfare Reform Act 2007;

(f) the person is in receipt of universal credit under Part 1 of the Welfare Reform Act 2012; or

(g) the person or the person's partner has, within the period of 3 months prior to the date the specified fee would be payable but for this exemption, received financial or other assistance under the Welfare Funds (Scotland) Act 2015.

Exemptions for applicants for certain interdicts and orders

6.—(1) The fees provided for by this Order are not payable by a person applying for a specified interdict or for an exclusion order. **C3.9**

(2) In this article—

(a) "specified interdict" means an interdict or interim interdict that is—

(i) a matrimonial interdict within the meaning of section 14(2) of the Matrimonial Homes (Family Protection) (Scotland) Act 1981 (interdict competent where spouses live together);

(ii) a domestic interdict within the meaning of section 18A of that Act (meaning of "domestic interdict");

(iii) a relevant interdict under section 113(2) of the Civil Partnership Act 2004 (civil partners: competency of interdict); or

(iv) otherwise an interdict in respect of which there is an application for a power of arrest to be attached under section 1 of the Protection from Abuse (Scotland) Act 2001 (attachment of power of arrest to interdict); and

(b) "exclusion order" means an exclusion order under—

(i) section 4 of the Matrimonial Homes (Family Protection) (Scotland) Act 1981 (exclusion orders); or

(ii) section 104 of the Civil Partnership Act 2004 (exclusion orders).

(3) The exemption in paragraph (1) does not apply to a person applying for a principal remedy other than a specified interdict or exclusion order.

(4) The fees provided for by this Order are not payable by the applicant in any appeal in connection with proceedings in respect of which the applicant would not be required to pay fees by virtue of—

(a) paragraph (1); or

(b) article 12(1) of the Sheriff Court Fees Order 2018 (exemptions for applicants for certain interdicts and orders).

Exemption of certain motions from fees

7.—(1) This article applies to motions which are enrolled in the process of the cause or made orally at the bar in accordance with rule 23.2 of the Rules of Court (enrolment of motions). **C3.10**

(2) The fees specified in items B21 and C17 of the Table of Fees are not payable in respect of motions which operate solely so as to activate further steps of procedure and any opposition to such motions.

(3) Without prejudice to the generality of paragraph (2) above, a motion which is exempt from the payment of fees includes a motion under any of the following rules of the Rules of Court—

(a) rule 19.1 (decrees in absence);

(b) rule 22.3(5)(a) (closing record);

(c) rule 36.13 (death, disability, retiral, etc. of Lord Ordinary);

(d) rules 37.1(2)(b), 37.1(6) and 37.1(7) (applications for jury trial);

(e) rule 37.10 (application of verdicts); and

(f) rule 38.17(1) (amendment of pleadings in reclaiming motion).

Calculation of certain fees payable

C3.11 **8.**—(1) Subject to article 7, the fees specified in items B21 and C17 of the Table of Fees are payable in addition to those fees which are specified in items B2, B6 and C5 of the Table of Fees.

(2) The fees specified in items B21 and C17 of the Table of Fees are not payable in addition to those fees which are specified in items B9, B10 and B13 and C9 of the Table of Fees.

Revocations

C3.12 **9.** The Court of Session etc. Fees Order 2015 and the Court Fees (Miscellaneous Amendments) (Scotland) Order 2016 are revoked.

SCHEDULE 1

TABLE OF FEES

Article 3(2)(a)

C3.13

Payable from 25th April 2018[1]

Column 1 (Matters)	**Column 2 (Fee payable) £**	**Column 3 (Fee formerly Payable) £**
PART I – FEES IN THE CENTRAL OFFICE OF THE COURT A. SIGNETING Signeting of any writ or summons if attendance is necessary outwith normal office hours.	128	125
B. GENERAL DEPARTMENT 1. Appeal, application for leave or permission to appeal, summons, or other writ or step by which any cause or proceeding, other than a family action, is originated in either the Inner or Outer House (to include signeting in normal office hours).	307	300
2. Defences, answers or other writ (including a joint minute) or step in process or enrolment or opposition to a motion in a pending process by which a party other than an originating party first makes an appearance in a cause or proceeding, other than a family action.	307	300

[1] Column 3 shows the fees which were payable by virtue of Sched. 3 of S.S.I. 2015/261 (as substituted by Sched. 1 of S.S.I. 2016/332) immediately before the coming into force of this schedule.

Column 1 (Matters)	**Column 2 (Fee payable) £**	**Column 3 (Fee formerly Payable) £**
3. Writ by which a family action is originated (other than a simplified divorce or dissolution of a civil partnership application) – inclusive fee (to include signeting within normal office hours and, if applicable, issue to the pursuer of an extract in terms of item G5(a) of this Table, and to the defender, if appropriate, a duplicate thereof).	170	166
4. Simplified divorce or dissolution of a civil partnership application (inclusive of all procedure other than that specified in item B5 of this Table).	128	125
5. In relation to a simplified divorce or dissolution of a civil partnership application, citation of any persons under rule 16.1(1)(a)(i), (ii) or (iii), as applied by rule 49.76, of the Rules of Court, or intimation to any person or persons under rule 16.1(1)(a)(i), (ii) or (iii), as applied by rule 49.76 of those Rules, where such intimation is required.	13 plus messenger at arms fee to serve document	12 plus messenger at arms fee to serve document
6. Defences, answers or other writ (including a joint minute) or step in process or enrolment of or opposition to a motion in a pending process by which a party other than an originating party first makes appearance in a family action.	170	166
7. Initial lodging of affidavits in a family action where proof by affidavit evidence has been allowed.	73	71
8. Special case— for each party; maximum fee payable (per case).	 109 445	 107 435
9. Application by minute or motion for variation of an order in a family action.	37	36
10. Answers or opposition to an application under item B9 of this Table.	37	36
11. Letter of request to a foreign court.	55	54
12. Citation of each jury, to include outlays incurred in citing and countermanding - payable on receipt of instruments for issue of precept.	305	298
13. Reclaiming motion - payable by party enrolling motion.	219	214

Column 1 (Matters)	Column 2 (Fee payable) £	Column 3 (Fee formerly Payable) £
14. Closed record – payable by each party on the lodging of the closed record or, where no closed record is lodged, when mode of enquiry is determined.	205	200
15. Allowing proof, etc. - payable by each party on diet of proof, jury trial, procedure roll or summar roll hearing being allowed.	60	59
16. Court hearing (in normal hours) before a bench of one or two judges – payable by each party for every 30 minutes or part thereof. *Note:* This fee does not apply to the first 30 minutes of the hearing of a motion.	205	200[1]
17. Court hearing (in normal hours) before 3 or more judges – payable by each party for every 30 minutes or part thereof. *Note:* This fee does not apply to the first 30 minutes of the hearing on the single bills.	512	500
18. Court hearing (out of hours) before a bench of one or two judges – payable by each party for every 30 minutes or part thereof.	246	240[2]
19. Court hearing (out of hours) before 3 or more judges – payable by each party for every 30 minutes or part thereof.	614	600
20. Cancellation of court hearing before 3 or more judges, by a party or parties, within 28 days of court hearing date – fee payable is shared equally between the parties.	50% of fee that would have been payable under this Table had the court hearing taken place as planned	50% of fee that would have been payable under this Table had the court hearing taken place as planned
21. Fee payable by any party enrolling a motion or making a motion orally at the bar and any party opposing any such motion.	102	100
C. PETITION DEPARTMENT		

[1] A different fee narrative for item B.16 has previously been applicable.
[2] A different fee narrative for item B.18 has previously been applicable.

Column 1 (Matters)	**Column 2 (Fee payable) £**	**Column 3 (Fee formerly Payable) £**
1. Petition of whatever nature presented to the Inner or Outer House other than a petition under item C3 or C4 of this Table, whether in respect of the first or any subsequent step of process, and any application for registration or recognition of a judgment under the Civil Jurisdiction and Judgments Act 1982.	307	300
2. Additional fee payable when a petition in terms of item C1 of this Table is presented outwith normal office hours.	128	125
3. Petition to be admitted as a notary public—for each applicant.	165	161
4. Petition to be admitted as a solicitor—for each applicant.	165	161
5. Answers, objection or other writ (including a joint minute) or step in process or enrolment or opposition to a motion in a pending process by which a party other than an originating party first makes appearance in a proceeding to which item C1 of this Table applies.	307	300
6. Caveat.	43	48
7. No fee.		-
8. Registering official copies of orders of courts in England and Wales or Northern Ireland.	19	18
9. Reclaiming motion – payable by party enrolling motion.	219	214
10. Closed record – payable by each party on the lodging of the closed record or, when no closed record is lodged, when mode of enquiry is determined.	205	200
11. Allowing proof, etc. – payable by each party on diet of proof, procedure roll, summar roll or judicial review hearing being allowed.	60	59
12. Court hearing (in normal hours) before a bench of one or two judges – payable by each party for every 30 minutes or part thereof. *Note:* This fee does not apply to the first 30 minutes of the hearing of a motion.	205	200[1]
13. Court hearing (in normal hours) before 3 or more judges – payable by each party for every 30 minutes or part thereof.	512	500

[1] A different fee narrative for item C.12 has previously been applicable.

Column 1 (Matters)	Column 2 (Fee payable) £	Column 3 (Fee formerly Payable) £
Note: This fee does not apply to the first 30 minutes of the hearing on the single bills.		
14. Court hearing (out of hours) before a bench of one or two judges – payable by each party for every 30 minutes or part thereof.	246	240[1]
15. Court hearing (out of hours) before 3 or more judges – payable by each party for every 30 minutes or part thereof.	614	600
16. Cancellation of court hearing before 3 or more judges, by a party or parties, within 28 days of court hearing date – fee payable is shared equally between parties.	50% of fee that would have been payable under this Table had the court hearing taken place as planned	50% of fee that would have been payable under this Table had the court hearing taken place as planned
17. Fee payable by any party enrolling a motion or making a motion orally at the bar and any party opposing any such motion.	102	100
18. Lodging of notice of appointment or intention to appoint an administrator out of court under the Insolvency Act 1986.	307	300
D. COURT FOR HEARING APPEALS RELATING TO THE REGISTRATION OF ELECTORS Appeal – inclusive fee.	307	300
E. ELECTION COURT 1. Parliamentary election petition.	307	300
2. Statement of matters.	19	18
3. Any other petition, application, answers or objections submitted to the court.	55	54
4. Certificate of judgment.	55	54
5. Court hearing (in normal hours) before a bench of one or two judges – payable by each party for every 30 minutes or part thereof. Note: This fee does not apply to the first 30 minutes of the hearing of a motion.	205	-
6. Court hearing (in normal hours) before 3 or more judges – payable by each party for every 30 minutes or part thereof.	512	-

[1] A different fee narrative for item C.14 has previously been applicable.

Column 1 (Matters)	Column 2 (Fee payable) £	Column 3 (Fee formerly Payable) £
Note: This fee does not apply to the first 30 minutes of the hearing on the single bills.		
7. Fee payable by any party enrolling a motion or making a motion orally at the bar and any party opposing any such motion.	102	-
F. LANDS VALUATION APPEAL COURT 1. Appeal – inclusive fee.	307	300
2. Answers – inclusive fee.	219	214
G. EXTRACTS DEPARTMENT 1. Extract decree following upon a summons, petition or appeal, or after protestation of a note, whether in absence or otherwise.	60	59
2. Extract of admission as a solicitor.	55	54
3. Extract of protestation.	55	54
4. Certificate under the Civil Jurisdiction and Judgments Act 1982.	55	54
5. Documentation evidencing divorce, nullity or dissolution of marriage or civil partnership including— (a) extract from Consistorial Register of Decrees of decree pronounced on or after 23rd September 1975 if not issued in terms of item B3 or B4 of this Table; (b) certificate of divorce in decree pronounced prior to 23rd September 1975; (c) certified copy interlocutor in decree pronounced prior to 23rd September 1975.	31	30
6. Extract from the Register of Acts and Decrees – per sheet or part thereof.	31	30
7. Sealing and certifying any document for exhibition in a foreign jurisdiction or otherwise.	31	30
8. Acknowledgement of receipt of a notice under section 19(6) or 21(2) of the Conveyancing and Feudal Reform (Scotland) Act 1970.	55	54
PART II – FEES IN THE OFFICE OF THE ACCOUNTANT OF COURT H. OFFICE OF THE ACCOUNTANT OF COURT *I. In Factories* 1. Registering case and receiving and delivering up bond of caution.	23	22

Column 1 (Matters)	**Column 2 (Fee payable) £**	**Column 3 (Fee formerly Payable) £**
2. Examining factor's inventory – 0.333% of the value of the estate as disclosed		
(a) minimum fee payable;	31	30
(b) maximum fee payable.	738	721
3. Auditing each account, based on estate value—		
(a) £0 - £30,000;	115	112
(b) £30,001 - £50,000;	230	225
(c) £50,001 - £250,000;	575	562
(d) £250,001 - £500,000;	864	845
(e) £500,001 and above.	1,152	1,126
4. Reporting with regard to discharge, special powers, other special matters, surplus estate or scheme of division.	57	56
5. For certificate under seal.	18	17
II. In Consignations		
6. Lodging consignation.	33	32
7. Producing or delivering up consignation, based on consignation value—		
(a) consignation value £0 - £50 and less than 7 years since lodged;	No charge	No charge
(b) consignation value over £50 and less than 7 years since lodged;	33	32
(c) consignation value £0 - £70 and over 7 years since lodged;	No charge	No charge
(d) consignation value over £70 and over 7 years since lodged.	54	53
PART III – FEES IN THE OFFICE OF THE AUDITOR OF THE COURT OF SESSION		
I. OFFICE OF THE AUDITOR OF THE COURT OF SESSION		
1. Taxing accounts of expenses incurred in judicial proceedings (including proceedings in the High Court of Justiciary) remitted to the Auditor of the Court of Session for taxation—		
(a) on lodging account for taxation;	44	43
(b) taxing accounts for expenses etc.—		
(i) up to £400;	21	20
(ii) for every additional £100 or part thereof.	5	5
Note: fee to be determined by the Auditor of the Court of Session on amount of account as submitted.		

Column 1 (Matters)	Column 2 (Fee payable) £	Column 3 (Fee formerly Payable) £
2. Fee for assessing account remitted to the Auditor to determine whether an additional fee should be paid.	294	287
3. Fee for cancellation of diet of taxation—		
(a) where written notice of cancellation received from receiving party after 4.00 pm on the fourth working day before the day of the diet of taxation;	50% of fee that would be payable under item I1(b) of this Table	50% of fee that would be payable under item I1(b) of this Table
(b) where written notice of cancellation received from receiving party after 4.00 pm on the second working day before the day of the diet of taxation.	75% of fee that would be payable under item I1(b) of this Table	75% of fee that would be payable under item I1(b) of this Table
PART IV – FEES COMMON TO ALL OFFICES		
J. MISCELLANEOUS		
1. Certified copy of proceedings for appeal to the Supreme Court.	219	214
2. Certifying of any other document (plus copying charges if necessary).	19	18
3. Recording, engrossing, extracting, printing or copying of all documents (exclusive of search fee)—		
(a) by photocopying or otherwise producing a printed or typed copy—		
(i) up to 10 pages;	7	6
(ii) each page or part thereof in excess of 10 pages;	0.50	0.50
(b) for a copy of each document in electronic form.	7	6
4. Any search of records or archives, per 30 minutes or part thereof.	13	12
In addition, correspondence fee where applicable.	13	12
5. Captions—		
(a) marking caption when ordered;	13	12
(b) warrant for caption when issued.	13	12
6. Change of party name where more than 10 cases are registered – per case.	2	2

SCHEDULE 2

TABLE OF FEES

Article 3(2)(b)

C3.14

Payable from 1st April 2019

Column 1 (Matters)	**Column 2 (Fee payable) £**	**Column 3 (Fee formerly Payable)[1] £**
PART I – FEES IN THE CENTRAL OFFICE OF THE COURT A. SIGNETING Signeting of any writ or summons if attendance is necessary outwith normal office hours.	131	128
B. GENERAL DEPARTMENT 1. Appeal, application for leave or permission to appeal, summons, or other writ or step by which any cause or proceeding, other than a family action, is originated in either the Inner or Outer House (to include signeting in normal office hours).	313	307
2. Defences, answers or other writ (including a joint minute) or step in process or enrolment or opposition to a motion in a pending process by which a party other than an originating party first makes an appearance in a cause or proceeding, other than a family action.	313	307
3. Writ by which a family action is originated (other than a simplified divorce or dissolution of a civil partnership application) – inclusive fee (to include signeting within normal office hours and, if applicable, issue to the pursuer of an extract in terms of item G5(a) of this Table, and to the defender, if appropriate, a duplicate thereof).	173	170
4. Simplified divorce or dissolution of a civil partnership application (inclusive of all procedure other than that specified in item B5 of this Table).	131	128

[1] Column 3 shows the fees which were payable by virtue of Sched. 1 of this Order immediately before the coming into force of this schedule.

Column 1 (Matters)	Column 2 (Fee payable) £	Column 3 (Fee formerly Payable)[1] £
5. In relation to a simplified divorce or dissolution of a civil partnership application, citation of any persons under rule 16.1(1)(a)(i), (ii) or (iii), as applied by rule 49.76, of the Rules of Court, or intimation to any person or persons under rule 16.1(1)(a)(i), (ii) or (iii), as applied by rule 49.76 of those Rules, where such intimation is required.	13 plus messenger at arms fee to serve document	13 plus messenger at arms fee to serve document
6. Defences, answers or other writ (including a joint minute) or step in process or enrolment of or opposition to a motion in a pending process by which a party other than an originating party first makes appearance in a family action.	173	170
7. Initial lodging of affidavits in a family action where proof by affidavit evidence has been allowed.	74	73
8. Special case—		
for each party;	111	109
maximum fee payable (per case).	454	445
9. Application by minute or motion for variation of an order in a family action.	38	37
10. Answers or opposition to an application under item B9 of this Table.	38	37
11. Letter of request to a foreign court.	56	55
12. Citation of each jury, to include outlays incurred in citing and countermanding - payable on receipt of instruments for issue of precept.	311	305
13. Reclaiming motion - payable by party enrolling motion.	223	219
14. Closed record – payable by each party on the lodging of the closed record or, where no closed record is lodged, when mode of enquiry is determined.	209	205
15. Allowing proof, etc. - payable by each party on diet of proof, jury trial, procedure roll or summar roll hearing being allowed.	61	60
16. Court hearing (in normal hours) before a bench of one or two judges – payable by each party for every 30 minutes or part thereof. *Note:* This fee does not apply to the first 30 minutes of the hearing of a motion.	209	205

Column 1 (Matters)	Column 2 (Fee payable) £	Column 3 (Fee formerly Payable)[1] £
17. Court hearing (in normal hours) before 3 or more judges – payable by each party for every 30 minutes or part thereof. *Note:* This fee does not apply to the first 30 minutes of the hearing on the single bills.	522	512
18. Court hearing (out of hours) before a bench of one or two judges – payable by each party for every 30 minutes or part thereof.	251	246
19. Court hearing (out of hours) before 3 or more judges – payable by each party for every 30 minutes or part thereof.	626	614
20. Cancellation of court hearing before 3 or more judges, by a party or parties, within 28 days of court hearing date – fee payable is shared equally between the parties.	50% of fee that would have been payable under this Table had the court hearing taken place as planned	50% of fee that would have been payable under this Table had the court hearing taken place as planned
21. Fee payable by any party enrolling a motion or making a motion orally at the bar and any party opposing any such motion.	104	102
C. PETITION DEPARTMENT 1. Petition of whatever nature presented to the Inner or Outer House other than a petition under item C3 or C4 of this Table, whether in respect of the first or any subsequent step of process, and any application for registration or recognition of a judgment under the Civil Jurisdiction and Judgments Act 1982.	313	307
2. Additional fee payable when a petition in terms of item C1 of this Table is presented outwith normal office hours.	131	128
3. Petition to be admitted as a notary public—for each applicant.	168	165
4. Petition to be admitted as a solicitor—for each applicant.	168	165
5. Answers, objection or other writ (including a joint minute) or step in process or enrolment or opposition to a motion in a pending process by which a party other than an originating party first makes appearance in a proceeding to which item C1 of this Table applies.	313	307

Column 1 (Matters)	Column 2 (Fee payable) £	Column 3 (Fee formerly Payable)[1] £
6. Caveat.	44	43
7. No fee.	-	-
8. Registering official copies of orders of courts in England and Wales or Northern Ireland.	19	19
9. Reclaiming motion – payable by party enrolling motion.	223	219
10. Closed record – payable by each party on the lodging of the closed record or, when no closed record is lodged, when mode of enquiry is determined.	209	205
11. Allowing proof, etc. – payable by each party on diet of proof, procedure roll, summar roll or judicial review hearing being allowed.	61	60
12. Court hearing (in normal hours) before a bench of one or two judges – payable by each party for every 30 minutes or part thereof. *Note:* This fee does not apply to the first 30 minutes of the hearing of a motion.	209	205
13. Court hearing (in normal hours) before 3 or more judges – payable by each party for every 30 minutes or part thereof. *Note:* This fee does not apply to the first 30 minutes of the hearing on the single bills.	522	512
14. Court hearing (out of hours) before a bench of one or two judges – payable by each party for every 30 minutes or part thereof.	251	246
15. Court hearing (out of hours) before 3 or more judges – payable by each party for every 30 minutes or part thereof.	626	614
16. Cancellation of court hearing before 3 or more judges, by a party or parties, within 28 days of court hearing date – fee payable is shared equally between parties.	50% of fee that would have been payable under this Table had the court hearing taken place as planned	50% of fee that would have been payable under this Table had the court hearing taken place as planned
17. Fee payable by any party enrolling a motion or making a motion orally at the bar and any party opposing any such motion.	104	102

Column 1 (Matters)	Column 2 (Fee payable) £	Column 3 (Fee formerly Payable)[1] £
18. Lodging of notice of appointment or intention to appoint an administrator out of court under the Insolvency Act 1986.	313	307
D. COURT FOR HEARING APPEALS RELATING TO THE REGISTRATION OF ELECTORS Appeal – inclusive fee.	313	307
E. ELECTION COURT 1. Parliamentary election petition.	313	307
2. Statement of matters.	19	19
3. Any other petition, application, answers or objections submitted to the court.	56	55
4. Certificate of judgment.	56	55
5. Court hearing (in normal hours) before a bench of one or two judges – payable by each party for every 30 minutes or part thereof. Note: This fee does not apply to the first 30 minutes of the hearing of a motion.	209	205
6. Court hearing (in normal hours) before 3 or more judges – payable by each party for every 30 minutes or part thereof. Note: This fee does not apply to the first 30 minutes of the hearing on the single bills.	522	512
7. Fee payable by any party enrolling a motion or making a motion orally at the bar and any party opposing any such motion.	104	102
F. LANDS VALUATION APPEAL COURT 1. Appeal - inclusive fee.	313	307
2. Answers - inclusive fee.	223	219
G. EXTRACTS DEPARTMENT 1. Extract decree following upon a summons, petition or appeal, or after protestation of a note, whether in absence or otherwise.	61	60
2. Extract of admission as a solicitor.	56	55
3. Extract of protestation.	56	55
4. Certificate under the Civil Jurisdiction and Judgments Act 1982.	56	55
5. Documentation evidencing divorce, nullity or dissolution of marriage or civil partnership including—	32	31

Column 1 (Matters)	Column 2 (Fee payable) £	Column 3 (Fee formerly Payable)[1] £
(a) extract from Consistorial Register of Decrees of decree pronounced on or after 23rd September 1975 if not issued in terms of item B3 or B4 of this Table; (b) certificate of divorce in decree pronounced prior to 23rd September 1975; (c) certified copy interlocutor in decree pronounced prior to 23rd September 1975.		
6. Extract from the Register of Acts and Decrees – per sheet or part thereof.	32	31
7. Sealing and certifying any document for exhibition in a foreign jurisdiction or otherwise.	32	31
8. Acknowledgement of receipt of a notice under section 19(6) or 21(2) of the Conveyancing and Feudal Reform (Scotland) Act 1970.	56	55
PART II – FEES IN THE OFFICE OF THE ACCOUNTANT OF COURT H. OFFICE OF THE ACCOUNTANT OF COURT *I. In Factories* 1. Registering case and receiving and delivering up bond of caution.	23	23
2. Examining factor's inventory – 0.333% of the value of the estate as disclosed (a) minimum fee payable; (b) maximum fee payable.	 32 753	 31 738
3. Auditing each account, based on estate value— (a) £0 - £30,000; (b) £30,001 - £50,000; (c) £50,001 - £250,000; (d) £250,001 - £500,000; (e) £500,001 and above.	 117 235 587 881 1,175	 115 230 575 864 1,152
4. Reporting with regard to discharge, special powers, other special matters, surplus estate or scheme of division.	58	57
5. For certificate under seal.	18	18
II. In Consignations 6. Lodging consignation.	34	33
7. Producing or delivering up consignation, based on consignation value—		

Column 1 (Matters)	**Column 2 (Fee payable) £**	**Column 3 (Fee formerly Payable)[1] £**
(a) consignation value £0 - £50 and less than 7 years since lodged;	No charge	No charge
(b) consignation value over £50 and less than 7 years since lodged;	34	33
(c) consignation value £0 - £70 and over 7 years since lodged;	No charge	No charge
(d) consignation value over £70 and over 7 years since lodged.	55	54
PART III – FEES IN THE OFFICE OF THE AUDITOR OF THE COURT OF SESSION		
I. OFFICE OF THE AUDITOR OF THE COURT OF SESSION		
1. Taxing accounts of expenses incurred in judicial proceedings (including proceedings in the High Court of Justiciary) remitted to the Auditor of the Court of Session for taxation—		
(a) on lodging account for taxation;	45	44
(b) taxing accounts for expenses etc.—		
(i) up to £400;	21	21
(ii) for every additional £100 or part thereof.	5	5
Note: fee to be determined by the Auditor of the Court of Session on amount of account as submitted.		
2. Fee for assessing account remitted to the Auditor to determine whether an additional fee should be paid.	300	294
3. Fee for cancellation of diet of taxation—		
(a) where written notice of cancellation received from receiving party after 4.00 pm on the fourth working day before the day of the diet of taxation;	50% of fee that would be payable under item I1(b) of this Table	50% of fee that would be payable under item I1(b) of this Table
(b) where written notice of cancellation received from receiving party after 4.00 pm on the second working day before the day of the diet of taxation.	75% of fee that would be payable under item I1(b) of this Table	75% of fee that would be payable under item I1(b) of this Table
PART IV – FEES COMMON TO ALL OFFICES		
J. MISCELLANEOUS		
1. Certified copy of proceedings for appeal to the Supreme Court.	223	219

Column 1 (Matters)	Column 2 (Fee payable) £	Column 3 (Fee formerly Payable)[1] £
2. Certifying of any other document (plus copying charges if necessary).	19	19
3. Recording, engrossing, extracting, printing or copying of all documents (exclusive of search fee)—		
(a) by photocopying or otherwise producing a printed or typed copy—		
(i) up to 10 pages;	7	7
(ii) each page or part thereof in excess of 10 pages;	0.50	0.50
(b) for a copy of each document in electronic form.	7	7
4. Any search of records or archives, per 30 minutes or part thereof.	13	13
In addition, correspondence fee where applicable.	13	13
5. Captions—		
(a) marking caption when ordered;	13	13
(b) warrant for caption when issued.	13	13
6. Change of party name where more than 10 cases are registered – per case.	2	2

SCHEDULE 3

TABLE OF FEES

Article 3(2)(c)

C3.15

Payable from 1st April 2020

Column 1 (Matters)	Column 2 (Fee payable) £	Column 3 (Fee formerly Payable)[1] £
PART I – FEES IN THE CENTRAL OFFICE OF THE COURT		
A. SIGNETING		
Signeting of any writ or summons if attendance is necessary outwith normal office hours.	134	131

[1] Column 3 shows the fees which were payable by virtue of Sched. 2 of this Order immediately before the coming into force of this schedule.

Column 1 (Matters)	Column 2 (Fee payable) £	Column 3 (Fee formerly Payable)[1] £
B. GENERAL DEPARTMENT 1. Appeal, application for leave or permission to appeal, summons, or other writ or step by which any cause or proceeding, other than a family action, is originated in either the Inner or Outer House (to include signeting in normal office hours).	319	313
2. Defences, answers or other writ (including a joint minute) or step in process or enrolment or opposition to a motion in a pending process by which a party other than an originating party first makes an appearance in a cause or proceeding, other than a family action.	319	313
3. Writ by which a family action is originated (other than a simplified divorce or dissolution of a civil partnership application) – inclusive fee (to include signeting within normal office hours and, if applicable, issue to the pursuer of an extract in terms of item G5(a) of this Table, and to the defender, if appropriate, a duplicate thereof).	176	173
4. Simplified divorce or dissolution of a civil partnership application (inclusive of all procedure other than that specified in item B5 of this Table).	134	131
5. In relation to a simplified divorce or dissolution of a civil partnership application, citation of any persons under rule 16.1(1)(a)(i), (ii) or (iii), as applied by rule 49.76, of the Rules of Court, or intimation to any person or persons under rule 16.1(1)(a)(i), (ii) or (iii), as applied by rule 49.76 of those Rules, where such intimation is required.	13 plus messenger at arms fee to serve document	13 plus messenger at arms fee to serve document
6. Defences, answers or other writ (including a joint minute) or step in process or enrolment of or opposition to a motion in a pending process by which a party other than an originating party first makes appearance in a family action.	176	173
7. Initial lodging of affidavits in a family action where proof by affidavit evidence has been allowed.	75	74
8. Special case— for each party; maximum fee payable (per case).	 113 463	 111 454

Column 1 (Matters)	Column 2 (Fee payable) £	Column 3 (Fee formerly Payable)[1] £
9. Application by minute or motion for variation of an order in a family action.	39	38
10. Answers or opposition to an application under item B9 of this Table.	39	38
11. Letter of request to a foreign court.	57	56
12. Citation of each jury, to include outlays incurred in citing and countermanding - payable on receipt of instruments for issue of precept.	317	311
13. Reclaiming motion - payable by party enrolling motion.	227	223
14. Closed record – payable by each party on the lodging of the closed record or, where no closed record is lodged, when mode of enquiry is determined.	213	209
15. Allowing proof, etc. - payable by each party on diet of proof, jury trial, procedure roll or summar roll hearing being allowed.	62	61
16. Court hearing (in normal hours) before a bench of one or two judges – payable by each party for every 30 minutes or part thereof. *Note:* This fee does not apply to the first 30 minutes of the hearing of a motion.	213	209
17. Court hearing (in normal hours) before 3 or more judges – payable by each party for every 30 minutes or part thereof. *Note:* This fee does not apply to the first 30 minutes of the hearing on the single bills.	532	522
18. Court hearing (out of hours) before a bench of one or two judges – payable by each party for every 30 minutes or part thereof.	256	251
19. Court hearing (out of hours) before 3 or more judges – payable by each party for every 30 minutes or part thereof.	639	626
20. Cancellation of court hearing before 3 or more judges, by a party or parties, within 28 days of court hearing date – fee payable is shared equally between the parties.	50% of fee that would have been payable under this Table had the court hearing taken place as planned	50% of fee that would have been payable under this Table had the court hearing taken place as planned

Column 1 (Matters)	Column 2 (Fee payable) £	Column 3 (Fee formerly Payable)[1] £
21. Fee payable by any party enrolling a motion or making a motion orally at the bar and any party opposing any such motion.	106	104
C. PETITION DEPARTMENT 1. Petition of whatever nature presented to the Inner or Outer House other than a petition under item C3 or C4 of this Table, whether in respect of the first or any subsequent step of process, and any application for registration or recognition of a judgment under the Civil Jurisdiction and Judgments Act 1982.	319	313
2. Additional fee payable when a petition in terms of item C1 of this Table is presented outwith normal office hours.	134	131
3. Petition to be admitted as a notary public— for each applicant.	171	168
4. Petition to be admitted as a solicitor— for each applicant.	171	168
5. Answers, objection or other writ (including a joint minute) or step in process or enrolment or opposition to a motion in a pending process by which a party other than an originating party first makes appearance in a proceeding to which item C1 of this Table applies.	319	313
6. Caveat.	45	44
7. No fee.	-	-
8. Registering official copies of orders of courts in England and Wales or Northern Ireland.	19	19
9. Reclaiming motion – payable by party enrolling motion.	227	223
10. Closed record – payable by each party on the lodging of the closed record or, when no closed record is lodged, when mode of enquiry is determined.	213	209
11. Allowing proof, etc. – payable by each party on diet of proof, procedure roll, summar roll or judicial review hearing being allowed.	62	61
12. Court hearing (in normal hours) before a bench of one or two judges – payable by each party for every 30 minutes or part thereof. *Note:* This fee does not apply to the first 30 minutes of the hearing of a motion.	213	209

Column 1 (Matters)	Column 2 (Fee payable) £	Column 3 (Fee formerly Payable)[1] £
13. Court hearing (in normal hours) before 3 or more judges – payable by each party for every 30 minutes or part thereof. *Note:* This fee does not apply to the first 30 minutes of the hearing on the single bills.	532	522
14. Court hearing (out of hours) before a bench of one or two judges – payable by each party for every 30 minutes or part thereof.	256	251
15. Court hearing (out of hours) before 3 or more judges – payable by each party for every 30 minutes or part thereof.	639	626
16. Cancellation of court hearing before 3 or more judges, by a party or parties, within 28 days of court hearing date – fee payable is shared equally between parties.	50% of fee that would have been payable under this Table had the court hearing taken place as planned	50% of fee that would have been payable under this Table had the court hearing taken place as planned
17. Fee payable by any party enrolling a motion or making a motion orally at the bar and any party opposing any such motion.	106	104
18. Lodging of notice of appointment or intention to appoint an administrator out of court under the Insolvency Act 1986.	319	313
D. COURT FOR HEARING APPEALS RELATING TO THE REGISTRATION OF ELECTORS Appeal – inclusive fee.	319	313
E. ELECTION COURT 1. Parliamentary election petition.	319	313
2. Statement of matters.	19	19
3. Any other petition, application, answers or objections submitted to the court.	57	56
4. Certificate of judgment.	57	56
5. Court hearing (in normal hours) before a bench of one or two judges – payable by each party for every 30 minutes or part thereof. Note: This fee does not apply to the first 30 minutes of the hearing of a motion.	213	209

Column 1 (Matters)	Column 2 (Fee payable) £	Column 3 (Fee formerly Payable)[1] £
6. Court hearing (in normal hours) before 3 or more judges – payable by each party for every 30 minutes or part thereof. Note: This fee does not apply to the first 30 minutes of the hearing on the single bills.	532	522
7. Fee payable by any party enrolling a motion or making a motion orally at the bar and any party opposing any such motion.	106	104
F. LANDS VALUATION APPEAL COURT 1. Appeal - inclusive fee.	319	313
2. Answers - inclusive fee.	227	223
G. EXTRACTS DEPARTMENT 1. Extract decree following upon a summons, petition or appeal, or after protestation of a note, whether in absence or otherwise.	62	61
2. Extract of admission as a solicitor.	57	56
3. Extract of protestation.	57	56
4. Certificate under the Civil Jurisdiction and Judgments Act 1982.	57	56
5. Documentation evidencing divorce, nullity or dissolution of marriage or civil partnership including— (a) extract from Consistorial Register of Decrees of decree pronounced on or after 23rd September 1975 if not issued in terms of item B3 or B4 of this Table; (b) certificate of divorce in decree pronounced prior to 23rd September 1975; (c) certified copy interlocutor in decree pronounced prior to 23rd September 1975.	33	32
6. Extract from the Register of Acts and Decrees – per sheet or part thereof.	33	32
7. Sealing and certifying any document for exhibition in a foreign jurisdiction or otherwise.	33	32
8. Acknowledgement of receipt of a notice under section 19(6) or 21(2) of the Conveyancing and Feudal Reform (Scotland) Act 1970.	57	56
PART II – FEES IN THE OFFICE OF THE ACCOUNTANT OF COURT H. OFFICE OF THE ACCOUNTANT OF COURT *I. In Factories*		

Column 1 (Matters)	Column 2 (Fee payable) £	Column 3 (Fee formerly Payable)[1] £
1. Registering case and receiving and delivering up bond of caution.	23	23
2. Examining factor's inventory – 0.333% of the value of the estate as disclosed (a) minimum fee payable; (b) maximum fee payable.	 33 768	 32 753
3. Auditing each account, based on estate value— (a) £0 - £30,000; (b) £30,001 - £50,000; (c) £50,001 - £250,000; (d) £250,001 - £500,000; (e) £500,001 and above.	 119 240 599 899 1,199	 117 235 587 881 1,175
4. Reporting with regard to discharge, special powers, other special matters, surplus estate or scheme of division.	59	58
5. For certificate under seal.	18	18
II. In Consignations 6. Lodging consignation.	 35	 34
7. Producing or delivering up consignation, based on consignation value— (a) consignation value £0 - £50 and less than 7 years since lodged; (b) consignation value over £50 and less than 7 years since lodged; (c) consignation value £0 - £70 and over 7 years since lodged; (d) consignation value over £70 and over 7 years since lodged.	 No charge 35 No charge 56	 No charge 34 No charge 55
PART III – FEES IN THE OFFICE OF THE AUDITOR OF THE COURT OF SESSION I. OFFICE OF THE AUDITOR OF THE COURT OF SESSION 1. Taxing accounts of expenses incurred in judicial proceedings (including proceedings in the High Court of Justiciary) remitted to the Auditor of the Court of Session for taxation— (a) on lodging account for taxation; (b) taxing accounts for expenses etc.— (i) up to £400; (ii) for every additional £100 or part thereof.	 46 21 5	 45 21 5

Column 1 (Matters)	Column 2 (Fee payable) £	Column 3 (Fee formerly Payable)[1] £
Note: fee to be determined by the Auditor of the Court of Session on amount of account as submitted.		
2. Fee for assessing account remitted to the Auditor to determine whether an additional fee should be paid.	306	300
3. Fee for cancellation of diet of taxation—		
(a) where written notice of cancellation received from receiving party after 4.00 pm on the fourth working day before the day of the diet of taxation;	50% of fee that would be payable under item I1(b) of this Table	50% of fee that would be payable under item I1(b) of this Table
(b) where written notice of cancellation received from receiving party after 4.00 pm on the second working day before the day of the diet of taxation.	75% of fee that would be payable under item I1(b) of this Table	75% of fee that would be payable under item I1(b) of this Table
PART IV – FEES COMMON TO ALL OFFICES		
J. MISCELLANEOUS		
1. Certified copy of proceedings for appeal to the Supreme Court.	227	223
2. Certifying of any other document (plus copying charges if necessary).	19	19
3. Recording, engrossing, extracting, printing or copying of all documents (exclusive of search fee)—		
(a) by photocopying or otherwise producing a printed or typed copy—		
(i) up to 10 pages;	7	7
(ii) each page or part thereof in excess of 10 pages;	0.50	0.50
(b) for a copy of each document in electronic form.	7	7
4. Any search of records or archives, per 30 minutes or part thereof.		
In addition, correspondence fee where applicable.	13	13
5. Captions—		
(a) marking caption when ordered;	13	13
(b) warrant for caption when issued.	13	13

Column 1 (Matters)	**Column 2 (Fee payable) £**	**Column 3 (Fee formerly Payable)[1] £**
6. Change of party name where more than 10 cases are registered – per case.	2	2

DIRECTIONS

NO. 3 OF 1994: PRODUCTIONS WHICH MAY BE SENT BY FACSIMILE TRANSMISSION

I, the Lord President of the Court of Session, under and by virtue of the powers conferred on me by rule 23.2(4)(a)(iv) (documents which may be transmitted by facsimile) of the Rules of the Court of Session 1994, hereby make the following direction: C4.1

1. A production may not be sent to the court and lodged in process by facsimile transmission except as permitted under this direction.

2. Subject to paragraph 3 below, where a motion mentioned in column 1 of the following table is enrolled by facsimile transmission, a document mentioned in column 2 of that table which is to be referred to solely in support of the motion may be sent by facsimile transmission with an Inventory of Productions.

Table

Column 1	**Column 2 Supporting document**
1. Assessment of liability for expenses under or by virtue of the Legal Aid (Scotland) Act 1967 or the Legal Aid (Scotland) Act 1986	Minute of assessment
2. Commission to take evidence of witness	Medical certificate
3. Interim aliment	Wage certificate etc.
4. To open confidential envelope	Copy of letter of intimation of motion to haver
5. Loosing, restriction or recall of arrestment or recall of inhibition	Copy of letter of intimation of motion

3. Where—

(a) a motion to which paragraph 2 applies is opposed, or

(b) the court requests,

the original of a document transmitted under paragraph 1 above shall be lodged in process as a production.

4. This direction shall come into force on 5th September 1994.

28th June 1994

No. 3 of 1994: PRODUCTIONS WHICH MAY BE SENT BY FACSIMILE TRANSMISSION

The Lord President, at the Court of Session, under and by virtue of the powers conferred on him by rule 4.7(1)(b) (documents which may be transmitted by facsimile) of the Rules of the Court of Session 1994, hereby makes the following direction:

1. A production may not be sent to the court and to other parties by facsimile transmission except as permitted under this direction.

2. Subject to paragraph 3 below, where a motion mentioned in column 1 of the following table is applied for by facsimile transmission, a production mentioned in column 2 of that table which is referred to or lodged in support of the motion may be sent by facsimile transmission with the motion.

Table

Column 1	Column 2 supporting documents
1. Assessment of liability for expenses under or by virtue of the Legal Aid (Scotland) Act 1986	Minute of assessment
2. Commission to take evidence of any witness	Medical certificate
3. Interim aliment	Wages certificate, etc.
4. To open confidential envelope	Copy of letter of intimation of motion to haver
5. Change, restriction or recall of arrestment or recall of inhibition	Copy of letter of intimation of motion

3. Where—
(a) a motion to which paragraph 2 above applies is opposed; or
(b) the court so directs,
the original of a document transmitted under paragraph 2 above shall be lodged in process as a production.

4. This direction shall come into force on 5th September 1994.

28th June 1994.

NO. 4 OF 1994: MOTIONS

[Revoked by Direction No. 3 of 2009.] **C4.2**

NO. 5 OF 1994: JUDGES FOR ELECTION COURT

I, the Lord President of the Court of Session, under and by virtue of the power conferred on me by section 44 of the Court of Session Act 1988, do hereby make the following direction— C4.3

1. The judges to be placed on the rota for the trial of parliamentary election petitions under Part III of the Representation of the People Act 1983 for the remainder of 1994 and for 1995 shall be the Honourable Lord Morison and the Honourable Lord Sutherland.
2. Direction No. 2 of 1989 (Rota of Judges for Election Court) is hereby revoked.

1st October 1994

NO. 2 OF 1995: MOTIONS IN COMMERCIAL ACTIONS

[Revoked by Direction No.3 of 2010.] **C4.4**

NO. 4 OF 1999: THE ADVOCATE GENERAL FOR SCOTLAND

I, the Lord President of the Court of Session, under and by virtue of the powers conferred on me by rule 1.4 of the Rules of the Court of Session 1994, hereby make the following direction:— **C4.5**

When appearing in the Court of Session, the Advocate General for Scotland shall be entitled to sit at the table within the Bar, immediately below the Bench at the left hand side of the chair.

19th May 1999

NO. 2 OF 2000: ROTA OF JUDGES FOR ELECTION COURT

I, the Lord President of the Court of Session, under and by virtue of the power conferred on me by section 44 of the Court of Session Act 1988(a), do hereby make the following direction— **C4.6**

1. The judges to be placed on the rota for the trial of parliamentary election petitions under Part III of the Representation of the People Act 1983(b) for the remainder of 2000 shall be the Honourable Lord Kirkwood and the Honourable Lord Milligan.
2. Direction No 2 of 1997 (Rota of Judges for Election Court) is hereby revoked.

29th February 2000

NO. 2 OF 2004: SITTINGS OF THE COURT OF SESSION FOR THE LEGAL YEARS 2004/2005; 2005/2006; AND 2006/2007

I, the Lord President of the Court of Session, under and by virtue of the powers conferred on me by rules 10.1, 10.2(2), 10.3 and 10.4 of the Rules of the Court of Session 1994 hereby make the following direction— C4.7

1. Revocation of previous direction

Direction No. 1 of 2004 (sittings of the Court of Session for the legal years 2004/5; 2005/6; and 2006/7) is hereby revoked.

2. Sessions of court

Subject to paragraph 4 below, the court shall be in session from—

(a) Saturday 18th September 2004 to Monday 26th September 2005 ("legal year 2004/2005");

(b) Tuesday 27th September 2005 to Monday 25th September 2006 ("legal year 2005/2006"); and

(c) Tuesday 26th September 2006 to Monday 24th September 2007 ("legal year 2006/2007").

3.— Terms of court

(1) The terms of the court for the legal year 2004/2005 shall be as follows—

- (a) winter term - Tuesday 21st September 2004 to Friday 17th December 2004;
- (b) spring term - Thursday 6th January 2005 to Friday 18th March 2005; and
- (c) summer term - Tuesday 19th April 2005 to Friday 15th July 2005.

(2) The terms of the court for the legal year 2005/2006 shall be as follows—

- (a) winter term - Tuesday 27th September 2005 to Friday 23rd December 2005;
- (b) spring term - Thursday 5th January 2006 to Friday 24th March 2006; and
- (c) summer term - Tuesday 25th April 2006 to Friday 14th July 2006.

(3) The terms of the court for the legal year 2006/2007 shall be as follows—

- (a) winter term - Tuesday 26th September 2006 to Friday 22nd December 2006;
- (b) spring term - Thursday 4th January 2007 to Friday 23rd March 2007; and
- (c) summer term - Tuesday 24th April 2007 to Friday 13th July 2007.

4.— Vacation

(1) The court shall be in vacation from—

- (a) Saturday 18th December 2004 to Wednesday 5th January 2005;
- (b) Saturday 24th December 2005 to Wednesday 4th January 2006; and
- (c) Saturday 23rd December 2006 to Wednesday 3rd January 2007.

(2) Each Thursday during the periods mentioned in sub-paragraph (1) shall be a sederunt day.

5.— Public holidays

(1) Subject to rule 10.3(3) of the Rules of the Court of Session 1994, no Division, Lord Ordinary or Vacation Judge shall sit during the public holidays specified in sub-paragraphs (2) to (4).

(2) The public holidays for the legal year 2004/2005 shall be as follows—

the afternoon of Friday 24th December 2004;
Monday 27th December 2004;
Tuesday 28th December 2004;
Monday 3rd January 2005;
Tuesday 4th January 2005;
Friday 25th March 2005 (Good Friday);
Monday 28th March 2005 (Easter Monday);
Monday 18th April 2005 (Spring Holiday);
Monday 2nd May 2005 (May Day Holiday);
Monday 23rd May 2005 (Victoria Day Holiday); and
Monday 19th September 2005 (Autumn Holiday).

(3) The public holidays for the legal year 2005/2006 shall be as follows—

the afternoon of Friday 23rd December 2005;
Monday 26th December 2005;
Tuesday 27th December 2005;
Monday 2nd January 2006;
Tuesday 3rd January 2006;
Monday 10th April 2006 (Spring Holiday);
Friday 14th April 2006 (Good Friday);
Monday 17th April 2006 (Easter Monday);
Monday 1st May 2006 (May Day Holiday);
Monday 22nd May 2006 (Victoria Day Holiday); and
Monday 18th September 2006 (Autumn Holiday).

(4) The public holidays for the legal year 2006/2007 shall be as follows—

the afternoon of Friday 22nd December 2006;
Monday 25th December 2006;
Tuesday 26th December 2006;
Monday 1st January 2007;
Tuesday 2nd January 2007;
Friday 6th April 2007 (Good Friday);
Monday 9th April 2007 (Easter Monday);
Monday 16th April 2007 (Spring Holiday);
Monday 7th May 2007 (May Day Holiday);
Monday 21st May 2007 (Victoria Day Holiday); and
Monday 17th September 2007 (Autumn Holiday).

6. Court hours

In term, the court shall normally sit between the following hours, with an appropriate adjournment for luncheon—

(a) Inner House - 10.30 am and 4.00 pm; and
(b) Outer House - 10.00 am and 4.00 pm

17th March 2004

NO.1 OF 2005: HUMAN RIGHTS ACT 1998: DECLARATIONS OF INCOMPATIBILITY

I, the Lord President of the Court of Session, under and by virtue of the power conferred on me by rule 82.3 of the Rules of the Court of Session 1994, hereby make the following direction— **C4.8**

1. Direction No.2 of 2003 (intimation to the Crown in proceedings where the court is considering whether to make a declaration of incompatibility) is hereby revoked.
2. Where in any proceedings the court is considering whether to make a declaration of incompatibility within the meaning of section 4 of the Human Rights Act 1998, notice in Form 82.3-A of the Rules of the Court of Session 1994 shall be given to the following—

   (a) Solicitor to the Advocate General for Scotland,

   Victoria Quay,
   Edinburgh,
   EH6 6QQ

   (b) Solicitor to the Scottish Executive,

   Victoria Quay,
   Edinburgh,
   EH6 6QQ

13th April 2005

NO. 2 OF 2005: ROTA FOR TRIAL OF PARLIAMENTARY ELECTION PETITIONS

[Revoked by Direction No. 1 of 2012.] **C4.9**

NO. 3 OF 2005: MOTIONS IN CERTAIN INSOLVENCY AND COMPANIES ACTIONS

[Revoked by Direction No. 3 of 2010.] **C4.10**

NO. 2 OF 2006: SITTINGS OF THE COURT OF SESSION FOR THE LEGAL YEARS 2007/2008; 2008/2009; AND 2009/2010

I, the Lord President of the Court of Session, under and by virtue of the powers conferred on me by rules 10.1, 10.2(2), 10.3 and 10.4 of the Rules of the Court of Session 1994 hereby make the following direction— **C4.11**

1. Revocation of previous direction

Direction No. 1 of 2006 (sittings of the Court of Session for the legal years 2007/2008; 2008/2009; and 2009/2010) is hereby revoked.

2. Sessions of court

Subject to paragraph 4 below, the court shall be in session from—

(a) Tuesday 25th September 2007 to Monday 22nd September 2008 ("legal year 2007/2008");

(b) Tuesday 23rd September 2008 to Monday 21st September 2009 ("legal year 2008/2009"); and

(c) Tuesday 22nd September 2009 to Monday 20th September 2010 ("legal year 2009/2010").

3.— Terms of court

(1) The terms of the court for the legal year 2007/2008 shall be as follows—

- (a) winter term—Tuesday 25th September 2007 to Friday 21st December 2007;
- (b) spring term—Friday 4th January 2008 to Thursday 20th March 2008; and
- (c) summer term—Tuesday 22nd April 2008 to Friday 11th July 2008.

(2) The terms of the court for the legal year 2008/2009 shall be as follows—

- (a) winter term—Tuesday 23rd September 2008 to Friday 19th December 2008;
- (b) spring term—Tuesday 6th January 2009 to Friday 20th March 2009; and
- (c) summer term—Tuesday 21st April 2009 to Friday 10th July 2009.

(3) The terms of the court for the legal year 2009/2010 shall be as follows—

- (a) winter term—Tuesday 22nd September 2009 to Friday 18th December 2009;
- (b) spring term—Wednesday 6th January 2010 to Friday 26th March 2010; and
- (c) summer term—Monday 26th April 2010 to Friday 16th July 2010.

4.— Vacation

(1) The court shall be in vacation from—

- (a) Saturday 22nd December 2007 to Thursday 3rd January 2008;
- (b) Saturday 20th December 2008 to Monday 5th January 2009; and
- (c) Saturday 19th December 2009 to Tuesday 5th January 2010.

(2) Each Thursday during the periods mentioned in sub-paragraph (1) shall be a sederunt day.

5.— Public holidays

(1) Subject to rule 10.3(3) of the Rules of the Court of Session 1994, no Division, Lord Ordinary or Vacation Judge shall sit during the public holidays specified in sub-paragraphs (2) to (4).

(2) The public holidays for the legal year 2007/2008 shall be as follows—

the afternoon of Monday 24th December 2007;
Tuesday 25th December 2007;
Wednesday 26th December 2007;
Tuesday 1st January 2008;
Wednesday 2nd January 2008;
Friday 21st March 2008 (Good Friday);
Monday 24th March 2008 (Easter Monday);
Monday 21st April 2008 (Spring Holiday);
Monday 5th May 2008 (May Day Holiday);
Monday 19th May 2008 (Victoria Day Holiday); and
Monday 15th September 2008 (Autumn Holiday).

(3) The public holidays for the legal year 2008/2009 shall be as follows—

the afternoon of Wednesday 24th December 2008;
Thursday 25th December 2008;
Friday 26th December 2008;
Thursday 1st January 2009;
Friday 2nd January 2009;
Friday 10th April 2009 (Good Friday);
Monday 13th April 2009 (Easter Monday);
Monday 20th April 2009 (Spring Holiday);
Monday 4th May 2009 (May Day Holiday);
Monday 18th May 2009 (Victoria Day Holiday); and
Monday 21st September 2009 (Autumn Holiday).

(4) The public holidays for the legal year 2009/2010 shall be as follows—

the afternoon of Thursday 24th December 2009;
Friday 25th December 2009;
Monday 28th December 2009;
Friday 1st January 2010;
Monday 4th January 2010;
Friday 2nd April 2010 (Good Friday);
Monday 5th April 2010 (Easter Monday);
Monday 19th April 2010 (Spring Holiday);
Monday 3rd May 2010 (May Day Holiday);
Monday 17th May 2010 (Victoria Day Holiday); and
Monday 20th September 2010 (Autumn Holiday).

6. Court hours

In term, the court shall normally sit between the following hours, with an appropriate adjournment for luncheon—

(a) Inner House—10.30 am and 4.00 pm; and
(b) Outer House—10.00 am and 4.00 pm.

November 2006

NO. 2 OF 2007: MOTIONS IN CERTAIN CAUSES

[*Revoked by Direction No. 3 of 2009.*] **C4.12**

NO. 2 OF 2009: SITTINGS OF THE COURT OF SESSION FOR THE LEGAL YEARS 2010/2011 AND 2011/2012

I, the Lord President of the Court of Session, under and by virtue of the powers conferred on me by rules 10.1, 10.2(2), 10.3 and 10.4 of the Rules of the Court of Session 1994 hereby make the following direction— **C4.13**

1. Sessions of court

Subject to paragraph 4 below, the court shall be in session from—

(a) Tuesday 21th September 2010 to Monday 26th September 2011 ("legal year 2010/2011");
and

(b) Tuesday 27th September 2011 to Monday 24th September 2012 ("legal year 2011/2012").

2.— Terms of court

(1) The terms of the court for the legal year 2010/2011 shall be as follows—

- (a) winter term—Tuesday 21st September 2010 to Friday 24th December 2010;
- (b) spring term—Thursday 6th January 2011 to Friday 25th March 2011; and
- (c) summer term—Tuesday 26th April 2011 to Friday 15th July 2011.

(2) The terms of the court for the legal year 2011/2012 shall be as follows—

- (a) winter term—Tuesday 27th September 2011 to Friday 23rd December 2011;
- (b) spring term—Thursday 5th January 2012 to Friday 23rd March 2012; and
- (c) summer term—Tuesday 24th April 2012 to Friday 13th July 2012.

3.— Vacation

(1) The court shall be in vacation from—

- (a) Saturday 25th December 2010 to Wednesday 5th January 2011; and
- (b) Saturday 24th December 2011 to Wednesday 4th January 2012.

(2) Each Thursday during the periods mentioned in subparagraph (1) shall be a sederunt day.

4.— Public holidays

(1) Subject to rule 10.3(3) of the Rules of the Court of Session 1994, no Division, Lord Ordinary or Vacation Judge shall sit during the public holidays specified in subparagraphs (2) and (3).

(2) The public holidays for the legal year 2010/2011 shall be as follows—

the afternoon of Friday 24th December 2010;
Monday 27th December 2010;
Tuesday 28th December 2010;
Monday 3rd January 2011;
Tuesday 4th January 2011;
Monday 18th April 2011 (Spring Holiday);
Friday 22nd April 2011 (Good Friday);
Monday 25tll April 2011 (Easter Monday);
Monday 2nd May 2011 (May Day Holiday);
Monday 3rd May 2011 (Victoria Day Holiday); and
Monday 19th September 2011 (Autumn Holiday).

(3) [1]The public holidays for the legal year 2011/2012 shall be as follows—

the afternoon of Friday 23rd December 2011;
Monday 26th December 2011;
Tuesday 27th December 2011;
Monday 2nd January 2012;
Tuesday 3rd January 2012;
Friday 6th April 2012 (Good Friday);
Monday 9th April 2012 (Easter Monday);
Monday 16th April 2012 (Spring Holiday);
Monday 7th May 2012 (May Day Holiday);
Monday 4th June 2012 (Victoria Day Holiday);
Tuesday 5th June (The Queen's Diamond Jubilee Holiday); and
Monday 17th September 2012 (Autumn Holiday).

5. Court hours

In term, the court shall normally sit between the following hours, with an appropriate adjournment for lunch—

(a) Inner House—10.30 am and 4.00 pm; and
(b) Outer House—10.00 am and 4.00 pm.

8th October 2009

Note:

Direction No.2 of 2006 was amended to include 30 November 2009 (St. Andrew's Day) in the list of public holidays when the court shall not sit. It has yet to be decided whether there is to be a day when the court shall not sit for St. Andrew's Day in the legal years fixed by this Direction. A decision will be taken in due course and an amendment made to this Direction if appropriate.

[1] As amended by P.N. No. 2 of 2011.

NO.3 OF 2009: MOTIONS INTIMATED AND ENROLLED BY MEANS OTHER THAN EMAIL

I, the Lord President of the Court of Session, under and by virtue of the powers conferred on me by rule 23.4(1)(a) (day and time for lodging notices of opposition to motions) and rule 23.6(1) (day of publication and hearing of motions) of the Rules of the Court of Session 1994, hereby make the following direction— **C4.14**

1. Subject to paragraph 2, this direction applies to a motion which is intimated and enrolled in accordance with Parts 3 and 4 of Chapter 23 of the Rules of the Court of Session 1994.
2. This direction does not apply to a motion under any of the following rules:
   (a) rule 23.8 (motions by pursuer before calling or petitioner before first order);
   (b) rule 23.9 (motions where caveat lodged);
   (c) rule 23.10 (motions by defender or other person before calling).
3. Where, after calling, a motion is enrolled during a term, the provisions of the following timetable shall apply subject to paragraph 4.

Timetable

Time for enrolment	Latest time for opposition	Day of publication	Day of court hearing in the rolls
Monday 4 p.m.	Tuesday 12.30 p.m.	Tuesday	Wednesday
Tuesday 4 p.m.	Wednesday 12.30 p.m.	Wednesday	Thursday
Wednesday 4 p.m.	Thursday 12.30 p.m.	Thursday	Friday
Thursday 4 p.m.	Monday 12.30 p.m.	Monday	Tuesday
Friday 4 p.m.	Monday 12.30 p.m.	Monday	Tuesday

4. Where, in the case of an opposed motion, it is not possible for the motion to be heard in accordance with the timetable in paragraph 3, the motion will be put out for hearing at another date and time convenient to the court and, where possible, to the parties. Urgent motions will be dealt with on a priority basis.
5. The Keeper of the Rolls or clerk to the court shall intimate the date and time mentioned in paragraph 4 to the parties.
6. Where a motion is enrolled in session outwith a term or in vacation, the timetable in paragraph 3 shall apply subject to the following provisions—
   (a) there shall be no publication in the rolls of the motion; and
   (b) where a motion enrolled in a cause in the Inner House is one which—
      (i) may not be heard by the Lord Ordinary or the vacation judge; and
      (ii) the day for hearing the motion would fall outwith a term or in vacation,

   the motion should be put out for hearing in the Single Bills on the earliest available day in the following term of the court.

7. Direction No. 4 of 1994 (Motions) and Direction No.2 of 2007 (Motions in Certain Causes) are hereby revoked.
8. This direction shall come into force on 1st February 2010.

16th December 2009

NO. 1 OF 2010: PUBLIC HOLIDAYS IN RESPECT OF ST ANDREW'S DAY

I, the Lord President of the Court of Session, under and by virtue of the powers conferred on me by rule 10.3 of the Rules of the Court of Session 1994, direct that Monday 29 November 2010 and Monday 28 November 2011 shall be public holidays on which the court shall not sit; and the lists of dates in paragraphs 4(2) and (3) of Direction No. 2 of 2009 are amended accordingly. **C4.15**

6th January 2010

NO. 2 OF 2010: PERSONAL INJURY ACTIONS RELATING TO THE DRUGS VIOXX AND CELEBREX

I, the Lord President of the Court of Session, under and by virtue of the powers conferred on me by paragraph (2) of rule 2.2 of the Rules of the Court of Session 1994, having consulted the parties of proceedings already raised to which this direction applies and being of the opinion mentioned in paragraph (1) of that rule, make the following direction. C4.16

1. This direction applies to actions for damages for, or arising from, personal injuries or death arising out of the taking of either of the drugs commonly known as Vioxx and Celebrex.
2. This direction applies to an action already raised as well as a new action.
3. Expressions used in this direction which are also used in the Rules of the Court of Session 1994 have the same meaning here as they have in those Rules.
4. Chapter 43 of the Rules of the Court of Session 1994 shall not apply; accordingly—
   (a) a new action shall be raised as an ordinary action; and
   (b) an action already raised shall proceed as an ordinary action without the need for further procedure.
5. Subject to the following provisions, actions shall proceed as ordinary actions and be subject to the rules which apply to such actions.
6. Subject to paragraph 7, by the due date the pursuer shall—
   (a) disclose to the defenders the identity of all medical practitioners or institutions from whom he or she has received medical treatment; and
   (b) produce all medical records relating to the pursuer.
7. The "due date" is—
   (a) in relation to an action raised before the date of this direction, the date falling 12 weeks after the date of this direction;
   (b) in relation to an action raised after the date of this direction, the date falling 4 weeks after the raising of the action.
8. Where the pursuer considers that any part of his or her medical records should not be disclosed under paragraph 7, that part is to be produced to the court in a sealed envelope together with a note setting out the reasons why they should not be disclosed. The court shall determine, on the application of any party, whether they should be disclosed.
9. Where paragraph 7 is not complied with, the court shall grant an appropriate order for the production of the medical records unless the pursuer shows special cause why such order should not be granted.
10. Defences require to be lodged by the date falling 12 weeks (or such longer period as the court may order on cause shown) after production of the relevant medical records by the pursuer.
11. The court will manage the actions with the aim of securing the efficient disposal of them.
12. To that end, the court shall have power to make appropriate orders, including—
    (a) the fixing of by order hearings;
    (b) determining further procedure;
    (b) setting timetables;
    (c) ordering disclosure of information;

(d) ordering the production and recovery of documents;
(e) ordering the production of expert reports (and rebuttal reports);
(f) ordering the production of affidavits;
(g) ordering the production of witness lists and notes of argument;
(h) ordering the appointment of actions to procedure roll hearings or proofs on all or any part of the action;
(j) ordering the use of information technology in the presentation of documents and the recording and presentation of evidence;
(k) ordering the reservation of dates in the court diary for hearings;
(l) sisting actions.

13. The court may make any of these orders at its own initiative or on the motion or one or more parties, but if acting on its own initiative it must (with the exception of fixing by order hearings) give the parties an opportunity to be heard before making an order.
14. So far as reasonably practicable, the court's management function will be discharged by Lord Drummond Young.
15. Lord Drummond Young shall give early to consideration to whether, in order to determine or give guidance on any generic issues in the actions, it is appropriate to identify a lead action or actions to be progressed at an advanced rate.

23 September 2010

NO. 3 OF 2010: MOTIONS IN COMMERCIAL ACTIONS AND CERTAIN INSOLVENCY AND COMPANIES ACTIONS

I, the Lord President of the Court of Session, under and by virtue of the powers conferred on me by rule 23.6(1) of the Rules of the Court of Session 1994 (day of publication and hearing of motions), hereby make the following direction: **C4.17**

1. This direction applies to a motion enrolled in—
   (a) an action within the meaning of rule 47.1(2) (definition of commercial action);
   (b) proceedings in the Outer House in a cause under or by virtue of the Insolvency Act 1986 or the Company Directors Disqualification Act 1986; and
   (c) proceedings in the Outer House in a cause under or by virtue of section 645 (application to court for order of confirmation), section 896 (court order for holding of meeting) or section 899 (court sanction for compromise or arrangement) of the Companies Act 2006.
2. This direction is intended to ensure that the substantive business scheduled to begin at 10 a.m. is not interrupted or delayed.
3. Direction No. 3 of 2009 (motions intimated and enrolled by means other than email) shall apply to such a motion subject to the following paragraph.
4. Any opposed motion, or a motion requiring explanation, will be put out for hearing at a date and time convenient to the court and, where possible, to the parties. Where a motion is opposed or otherwise starred, the clerk of court will fix a date for hearing and give intimation of that date to the parties. Urgent motions will be dealt with on a priority basis.
5. Direction No. 2 of 1995 (Motions in Commercial Actions) and Direction No. 3 of 2005 (Motions in certain insolvency and companies actions) are hereby revoked.
6. This direction comes into force on 1st November 2010.

14th October 2010

NO. 1 OF 2011: PUBLIC HOLIDAY IN RESPECT OF ROYAL WEDDING

I, the Lord President of the Court of Session, under and by virtue of the powers conferred on me by rule 10.3 of the Rules of the Court of Session 1994, direct that Friday 29 April 2011 shall be a public holiday on which the court shall not sit; and the list of dates in paragraph 4(2) of Direction No. 2 of 2009 is amended accordingly. **C4.18**

12th January 2011

NO. 2 OF 2011: PUBLIC HOLIDAYS IN RESPECT OF THE QUEEN'S DIAMOND JUBILEE

I, the Lord President of the Court of Session, under and by virtue of the powers conferred on me by rule 10.3 of the Rules of the Court of Session 1994, direct that: **C4.19**

(i) the public holiday (on which the court shall not sit) on Monday 21st May 2012 (Victoria Day Holiday) shall now take place on Monday 4th June 2012;
(ii) Tuesday 5th June 2012 (The Queen's Diamond Jubilee Holiday) shall be a public holiday on which the court shall not sit; and
(iii) the list of dates in paragraph 4(3) of Direction No. 2 of 2009 is amended accordingly.

8th August 2011

NO. 2 OF 2011: PUBLIC HOLIDAYS IN RESPECT OF THE QUEEN'S DIAMOND JUBILEE

The Lord President of the Court of Session, under and by virtue of the powers conferred on him by rule 10.5 of the Rules of the Court of Session 1994, directs that— C4.19

(i) the public holiday on which the court shall not sit on Monday 21st May 2012 (Victoria Day Holiday) shall not take place on Monday 21st May 2012;

(ii) Tuesday 5th June 2012 (The Queen's Diamond Jubilee Holiday) shall be a public holiday on which the court shall not sit; and

NO. 3 OF 2011: SITTINGS OF THE COURT OF SESSION FOR THE LEGAL YEARS 2012/2013, 2013/2014 AND 2014/2015

I, the Lord President of the Court of Session, under and by virtue of the powers conferred on me by rules 10.1, 10.2(2), 10.3 and 10.4 of the Rules of the Court of Session 1994 hereby make the following direction— **C4.20**

1. Sessions of court

Subject to paragraph 4 below, the court shall be in session from—

(a) Tuesday 25th September 2012 to Monday 23rd September 2013 ("legal year 2012/2013");

(b) Tuesday 24th September 2013 to Monday 22nd September 2014 ("legal year 2013/2014"); and

(c) Tuesday 23rd September 2014 to Monday 21st September 2015 ("legal year 2014/2015").

2.— Terms of court

(1) The terms of the court for the legal year 2012/2013 shall be as follows—

(a) winter term—Tuesday 25th September 2012 to Friday 21st December 2012;

(b) spring term—Tuesday 8th January 2013 to Friday 22nd March 2013; and

(c) summer term—Tuesday 23rd April 2013 to Friday 12th July 2013.

(2) The terms of the court for the legal year 2013/2014 shall be as follows—

(a) winter term—Tuesday 24th September 2013 to Friday 20th December 2013;

(b) spring term—Tuesday 7th January 2014 to Friday 21st March 2014; and

(c) summer term—Tuesday 22nd April 2014 to Friday 11th July 2014.

(3) The terms of the court for the legal year 2014/2015 shall be as follows—

(a) winter term—Tuesday 23rd September 2014 to Friday 19th December 2014;

(b) spring term—Tuesday 6th January 2015 to Friday 20th March 2015; and

(c) summer term—Tuesday 21st April 2015 to Friday 10th July 2015.

3.— Vacation

(1) The court shall be in vacation from—

(a) Saturday 22nd December 2012 to Monday 7th January 2013;

(b) Saturday 21st December 2013 to Monday 6th January 2014; and

(c) Saturday 20th December 2014 to Monday 5th January 2015.

(2) The sederunt days during the periods mentioned in subparagraph (1) shall be as follows:

(a) Friday 28th December 2012 and Friday 4th January 2013;

(b) Tuesday 31st December 2013; and

(c) Tuesday 30th December 2014.

4.— Public holidays

(1) Subject to rule 10.3(3) of the Rules of the Court of Session 1994, no Division, Lord Ordinary or Vacation Judge shall sit during the public holidays specified in subparagraphs (2) and (3).

(2) The public holidays for the legal year 2012/2013 shall be as follows:

Monday 3rd December 2012 (St. Andrew's Day);
the afternoon of Monday 24th December 2012;
Tuesday 25th December 2012;
Wednesday 26th December 2012;
Tuesday 1st January 2013;
Wednesday 2nd January 2013;
Friday 29th March 2013 (Good Friday);
Monday 1st April 2013 (Easter Monday);
Monday 15th April 2013 (Spring Holiday);
Monday 6th May 2013 (May Day Holiday);
Monday 20th May 2013 (Victoria Day Holiday); and
Monday 16th September 2013 (Autumn Holiday).

(3) The public holidays for the legal year 2013/2014 shall be as follows:

Monday 2nd December 2013 (St. Andrew's Day);
the afternoon of Tuesday 24th December 2013;
Wednesday 25th December 2013;
Thursday 26th December 2013;
Wednesday 1st January 2014;
Thursday 2nd January 2014;
Monday 14th April 2014 (Spring Holiday);
Friday 18th April 2014 (Good Friday);
Monday 21st April 2014 (Easter Monday);
Monday 5th May 2014 (May Day Holiday);
Monday 19th May 2014 (Victoria Day Holiday); and
Monday 15th September 2014 (Autumn Holiday).

(4) The public holidays for the legal year 2014/2015 shall be as follows:

Monday 1st December 2014 (St. Andrew's Day);
the afternoon of Wednesday 24th December 2014;
Thursday 25th December 2014;
Friday 26th December 2014;
Thursday 1st January 2015;
Friday 2nd January 2015;
Friday 3rd April 2015 (Good Friday);
Monday 6th April 2015 (Easter Monday);
Monday 20th April 2015 (Spring Holiday);
Monday 4th May 2015 (May Day Holiday);
Monday 18th May 2015 (Victoria Day Holiday); and
Monday 21st September 2015 (Autumn Holiday).

5. Court hours

In term, the court shall normally sit between the following hours, with an appropriate adjournment for lunch—

(a) Inner House—10.00 am and 4.00 pm; and
(b) Outer House—10.00 am and 4.00 pm.

8th August 2011

NO. 1 OF 2012: ROTA FOR TRIAL OF PARLIAMENTARY ELECTION PETITIONS

I, the Lord President of the Court of Session, under and by virtue of the power conferred on me by section 44 of the Court of Session Act 1988, hereby make the following direction— **C4.21**

1. The judges to be placed on the rota for the trial of parliamentary election petitions under Part III of the Representation of the People Act 1983 for the remainder of 2012 and for 2013 shall be the Right Honourable Lord Eassie and the Right Honourable Lady Paton.

2. Direction No. 2 of 2005 (Rota for trial of parliamentary election petitions) is hereby revoked.

7 June 2012

NO. 2 OF 2012: PERSONAL INJURY ACTIONS IN RESPECT OF PLEURAL PLAQUES AND THE DAMAGES (ASBESTOS-RELATED CONDITIONS) (SCOTLAND) ACT 2009

I, the Lord President of the Court of Session, under and by virtue of the powers conferred on me by paragraph (2) of rule 2.2 of the Rules of the Court of Session 1994, having consulted the parties of proceedings already raised to which this direction applies and being of the opinion mentioned in paragraph (1) of that rule, make the following direction. C4.22

1. This direction applies to actions for damages arising out of the exposure to asbestos and the resulting development of pleural plaques and hitherto no other asbestos-related condition.

2. This direction applies to an action already raised as well as a new action.

3. Expressions used in this direction which are also used in the Rules of the Court of Session 1994 have the same meaning here as they have in those Rules. Chapter 43 of the Rules of the Court of Session 1994 shall apply, except as modified by this Direction.

4. An action already raised and sisted will remain sisted and a new action will be sisted immediately after calling on the authority of the court without the need for further procedure until the parties have complied with the following provisions.

5. The pursuer will assemble and deliver to the defender or each of the defenders a "pursuer's pack" which includes the following:

- (a) A summary of the employment history of the pursuer and evidence of that history;
- (b) An explanation of the pursuer's trade or other employment activity which exposed him to asbestos;
- (c) A copy of the pursuer's up-to-date medical records.

The pursuer will intimate to the General Department by email or letter the date of delivery of the pursuer's pack.

6. A defender will within eight weeks of the receipt of the pursuer's pack intimate to the pursuer whether it proposes to settle the pursuer's claim.

7. If a defender elects to pursue settlement the parties will have four weeks from the date of intimation under paragraph 6 above to agree the terms of the settlement and to produce a Joint Minute disposing of the action.

8. If a defender fails to respond to the pursuer's pack in accordance with paragraph 6 above or if it intimates that it does not propose to settle the claim, the pursuer may apply by motion for the recall of the sist. On receipt of that motion the case will be sent to a by order hearing before the nominated judge.

9. The nominated judge will be Lady Clark of Calton. So far as reasonably practicable she will discharge the court's management function. In her absence her functions may be discharged by another Lord Ordinary.

10. The nominated judge or her substitute will manage the actions in which a sist is recalled with the aim of securing their efficient disposal.

11. To that end the court shall have power to make appropriate orders including:

- (a) the fixing of by order hearings;
- (b) instructing the lodging of defences;
- (c) determining further procedure;

(d) after consultation with the Keeper of the Rolls, allocating a diet of proof and issuing a timetable for the progression of the action by adapting the timetable set out in rule 43.6 of the Rules of the Court of Session 1994 to the circumstances of the particular case;
(e) ordering the appointment of actions to procedure roll hearings;
(f) ordering disclosure of information;
(g) ordering the production and recovery of documents;
(h) ordering the production of expert reports;
(i) ordering each party to produce a statement of valuation of claim;
(j) varying the timetable issued under (d) above.

12. The court may make any of these orders at its own initiative or on the motion of one or more parties, but if acting on its own initiative it must (with the exception of fixing by order hearings) give the parties an opportunity to be heard before making an order.

13. Lady Clark of Calton shall give early consideration to whether it is appropriate to identify a lead action or actions to be progressed at an advanced rate in order to determine or give guidance on any generic issues in the actions.

14. Lady Clark of Calton will also review the actions which remain sisted on a regular basis and not less than every six months in order to avoid unnecessary delay in the determination of those actions and to that end will have power to recall a sist and fix a by order hearing.

27 August 2012

NO. 1 OF 2013: PERSONAL INJURY ACTIONS RELATING TO ALLEGED GROUND CONTAMINATION AT THE WATLING STREET DEVELOPMENT IN MOTHERWELL

I, the Lord President of the Court of Session, under and by virtue of the powers conferred on me by paragraph (2) of rule 2.2 of the Rules of the Court of Session 1994, having consulted the parties of proceedings already raised to which this direction applies and being of the opinion mentioned in paragraph (1) of that rule, make the following direction. **C4.23**

1. This direction applies to actions by residents or former residents of properties situated in Tiber Avenue, Empire Way, Forum Place, Romulus Court, Marius Crescent, Senate Place, Constantine Way, and Cornelia Street in Motherwell for damages arising out of alleged exposure to contaminants.

2. This direction applies to any actions already raised as well as to any new actions and has effect from 11 March 2013.

3. Expressions used in this direction which are also used in the Rules of the Court of Session 1994 have the same meaning here as they have in those Rules.

4. Chapter 43 of the Rules of the Court of Session 1994 shall not apply. Any new action shall be raised as an ordinary action. Any action raised under Chapter 43 shall proceed as an ordinary action without the need for further procedure.

5. Subject to the following provisions or any specific orders of the court, actions shall proceed as ordinary actions and be subject to the rules which apply to such actions.

6. The pursuer shall by the due date set out in paragraph 7:
(a) disclose to the defenders the identity of all medical practitioners or institutions from whom he or she has received medical treatment; and
(b) provide a mandate to the defenders for recovery of all his or her medical records.

7. For any particular action, the "due date" will be the latest of the following:
(a) the date falling 4 weeks from the date of this practice direction;
(b) the date falling 4 weeks from the date of raising the action; or
(c) for actions that remain or are subsequently sisted, the date falling 4 weeks from the date of recall of the sist.

8. If the pursuer considers that any part of his or her medical records should not be disclosed under paragraph 6, that part is to be produced to the court in a sealed envelope together with a note setting out the reasons why it should not be disclosed. The court shall determine, on the application of any party, whether that part of the records should be disclosed.

9. If paragraph 6 is not complied with, the court shall grant an appropriate order for the production of the pursuer's medical records unless the pursuer shows special cause why such an order should not be granted.

10. So far as reasonably practicable, the nominated judge will discharge the court's management function with the aim of securing the efficient disposal of the actions. To that end, the court shall have the power to make the following orders:
(a) fixing of by order hearings;
(b) setting or varying timetables;
(c) determining further procedure;

(d) ordering disclosure of information;
(e) ordering the production and recovery of documents;
(f) ordering the production of the reports of skilled persons;
(g) ordering the sharing of medical records or other information and documents disclosed by one party among other parties;
(h) ordering the production of affidavits;
(i) ordering the lodging of witness lists (including the time estimated for each witness and the matters to which they will speak);
(j) ordering the lodging of notes of argument;
(k) ordering each party to produce a statement of valuation of claim;
(l) ordering the appointment of actions to procedure roll hearings or proofs on all or any parts of the action;
(m) ordering the use of information technology in the presentation of documents and other evidence;
(n) ordering the reservation of dates in the court diary for hearings;
(o) sisting actions; or
(p) such other order as it thinks fit for the speedy determination of the actions.

11. The court may make any of these orders at its own initiative or on the motion of one or more parties, but if acting on its own initiative it must (with the exception of fixing by order hearings) give the parties an opportunity to be heard before making an order.

12. The timetable mentioned in paragraph 10(b) may require the pursuer to:
(a) provide to the defenders all expert reports showing or tending to show the presence of contaminants, the location of those contaminants, and concentration levels of the contaminants;
(b) disclose to the defenders his or her employment history and absence records; and
(c) provide to the defenders vouching for any pecuniary losses, in particular any prescription costs and alternative accommodation costs.

13. The nominated judge shall give early consideration to whether in order to determine or give guidance on any generic issues in the actions, the lead actions which the parties have identified are appropriate to be progressed at an advanced rate.

14. The nominated judge will review any actions which remain sisted on a regular basis and not less than every six months in order to avoid unnecessary delay in the determination of those actions and to that end will have power to recall a sist and fix a by order hearing.

15. The nominated judge will be Lord Doherty. In his absence the court's management function may be discharged by another Lord Ordinary.

26th February 2013

NO.2 OF 2013

SITTINGS OF THE COURT OF SESSION FOR THE LEGAL YEARS 2015/2016, 2016/2017 AND 2017/2018 **C4.24**

I, the Lord President of the Court of Session, under and by virtue of the powers conferred on me by rules 10.1, 10.2, 10.3 and 10.4 of the Rules of the Court of Session 1994 hereby make the following direction:

1. Sessions of court

Subject to paragraph 4 below, the court shall be in session from—

(a) Tuesday 22nd September 2015 to Monday 26th September 2016 ("legal year 2015/2016");
(b) Tuesday 27th September 2016 to Monday 25th September 2017 ("legal year 2016/2017"); and;
(c) Tuesday 26th September 2017 to Monday 24th September 2018 ("legal year 2017/2018").

2.— Terms of court

(1) The terms of the court for the legal year 2015/2016 shall be as follows:

(a) winter term - Tuesday 22nd September 2015 to Friday 18th December 2015;
(b) spring term - Thursday 7th January 2016 to Thursday 24th March 2016; and
(c) summer term - Tuesday 26th April 2016 to Friday 15th July 2016.

(2) The terms of the court for the legal year 2016/2017 shall be as follows:

(a) winter term - Tuesday 27th September 2016 to Friday 23th December 2016;
(b) spring term - Tuesday 10th January 2017 to Friday 24th March 2017; and
(c) summer term - Tuesday 25th April 2017 to Friday 14th July 2017.

(3) The terms of the court for the legal year 2017/2018 shall be as follows:

(a) winter term - Tuesday 26th September 2017 to Friday 22nd December 2017;
(b) spring term - Tuesday 9th January 2018 to Friday 23rd March 2018; and
(c) summer term - Tuesday 24th April 2018 to Friday 13th July 2018.

3.— Vacation

(1) The court shall be in vacation from—

(a) Saturday 19th December 2015 to Wednesday 6th January 2016;
(b) Saturday 24th December 2016 to Monday 9th January 2017; and
(c) Saturday 23rd December 2017 to Monday 8th January 2018.

(2) The sederunt days during the periods mentioned in subparagraph (1) shall be as follows:

(a) Wednesday 23rd December 2015 and Wednesday 30th December 2015;
(b) Thursday 29th December 2016 and Thursday 5th January 2017; and
(c) Thursday 28th December 2017 and Thursday 4th January 2018.

4.— Public holidays

(1) Subject to rule 10.3(3) and rule 10.5(2) of the Rules of the Court of Session 1994, no Division, Lord Ordinary or Vacation Judge shall sit during the public

holidays specified in subparagraphs (2), (3) and (4).

(2) The public holidays for the legal year 2015/2016 shall be as follows:

Monday 30th November 2015 (St. Andrew's Day);
the afternoon of Thursday 24th December 2015;
Friday 25th December 2015;
Monday 28th December 2015;
Friday 1st January 2016;
Monday 4th January 2016;
Friday 25th March 2016 (Good Friday);
Monday 28th March 2016 (Easter Monday);
Monday 18th April 2016 (Spring Holiday);
Monday 2nd May 2016 (May Day Holiday);
Monday 23rd May 2016 (Victoria Day Holiday); and
Monday 19th September 2016 (Autumn Holiday).

(3) The public holidays for the legal year 2016/2017 shall be as follows:

Monday 28th November 2016 (St. Andrew's Day);
the afternoon of Friday 23rd December 2016;
Monday 26th December 2016;
Tuesday 27th December 2016;
Monday 2nd January 2017;
Tuesday 3rd January 2017;
Monday 10th April 2017 (Spring Holiday);
Friday 14th April 2017 (Good Friday);
Monday 17th April 2017 (Easter Monday);
Monday 1st May 2017 (May Day Holiday);
Monday 22nd May 2017 (Victoria Day Holiday); and
Monday 18th September 2017 (Autumn Holiday).

(4) The public holidays for the legal year 2017/2018 shall be as follows:

Monday 27th November 2017 (St. Andrew's Day);
the afternoon of Friday 22nd December 2017;
Monday 25th December 2017;
Tuesday 26th December 2017;
Monday 1st January 2018;
Tuesday 2nd January 2018;
Friday 30th March 2018 (Good Friday);
Monday 2nd April 2018 (Easter Monday);
Monday 16th April 2018 (Spring Holiday);
Monday 7th May 2018 (May Day Holiday);
Monday 21st May 2018 (Victoria Day Holiday); and
Monday 17th September 2018 (Autumn Holiday).

5. Court hours

In term, the court shall normally sit between the following hours, with an appropriate adjournment for lunch:

(a) Inner House—10.00 am and 4.00 pm; and
(b) Outer House—10.00 am and 4.00 pm.

8 October 2013

NO. 1 OF 2014: ROTA FOR TRIAL OF PARLIAMENTARY ELECTION PETITIONS

I, the Lord President of the Court of Session, under and by virtue of the power conferred on me by section 44 of the Court of Session Act 1988, hereby make the following direction:- **C4.25**

1. The judges to be placed on the rota for the trial of parliamentary election petitions under Part III of the Representation of the People Act 1983 for the remainder of 2014 and for 2015 shall be the Right Honourable Lord Eassie and the Right Honourable Lady Paton.

2. Direction No. 1 of 2012 (Rota for trial of parliamentary election petitions) is hereby revoked.

1 July 2014

NO.1 OF 2015: ROTA FOR TRIAL OF PARLIAMENTARY ELECTION PETITIONS

In exercise of the Lord President's functions under section 4(2) of the Judiciary and Courts (Scotland) Act 2008, and by virtue of the power conferred on the Lord President by section 44 of the Court of Session Act 1988, I hereby make the following direction:- **C4.26**

1. The judges to be placed on the rota for the trial of parliamentary election petitions under Part III of the Representation of the People Act 1983 for the remainder of 2015 and for 2016 shall be the Right Honourable Lady Paton and the Right Honourable Lord Matthews.

2. Direction No.1 of 2014 (Rota for trial of parliamentary election petitions) is hereby revoked.

Colin Sutherland
Lord Justice Clerk

Edinburgh
7 July 2015

NO.2 OF 2015: PERSONAL INJURY AND/OR PRODUCT LIABILITY ACTIONS RELATING TO THE USE OF VAGINAL TAPE & MESH

In exercise of the Lord President's functions under section 4(2) of the Judiciary and Courts (Scotland) Act 2008, and by virtue of the powers conferred on the Lord President by paragraph (2) of rule 2.2 of the Rules of the Court of Session 1994, having consulted the parties to proceedings already raised to which the direction applies and being of the opinion mentioned in paragraph (1) of that rule, I hereby make the following direction. **C4.27**

1. This direction applies to all actions for damages arising from the use of vaginal tape and female pelvic mesh to treat stress urinary incontinence and pelvic organ prolapses.

2. This direction applies to any actions already raised as well as to any new actions and has effect from 22 September 2015.

3. Expressions used in this direction which are also used in the Rules of the Court of Session 1994 have the same meaning here as they have in those Rules.

4. At the coming into effect of this direction, all actions already raised under the provisions of Chapter 43 of the Rules of the Court of Session 1994 are deemed to be appointed by the Lord Ordinary to the procedure in Chapter 42A, in terms of Rule of Court 42A.1.(2). The pursuer in any new action shall be deemed to have been granted authority for the cause to proceed as an ordinary action to which Chapter 42A applies, in terms of Rule of Court 43.1A.(3)(a), without the necessity of applying by motion for such authority, in terms of Rule of Court 43.1A.(1).

5. The provisions set out in this direction apply to the period *up to* the closing of the record.

6. Following the entering of appearance on behalf of the defenders, the pursuer shall enrol a motion to sist the action for six months. If the pursuer wishes the action to remain sisted after the expiry of six months - and the pursuer has obtained the consent of each of the defenders - the pursuer may, immediately prior to the expiry of the six month period, lodge a letter in the general department that:

- (a) confirms that all of the defenders' consent;
- (b) confirms the period sought, up to a maximum of six months;
- (c) sets out the progress in assembling the pursuer's pack (see paragraph 7);
- (d) states any difficulties encountered in obtaining the required information for the pack;
- (e) confirms the likely time needed to complete the pack;
- (f) states any other reason why the action should remain sisted.

That action may remain sisted for the period agreed among the parties and on the authority of the court without need for further procedure. Any party may seek recall of the sist on cause shown.

These procedures shall also apply to any existing action in which the defenders have entered appearance.

7. During the period of sist, the pursuer shall assemble and deliver to each of the defenders the "pursuer's pack". This shall comprise:

- (a) A document identifying all medical practitioners or institutions from whom the pursuer has received treatment;
- (b) A copy of the pursuer's complete up-to-date medical records, scans and x-rays;

(c) In respect of those actions that are based solely on, or include allegations of, product liability:

(i) copies of any product identification labels for any tape or mesh product in respect of which an action has been brought or, where such a label is not available, evidence of the identity of the type of product alleged to have been used;

(ii) a document confirming whether any of the product has been explanted, whether any of the product has been retained and, if so, its whereabouts;

(d) Where relevant and insofar as not already specified in the summons, a note of adjustments specifying:

(i) the advice, warnings and/or counselling which the pursuer contends were given to her;

(ii) the advice, warnings and/or counselling which the pursuer contends should have been given to her;

(iii) the decision which the pursuer would have made had she been given advice, warnings and/or counselling in the terms specified;

(iv) the detailed basis of the pursuer's statutory case or cases including a full description of any defect alleged in the product;

(v) the basis of the pursuer's common law case against the defenders involved in the case; and

(vi) the pursuer's case on how the alleged defect and/or negligence caused the pursuer's alleged injuries.

8. The pursuer shall thereafter within seven days enrol a motion to recall the sist in that action.

9. In the case of actions which have been raised and are sisted when this Direction comes into force, the pursuer's pack shall be assembled and delivered to each of the defenders within six months of the date on which this Direction comes into force.

10. Substantive defences shall require to be lodged in the action by the date six months (or such longer period as the court may order on cause shown) after the date on which the sist is recalled. Skeletal defences will not be acceptable.

11. If the pursuer considers that any part of her medical records (including scans and x-rays) should not be disclosed as part of the pursuer's pack, the pursuer shall: (a) include in the pursuer's pack only such records as the pursuer considers should be disclosed; and (b) intimate to the defenders that the pursuer has withheld a portion of the records. The records withheld shall be produced to the court in an electronic folder marked "confidential medical records" when the motion to recall the sist is enrolled, with a note setting out the reasons why the records have been withheld. The court shall determine, on the application of any party, whether that part of the records should be disclosed.

12. So far as reasonably practicable, the nominated judge will discharge the Court's management function with the aim of securing the efficient disposal of the action.

13. The nominated judge shall give early consideration to whether it is appropriate to identify a lead action or actions to be progressed at an advanced rate in order to give guidance on any generic issues in the actions. The nominated judge will not identify such action or actions without first giving all interested parties the opportunity to appear and make representations.

14. On a regular basis, and not less than every six months, the nominated judge will review any action that remains sisted, in order to avoid unnecessary delay in the determination of those actions.

Edinburgh
2 September 2015

CJM Sutherland
Lord Justice Clerk

DIRECTION NO. 1 OF 2016 SITTINGS OF THE COURT OF SESSION FOR THE LEGAL YEARS 2016/2017, 2017/2018, 2018/19 AND 2019/2020

I, the Lord President of the Court of Session, under and by virtue of the powers conferred on me by rules 10.1 , 10.2 , 10.3 and 10.4 of the Rules of the Court of Session 1994 hereby make the following direction. **C4.28**

Partial revocation of previous direction

1. The following paragraphs of Direction No. 2 of 2013 (sittings of the Court of Session for the Legal Years 2015/2016, 2016/2017 and 2017/2018) are hereby revoked:

(a) paragraph 1.(b) and (c);
(b) paragraph 2.(2) and (3);
(c) paragraphs 3.(1)(b) and (c), and (2)(b) and (c); and
(d) paragraph 4.(3) and (4).

Sessions of court

2. Subject to paragraph 4 below, the court shall be in session from—

(a) Tuesday 27th September 2016 to Friday 22nd September 2017 ("legal year 2016/2017");
(b) Monday 25th September 2017 to Friday 21st September 2018 ("legal year 2017/18");
(c) Monday 24th September 2018 to Friday 20th September 2019 ("legal year 2018/2019"); and
(d) Monday 23rd September 2019 to Friday 18th September 2020 ("legal year 2019/2020").

Terms of court

3.—(1) The terms of the court for the legal year 2016/2017 shall be as follows:–

(a) winter term – Tuesday 27th September 2016 to Friday 23rd December 2016;
(b) spring term – Monday 9th January 2017 to Friday 24th March 2017; and
(c) summer term – Monday 24th April 2017 to Friday 14th July 2017.

(2) The terms of the court for the legal year 2017/2018 shall be as follows—

(a) winter term – Monday 25th September 2017 to Friday 22nd December 2017;
(b) spring term – Monday 8th January 2018 to Friday 23rd March 2018; and
(c) summer term – Monday 9th April 2018 to Friday 21st September 2018.

(3) The terms of the court for the legal year 2018/2019 shall be as follows—

(a) winter term – Monday 24th September 2018 to Friday 21st December 2018;
(b) spring term – Monday 7th January 2019 to Friday 12th April 2019; and
(c) summer term – Monday 29th April 2019 to Friday 20th September 2019.

(4) The terms of the court for the legal year 2019/2020 shall be as follows—

(a) winter term – Monday 23rd September 2019 to Friday 20th December 2019;
(b) spring term – Monday 6th January 2020 to Friday 3rd April 2020; and
(c) summer term – Monday 20th April 2020 to Friday 18th September 2020.

Vacation

4.—(1) The court shall be in vacation from—

(a) Saturday 24th December 2016 to Friday 6th January 2017;
(b) Saturday 23rd December 2017 to Friday 5th January 2018;
(c) Saturday 24th March 2018 to Friday 6th April 2018;
(d) Saturday 22nd December 2018 to Friday 4th January 2019;
(e) Saturday 13th April 2019 to Friday 26th April 2019;
(f) Saturday 21st December 2019 to Friday 3rd January 2020; and
(g) Saturday 4th April 2020 to Friday 17th April 2020.

(2) The sederunt days during the periods mentioned in subparagraph (1) shall be as follows—

(a) Thursday 29th December 2016 and Thursday 5th January 2017;
(b) Thursday 28th December 2017 and Thursday 4th January 2018;
(c) Wednesday 28th March 2018 and Wednesday 4th April 2018;
(d) Friday 28th December 2018 and Friday 4th January 2019;
(e) Wednesday 17th April 2019 and Wednesday 24th April 2019;
(f) Tuesday 31st December 2019; and
(g) Wednesday 8th April 2020 and Wednesday 15th April 2020.

Public holidays

5.—(1) Subject to rule 10.3(3) and rule 10.5(2) of the Rules of the Court of Session 1994 , no Division, Lord Ordinary or Vacation Judge shall sit during the public holidays specified in subparagraphs (2), (3), (4) and (5).

(2) The public holidays for the legal year 2016/2017 shall be as follows:–

Monday 28th November 2016 (St. Andrew's Day);
the afternoon of Friday 23rd December 2016;
Monday 26th December 2016;
Tuesday 27th December 2016;
Monday 2nd January 2017;
Tuesday 3rd January 2017;
Monday 10th April 2017 (Spring Holiday);
Friday 14th April 2017 (Good Friday);
Monday 17th April 2017 (Easter Monday);
Monday 1st May 2017 (May Day Holiday);
Monday 22nd May 2017 (Victoria Day Holiday); and
Monday 18th September 2017 (Autumn Holiday).

(3) The public holidays for the legal year 2017/2018 shall be as follows:–

Monday 27th November 2017 (St. Andrew's Day);
the afternoon of Friday 22nd December 2017;
Monday 25th December 2017;
Tuesday 26th December 2017;
Monday 1st January 2018;
Tuesday 2nd January 2018;
Friday 30th March 2018 (Good Friday);
Monday 2nd April 2018 (Easter Monday);
Monday 16th April 2018 (Spring Holiday);
Monday 7th May 2018 (May Day Holiday);
Monday 21st May 2018 (Victoria Day Holiday); and
Monday 17th September 2018 (Autumn Holiday).

(4) The public holidays for the legal year 2018/2019 shall be as follows—

Monday 3rd December 2018 (St. Andrew's Day);
the afternoon of Monday 24th December 2018;
Tuesday 25th December 2018;
Wednesday 26th December 2018;
Tuesday 1st January 2019;
Wednesday 2nd January 2019;
Monday 15th April 2019 (Spring Holiday);
Friday 19th April 2019 (Good Friday);
Monday 22nd April 2019 (Easter Monday);
Monday 6th May 2019 (May Day Holiday);
Monday 20th May 2019 (Victoria Day Holiday); and
Monday 16th September 2019 (Autumn Holiday).

(5) The public holidays for the legal year 2019/2020 shall be as follows—

Monday 2nd December 2019 (St. Andrew's Day);
the afternoon of Tuesday 24th December 2019;
Wednesday 25th December 2019;
Thursday 26th December 2019;
Wednesday 1st January 2020;
Thursday 2nd January 2020;
Friday 10th April 2020 (Good Friday);
Monday 13th April 2020 (Easter Monday);
Monday 20th April 2020 (Spring Holiday);
Monday 4th May 2020 (May Day Holiday);
Monday 18th May 2020 (Victoria Day Holiday); and
Monday 14th September 2020 (Autumn Holiday).

Court hours

6. In term, the court shall normally sit between the following hours, with an appropriate adjournment for lunch—

(a) Inner House – 10.00 am and 4.00 pm; and
(b) Outer House – 10.00 am and 4.00 pm.

CJM Sutherland

Lord President of the Court of Session

Edinburgh,

26 September 2016

DIRECTION NO. 2 OF 2016 PERSONAL INJURY AND/OR PRODUCT LIABILITY ACTIONS RELATING TO THE USE OF VAGINAL TAPE & MESH

I, the Lord President of the Court of Session, under and by virtue of the powers conferred on me by paragraph (2) of rule 2.2 of the Rules of the Court of Session 1994 , having consulted the parties to proceedings already raised to which this Direction applies and being of the opinion mentioned in paragraph (1) of that rule, make the following Direction. **C4.29**

1. This Direction applies to those actions for damages arising from the use of vaginal tape or female pelvic mesh to treat stress urinary incontinence and pelvic organ prolapse in which, as at today's date, defences have been lodged.
2. Expressions used in this Direction which are also used in the Rules of the Court of Session 1994 have the same meaning here as they have in those Rules.
3. The provisions of Direction No. 2 of 2015 shall continue to apply in so far as not inconsistent with the provisions of this Direction.
4. Within the period of 6 weeks from the date of this Direction, those acting for the pursuers will produce a note of proposals ('the lead actions proposals') on the matter of the identification of 20 actions, or such greater or lesser number as is considered by them appropriate, as possible lead actions, based on such common significant issues as arise in all the actions in respect of which, by the date of this Direction, defences have been lodged.
5. Said note will be intimated to those acting for the defenders and to the court. Those acting for the defenders will consider whether consensus may be achieved on the lead actions proposals. In the event of failure to achieve consensus, those acting for the defenders who dissent from the lead actions proposals, to whatever extent, will intimate a note of corresponding positive counter-proposals as to the selection of alternative lead actions. Those acting for the defenders will intimate their position and any counter-proposals to the pursuers and to the court within a period of 3 weeks of the date of intimation to them of the pursuers' note.
6. An informal meeting of those acting for the parties will be held on a date to be fixed not less than 10 weeks from the date of this Direction for discussion before the nominated judge of the lead actions proposals and any counter-proposals.
7. In making any ruling as to the actions to be treated as lead actions or on any related matters, the nominated judge will take into account the proposals and any counter-proposals referred to in paragraphs 4 and 5 above.

CJM Sutherland

Lord President

Edinburgh

28 September 2016

DIRECTION NO. 2 OF 2016 PERSONAL INJURY AND/OR PRODUCT LIABILITY ACTIONS RELATING TO THE USE OF VAGINAL TAPE & MESH

The Lord President of the Court of Session, under and by virtue of the powers conferred on him by paragraph (2) of rule 2.2 of the Rules of the Court of Session 1994, having consulted the parties to proceedings already raised to which this Direction applies and being of the opinion mentioned in paragraph (1) of that rule, makes the following Direction:

1. This Direction applies to those actions for damages arising from the use of vaginal tape or mesh in pelvic floor surgery to treat stress urinary incontinence and pelvic organ prolapse in which, as at today's date, defences have been lodged.

2. Expressions used in this Direction which are also used in the Rules of the Court of Session 1994 have the same meaning here as they have in those Rules.

3. The provisions of Direction No. 2 of 2015 shall continue to apply, but only to the extent not inconsistent with the provisions of this Direction.

4. Within the period of 6 weeks from the date of this Direction, those acting for the pursuers will produce a note of proposals (the lead actions proposals) for the matter of the identification of 20 actions, or such greater or lesser number as is considered by them appropriate, as possible lead actions based on such common significant issues as arise in all the actions in respect of which, by the date of this Direction, defences have been lodged.

5. Such note will be intimated to those acting for the defenders and to the court. Those acting for the defenders will consider which questions may be resolved in the lead actions proposals in the event of failure to achieve consensus. Those acting for the defenders who dissent from the lead actions proposals, as they may be, will intimate a note of any corresponding alternative counter-proposals as to the selection of alternative lead actions. Those acting for the defenders will intimate their position and any counter-proposals to the pursuers and to the court within a period of 4 weeks of the date of intimation to them of the pursuers' note.

6. An informal meeting of those acting for the parties will be held on a date to be fixed not less than 10 weeks from the date of this Direction for discussion before the nominated judge of the lead actions proposals and any counter-proposals.

7. In deciding any future orders as to the actions to be treated as lead actions (or on any related matters), the nominated judge will take into account the proposals and any counter-proposals referred to in paragraphs 4 and 5 above.

CJM Sutherland

Lord President

Edinburgh

13 September 2016

PRACTICE NOTES

23RD JULY 1952: DESIGNATION OF DEFENDER IN DIVORCE SUMMONSES

Cases have been occurring in which Divorce Summonses have designed the defender as "at present a prisoner in" a named prison. This designation enters the Minute Book and if, as frequently happens after a long interval, a certificate or extract is required of the decree of divorce, the designation will re-appear. It is suggested to solicitors that, subject to suitable arrangements being made to secure that service is duly made, it is undesirable that the instance of the Summons should needlessly place on permanent record the fact that the defender was at the time temporarily in custody. **C5.1**

16TH APRIL 1953: LODGING CERTIFICATE OF SEARCH FOR DECLARATOR OF MARRIAGE

A case having occurred in which two decrees of declarator of marriage were pronounced relating to the same irregular marriage, the parties having lost touch with each other, arrangements have been made that in all such cases the Registrar General will be prepared on application to state whether a previous declarator has been granted and recorded in his Registers, and a letter from him certifying the result of his search should be lodged in process before the proof. **C5.2**

28TH SEPTEMBER 1956: COPIES OF ENTRIES IN REGISTER OF BIRTHS

It has been arranged that photostatic copies of entries in the Register of Births will be treated by the court as equivalent to the principals. In Scotland, applications for such photostatic copies should be made to the Registrar General of Births, Deaths and Marriages for Scotland, who holds duplicate originals of all entries, but in England where the system is different, applications should be made to the local Registrars. **C5.3**

15TH NOVEMBER 1957: CARE OF HOSPITAL REPORTS AND X-RAYS

The attention of all members of the legal profession is drawn to complaints which have been received from hospital boards regarding the condition in which hospital reports and X-ray plates, produced for use in the courts, have been returned to hospitals on the termination of proceedings. It is reported that X-ray plates in particular have been returned so folded and cracked that their value has been most seriously affected when the condition of the patient has required further examination of the plates. **C5.4**

It is hoped that in future the greatest care will be used in dealing with such productions, especially in guarding them from damage during transmission.

6TH JUNE 1968: SOUL AND CONSCIENCE MEDICAL CERTIFICATES

It shall no longer be necessary, in connection with any action pending before the Court of Session, that a medical certificate should bear the words "on soul and conscience." **C5.5**

6TH JUNE 1968: REPORT UNDER SECTION 11(1) OF THE MATRIMONIAL PROCEEDINGS (CHILDREN) ACT 1958

An Officer who has furnished a Report to the Court under subsection (1) of section 11 of the Matrimonial Proceedings (Children) Act 1958 shall not be cited as a witness unless, in terms of subsection (4) of said section, the Court, on consideration of such a Report, either *ex proprio motu* or on the application of any person interested requires the person who furnished the Report to appear and be examined on oath regarding any matter dealt with in the Report, and such person may be examined or cross-examined accordingly. **C5.6**

18TH JULY 1969: FEE FUND DUES ON ACCOUNT OF EXPENSES

With effect from 1st August 1969, the amount of the Fee Fund Dues which are payable when lodging an Account of Expenses in process should not be included as an outlay in the Account. The sum paid for these Fee Fund Dues will be added to the total amount of the Account by the Auditor. **C5.7**

14TH MAY 1970: RIGHT OF REPLY AT CONCLUSION OF PROOF

This Note is issued to confirm the practice that it is in the discretion of the Lord Ordinary to grant a right of reply to the defender's speech made at the conclusion of a proof. C5.8

14TH DECEMBER 1972: AVAILABILITY OF MEDICAL RECORDS FOR PARTY'S MEDICAL ATTENDANT

Medical records required for the purposes of a court action should at all times be available to a party's medical attendant.[1] With effect from this date it will be the duty of the solicitor concerned immediately on receipt by him of such records to furnish the medical attendant with a copy thereof. If medical records are received by the court marked "confidential" it will be the duty of the solicitor concerned immediately to enrol a motion to have the envelope containing such records opened up and, if the court admits the same, to transmit a copy thereof without delay to the medical attendant. **C5.9**

[1] "Medical attendant" means "general practitioner." The practice note does not refer to hospital records.

14TH APRIL 1973: OFFICE OF AUDITOR OF COURT OF SESSION: VALUE ADDED TAX; TAXATION OF EXPENSES IN (1) CIVIL PROCEEDINGS; (2) CRIMINAL PROCEEDINGS AND (3) GENERAL BUSINESS: OFFICE OF AUDITOR OF COURT OF SESSION: VALUE ADDED TAX; TAXATION OF EXPENSES IN (1) CIVIL PROCEEDINGS; (2) CRIMINAL PROCEEDINGS AND (3) GENERAL BUSINESS

R.C.S. 1994, r. 42.12(1), authorises solicitors to make an addition to fees, where appropriate, of such amount as is equal to the amount of value added tax. **C5.10**

Value added tax was introduced by the Finance Act 1972. Every taxable person as defined by the Act must be registered and in general terms (and subject to the exceptions set out in the Act) whenever a taxable person supplies goods or services in the United Kingdom in the course of business a liability to tax arises.

Responsibility for making a charge for VAT in a proper case and for accounting to Customs and Excise for the proper amount of VAT is solely that of the registered person concerned.

The following directions will apply to all accounts lodged for taxation which include any charge for work done or services rendered on or after 1st April 1973, namely:—

1. Registered Number

The registered number allocated by Customs and Excise to every person registered under the Act must appear in a prominent place at the head of every Account of Expenses, Business Accounts, Note of Fee, account or voucher on which VAT is claimed or chargeable.

2. Action before Taxation

(a) If there is a possibility of a dispute as to whether any person claiming expenses is a taxable person or whether any service in respect of which a charge is proposed to be made in the account is zero rated or exempt, reference should be made to Customs and Excise, and wherever possible, a statement produced on taxation.

(b) Where VAT is claimed by a person who is engaged in business and the expenses of the proceedings to be submitted for taxation are chargeable as an expense of that business, then (unless the paying party agrees the basis on which VAT is claimed) a certificate must be produced on taxation that the receiving party is not entitled to recover, or is only entitled to recover a stated proportion of, the VAT claimed on such expenses as input tax in his VAT account with Customs and Excise. A form of certificate to be given by the Solicitor or accountant for the party receiving expenses is set out in the schedule hereto.

3. Form of Accounts

The form of accounts in practice will require amendment as follows:—

(a) Apportionment

The account must be divided into separate parts so as to show the work done on a day to day basis before and from 1st April 1973. Wherever a lump sum charge has been made for work, only part of which was performed by 31st March 1973, the lump sum or scale fee must also be apportioned.

(b) Disbursements

(i) VAT attributable to any disbursement must be shown stating it has been paid. This will consist of the VAT which has been paid at the time when the account is drawn and an amount in respect of any unpaid disbursement. These amounts may be shown in the disbursement column immediately below the disbursement to which it relates.

(ii) Posts and incidents should be charged with VAT even though they bear no tax when the Solicitor incurs them.

It is otherwise where the disbursement is normally charged as a specific disbursement to the client, e.g. the cost of travel by public transport on a specific journey for a particular client. Taxi fares, however, are subject to VAT.

The end of the account must show the total for VAT including the VAT on the fees and posts.

The fee fund dues on Auditor's fee will be calculated on the total of profit fees and disbursements as lodged without the VAT thereon.

(c) Legal Aid

In legal aid cases the account must be drawn so as to show the total VAT on counsel's fees as a separate item from the VAT on profit costs and other disbursements and must take account of the fact that VAT will only be payable on 90 per cent of the solicitor profit fees and counsel's fees (see para. 7 below).

4. Tax Invoice in Judicial Proceedings

The taxed account is always retained in process so that where a Solicitor waives his Solicitor and own client expenses and accepts the taxed expenses payable by the unsuccessful party in settlement it will be necessary for a short statement as to the amount of the taxed expenses and the VAT thereon to be prepared for use as the tax invoice.

5. Vouchers

Where receipted accounts for disbursement made by the solicitor or his client are retained as tax invoices a photostat copy of any such receipted account may be produced and will be accepted as sufficient evidence of payment when disbursements are vouched.

6. Rate of VAT

The rate of VAT which will be applied on taxation will be the rate at that date, save in respect of disbursements which have been paid when the rate will be the rate at the date of payment. Should there be a change in the rate applied on taxation between the date of taxation and the signing of the report of taxation, any interested party may apply for the taxation to be varied so as to take account of any increase or reduction in the amount of tax payable. Once the report of taxation has been signed no variation will be possible.

7. Calculation of VAT Recoverable by a Legally Aided Party

VAT will not be recoverable on the 10 per cent of the solicitor's fees and counsel's fees which is retained by the legal aid fund. Accordingly, the recoverable VAT must be calculated on 90 per cent of the Solicitor's fees and 90 per cent of counsel's fees. This will not apply to other disbursements, which are paid in full by the legal aid fund.

8. Auditor's Reports

In non legal aid cases the total VAT allowed will be shown as a separate item. In legal aid cases the VAT on counsel's fees will be shown separately from the remaining VAT.

9. Posts and Incidents

Posts and incidents must be shown separately at the different rates in operation before and after 1st April 1973. Posts and incidents are not chargeable on the 10 per cent increase in fees for VAT.

10. Fee Fund Dues and Auditor's Fees

The sums payable as fee fund dues on an account of expenses or as Auditor's fees should not be added to the account. The appropriate sum will be added to the account by the Auditor. When it is impossible to ascertain the correct sum payable as fee fund dues when lodging an account in process (e.g. where an additional fee is allowed under the Rules of Court 347(d)) arrangements may be made for the fee fund stamps to be affixed to the account after taxation.

11. Witnesses' Expenses

In cases where it is impossible, because of the incidence of VAT for witnesses to incur accounts for subsistence at or below the levels prescribed by the Act of Sederunt (Rules of Court Amendment No. 5) 1970, such higher sums may be allowed as the Auditor may determine as having been reasonably incurred.

Schedule

Form of Certificate

Address:

Date:

To: The Auditor of the Court of Session .... *A. v. B.C. Ltd*........... With reference to the pending taxation of the defender's .... (or as the case may be) fees and disbursements herein which are payable by the pursuer, or .... (as the case may be) we the undersigned as .... (solicitors to) (the auditors of) the above-named defender .... (or as the case may be) company, hereby certify that the defender .... (or as the case may be) company on the basis of its last completed VAT return would .... (not be entitled to recover) (be entitled to recover only .... per cent of the) value added tax on such fees and disbursements, as input tax pursuant to s. 3 of the Finance Act 1972.

(Signed) ....

Solicitor/Auditor, to/or (Defender) ....

Registered No. ....

be calculated on 90 per cent of the Solicitor's fees and 90 per cent of counsel's fees. This will not apply to other disbursements which are paid in full by the legal aid fund.

8. Auditor's Returns

In non-legal aid cases the total VAT allowed will be shown as a separate item. In legal aid cases the VAT on counsel's fees will be shown separately from the remaining VAT.

9. Posts and Incidents

Posts and incidents must be shown separately on the different rates in operation before and after 1st April 1973. Posts and incidents are not chargeable on the 10 per cent increase in fees for VAT.

10. Fee Fund Dues and Auditor's Fees

The sums payable as fee fund dues on an account of expenses or as Auditor's fees should not be added to the account. The appropriate sums will be added to the account by the Auditor. Where it is impossible to ascertain the correct sum payable as fee fund dues when lodging an account for taxation, e.g. where an additional fee is allowed under the Rules of Court 347(d) an appropriate entry may be made for the fee fund stamps to be affixed to the account after taxation.

11. Witnesses' Expenses

In cases where it is impossible, because of the incidence of VAT on witnesses' fees to limit, as formerly, witnesses' fees at or below the levels prescribed by the Act of Sederunt (Rules of Court Amendment No. 3) 1970, such higher sums may be allowed as the Auditor may determine as having been reasonably incurred.

Schedule

Form of Certificate

Case

Date

To the Auditor of the Court of Session .... A. v. B. C. (or as the case may be) With reference to the pending taxation of the Defender's .... (or as the case may be) fees and disbursements which are payable by the pursuer, ... (or as the case may be) We the undersigned as (Solicitors to) (the auditors of) the above-named Defender .... (or as the case may be) company hereby certify that the said .... (or as the case may be) company on the basis of its latest quarterly VAT return would .... not be entitled to recover (be entitled to recover only .... per cent of) the value added tax on such fees and disbursements as input tax pursuant to s 3 of the Finance Act 1972.

(Signed) ....

Solicitor/Auditor/Director (Defender) ....

Registered No. ....

17TH DECEMBER 1974: SUMMONS SERVED ON SOLDIERS IN NORTHERN IRELAND

A case arose recently where a copy Summons was posted to a member of Her Majesty's Forces whose address was a private billet in Northern Ireland. The envelope containing the copy Summons revealed his name, rank and number. In future, such information should be excluded from the address on the envelope, and the recipient should be addressed as if he were a private citizen. Where the address of the barracks to which the recipient is attached is known, any document should be sent there rather than to his private billet. **C5.11**

NO. 2 OF 1976: REPORTERS IN PETITIONS TO SANCTION A SCHEME OF ARRANGEMENT

Petition for sanction of schemes of arrangement under section 206 of the Companies Act 1948:—solicitors are advised that when they enrol a motion for a first order in such a petition they may at the same time enrol a separate motion of the same date for the appointment by the court of a reporter for the process. The person so appointed will be the same person to whom the court will ultimately remit the petition for report. **C5.12**

NO. 4 OF 1976: FEE FUND DUES

As solicitors will be aware, the Court of Session (Scotland) (Fees) Order 1976, made on 10th February 1976, enacted that as from 1st April 1976 all fees payable to the Court of Session will cease to be collected in stamps. It is recognised that the payment of many individual fees, whether by cheques or by cash, would present some inconvenience to practitioners and that even the physical transmission of funds would create security difficulties. It has accordingly been decided that the general interest would best be served by the introduction of a credit system, and the following arrangements will therefore apply as from 1st April 1976. **C5.13**

1. There will be a central cashier's office for the Court of Session which will in the meantime be situated in room J15.

2. No cash will be handed over in either the general or petition departments in respect of any fee which is payable there. Instead, any fee due to be paid in either of these departments by any solicitor will be debited by the cashier to the account of the appropriate firm. This will include fees due in respect of requests for certified copy interlocutors.

3. A statement of account will thereafter be rendered to the appropriate firm weekly. This statement will show both the details of the individual items and the total due, and will be for immediate settlement which may be made by a single payment at the office of the cashier during business hours.

4. It is an essential feature of the scheme that all accounts be settled promptly and it is hoped that solicitors will co-operate with the departments in this respect.

5. The credit scheme will not in the meantime apply to payments falling to be made in the office of the extractor, in the opinions room, and in the teinds and the justiciary offices.

6. During the period from 1st April to 2nd May (when on the latter date the Court of Session will assume the duties of the signeting office) signeting dues will be payable in cash.

As solicitors will be aware, the Court of Session (Scotland) (Fees) Order 1976, made on 10th February 1976, enacted that as from 1st April 1976 all fees payable in the Court of Session will cease to be [illegible] means. It is recognised that the payment of new individual fees whether by cheque or by cash would present some inconvenience to practitioners and the [illegible] provision of [illegible] funds would [illegible] security difficulties. It has accordingly been decided that the [illegible] would be [illegible] by the introduction of a credit system, and the following arrangements will therefore apply as from 1st April 1976.

1. There will be a [illegible] ledger of fees for the Court of Session which will [illegible] be [illegible] to [illegible].

2. For each [illegible] of [illegible] to the [illegible] of [illegible] in respect of [illegible] which are payable [illegible] to [illegible] or [illegible] by any solicitor will be [illegible] the [illegible] of the appropriate [illegible]. [illegible] requests for [illegible] copy interlocutors.

3. Statements of account will [illegible] monthly. This statement will show both the details of the individual items and the total due and will be for [illegible] which may be made by cheque payment to the [illegible] Cashier [illegible].

4. [illegible] feature of the scheme that all accounts be settled [illegible], and [illegible] with the [illegible] in this respect.

5. The credit scheme will [illegible] the [illegible] to payments [illegible] to be made in the office of the [illegible] and in the [illegible].

6. [illegible] period from [illegible] on the [illegible] the Court of Session will [illegible] of the [illegible] will be [illegible].

NO. 3 OF 1977: RECONCILIATION IN BREAKDOWN OF MARRIAGES

1. The attention of practitioners is drawn to the provisions of section 2 of the Divorce (Scotland) Act 1976, and to the long title. **C5.14**

2. The provisions of section 2 are designed to facilitate and encourage the reconciliation of estranged spouses who are, or may become, involved in a consistorial action. By enacting those provisions, Parliament has emphasised the importance of exploring the possibility of effecting a reconciliation between the parties to a marriage which has not broken down irretrievably. Central and local government agencies have likewise sanctioned this policy by giving assistance in cash or in kind to voluntary organisations concerned with marriage counselling.

3. Experience shows that once an action has been raised, it is usually too late for the parties to attempt to effect a reconciliation, and it is not expected that the court will be frequently requested, or be in a position, to exercise the powers conferred on it by section 2(1) of the Act (power to continue an action to enable attempts to be made to effect a reconciliation). In these circumstances, in order to promote the success of the legislative policy, legal practitioners who are consulted about marital problems with a view to consistorial proceedings should try to identify, at as early a stage as possible, those cases in which the parties might benefit from the expert advice and guidance of a marriage counsellor, and in those cases should encourage the parties to seek such advice and guidance.

4. There are a number of voluntary organisations, some of them denominational, concerned with marriage counselling who have branch offices in Scotland. Direct liaison or referral by a solicitor will often not present any difficulty, but advice concerning the appropriate organisation may usually be obtained from the local citizens' advice bureau or social work department.

11th March 1977

NO. 3 OF 1977: RECONCILIATION IN BREAKDOWNS OF MARRIAGES

1. The attention of practitioners is drawn to the provisions of section 2 of the Divorce (Scotland) Act 1976, and to the [illegible]. C534

2. The provisions of section 2 are designed to facilitate and encourage the reconciliation of estranged spouses who are or may become involved in consistorial actions. By enacting these provisions Parliament has emphasised the importance of exploring the possibility of effecting a reconciliation between the parties to a marriage which has not in fact irretrievably broken down. Central and local government agencies have likewise sanctioned this policy by giving assistance [illegible] voluntary organisations concerned with marriage counselling.

3. Experience shows that once an action has been raised, it is usually too late for the parties to attempt to effect a reconciliation, and it is not expected that the court will be frequently requested, or be in a position, to exercise the powers conferred on it by section 2(2) of the Act, i.e. power to continue an action to enable attempts to be made to effect a reconciliation. In these circumstances, in order to promote the success of the legislative policy, legal practitioners who are consulted about marital problems with a view to consistorial proceedings should [illegible], at as early a stage as possible, those cases in which the parties might benefit from the expert advice and guidance of a marriage counsellor, and in those cases, should encourage the parties to seek such advice and guidance.

4. There are a number of voluntary organisations, some of them denominational, concerned with marriage counselling which have branches throughout Scotland. Direct liaison established by a solicitor will often not present any difficulty, but advice concerning the appropriate organisation may usually be obtained from the local citizens' advice bureau or social work department.

[illegible] March 1977

NO. 4 OF 1977: VALUE ADDED TAX; TAXATION OF EXPENSES IN (1) CIVIL PROCEEDINGS; (2) CRIMINAL PROCEEDINGS; AND (3) GENERAL BUSINESS

The Auditor refers to the above practice note.[1] Accounts are being lodged for taxation which do not conform to the directions or to the Act of Sederunt dated 28th February 1973. Solicitors are therefore requested to comply in order to save unnecessary time both in the auditor's office and at taxations. **C5.15**

For the guidance of solicitors it is explained that where the recoverable expenses of a legally aided party are paid by the Law Society of Scotland out of the legal aid fund without taxation, value added tax is not recoverable on the 10 per cent of solicitors' fees and counsel's fees which is retained by the legal aid fund. Attention is directed to paragraph 3(*c*) (forms of accounts) and paragraph 7 (calculation of VAT) in the above practice note.

An example of an abstract where a dual taxation has been carried out by the Auditor in any of the circumstances likely to be encountered is appended for reference.

[1] See Practice Note of 14th April 1973.

Abstract Party & Party, Legal Aid Fund—Pre- and Post-Legal Aid

TAXED OFF		LEGAL AID FUND			PARTY & PARTY		
P. & P.	L.A. PRE LEGAL AID—POST VAT	VAT	Disbs.	Fees and Posts	VAT	Disbs.	Fees and Posts
£10.00	£00.00				£0.80	£30.00	£60.00
	Taxed Off						10.00
							50.00
	Add 30% to 1/9/76						15.00
							65.00
	Add VAT on Solicitors' Fees and Posts						5.20
							70.20
	Add Disbursements						30.00
							£100.20
	Add VAT on Disbursements						80
							101.00
	Add Fee Fund Dues						2.00
							£103.00
	LEGAL AID—POST VAT						
£10.00	£15.00	£0.72	£20.00	£35.00	£4.04	£65.00	£140.00
	Taxed Off			15.00			10.00
				20.00			130.00
	Add VAT on 90% Solicitors' Fees and Posts			1.44			9.36
				21.44			139.36

TAXED OFF		LEGAL AID FUND			PARTY & PARTY		
P. & P.	L.A. PRE LEGAL AID—POST VAT	VAT	Disbs.	Fees and Posts	VAT	Disbs.	Fees and Posts
	Add disbursements			20.00			65.00
				41.44			204.36
	Add VAT on Disbursements			0.72			4.04
				42.16			208.40
	Add Fee Fund Dues			1.00			4.00
	TOTAL			£43.16			£212.40
	LEGAL AID ABSTRACT						
	Solicitors' Fees and Posts	£150.00					
	VAT on 90%	10.80					
	Counsel's Fees	55.00					
	VAT on 90%	3.96					
	Disbursements	35.00					
	VAT on 100%	0.80					
	TOTAL	£255.56					

21ST MARCH 1985: FORM OF EXTRACTS IN DECREES OF DIVORCE

The attention of solicitors is drawn to the fact that as the result of the recent extension of word processing facilities in the Court of Session now available to the Extracts Department, the form of extract in decrees of divorce will include (a) the divorce, (b) decrees for custody, access, aliment, periodical allowance, capital sum and expenses and (c) decrees for interdict and orders under the Matrimonial Homes (Family Protection) (Scotland) Act 1981. **C5.16**

10TH DECEMBER 1986: HEARING OF MOTIONS

1. All unopposed motions enrolled for hearing in the Outer House, other than those referred to in paragraph 9, shall *not*, in the first instance, require the appearance of counsel.[1] C5.17

Categories of unopposed motions

2. (1) Those motions which are according to present practice unstarred shall continue to be enrolled in the same manner as hitherto. (2) Those motions of a procedural nature, which have hitherto required the appearance of counsel, shall be dealt with by the clerk of court. (3) Those motions which have hitherto required the appearance of counsel and which will require to receive judicial consideration shall be dealt with by the judge in chambers.

3. Information to be supplied to the court

(1) Written reasons or explanations shall be incorporated in or produced as a paper apart along with motions categorised in paras. 2(2) and 2(3) and any relevant documentary evidence produced therewith where appropriate. (2) Details of the motions in the category referred to in para. 2(2), and illustrations of the information required, are set forth in appendix I to this practice note. (3) Similar details in respect of para. 2(3) are set forth in appendix II to this practice note. Details in this appendix are not exhaustive but practitioners should apply the principles illustrated therein to any motion which is not covered thereby.

4. Procedure in respect of disposal of motions

In regard to motions referred to in paras. 2(1) and 2(2) the following procedures shall apply: (1) Where the clerk of court is satisfied that any such motion may be granted he shall prepare and sign the appropriate interlocutor (subject to the provisions of Rule of Court 93A). (2) Where the clerk of court is not satisfied with the motion as enrolled, he shall either (a) where there is a defect of a technical nature (e.g. specification for the recovery of documents for which there is no call on record) which cannot be remedied immediately, drop the motion; or (b) consult with the practitioner to obtain any additional information which would allow the motion to be granted in full or in such restricted terms as may be agreed. (3) Where the clerk of court after such consultation is still not so satisfied, he shall either (a) of consent, drop the motion; or (b) arrange that the motion be put out starred in order that counsel may be heard thereon.

5. In regard to motions referred to in para. 2(3), the following procedures shall apply: (1) On receipt of such a motion, the terms thereof and any documentation relative thereto shall be examined by the clerk of court for any obvious errors or omissions. (2) Where any such error or omission is discovered, the clerk of court shall consult with the practitioner to obtain further information. (3) Where the clerk of court, with or without such consultation, is satisfied with the terms of and any documentation relative to such a motion, he shall present the papers to the Lord Ordinary in chambers. (4) After consideration of such papers the Lord Ordinary shall either (a) grant the motion in full; (b) grant the motion in such restricted terms as may be agreed after further consultation between the clerk of court and the practitioner; (c) of consent drop the motion; or (d) direct that the motion be put out starred in order that counsel may be heard thereon.

---

[1] As amended by P.N. No. 6 of 1994 with effect from 5th September 1994.

6. Where the Lord Ordinary has directed that a motion is to be put out starred in terms of paras. 4(3)(b) or 5(4)(d), the clerk of court, in consultation with the practitioner, shall arrange for such appearance in the motion roll on a mutually convenient date.

7. To facilitate consultation referred to in paras. 4 and 5 hereof, all motions shall include the name of the individual practitioner with whom contact should be made by the clerk of court.

8. Where, by 12.30 p.m. on the day the motion appears on the rolls, either (a) the clerk of court has been unable to consult with the practitioner through the absence of the individual or someone authorised to deputise for him; or (b) such additional information as has been sought is not available to the clerk of court, the clerk of court may drop the motion.

9. The present practice in regard to the appearance of counsel in (i) motions before calling; (ii) orders before service of a petition (which do not appear in the motion roll); and (iii) motions for interim orders under the Matrimonial Homes (Family Protection) (Scotland) Act 1981, shall continue to apply in the meantime.

1. N.B.

Practitioners who encounter problems in regard to the new procedure are requested to communicate with either of the deputy principal clerks, … who will be monitoring the procedure.

2. In an effort to ensure that motions are properly enrolled, the following are published as examples of motions and relative information which would be acceptable to the court. (1) "On behalf of the pursuer to allow a further continuation of the period of adjustment for four weeks in respect that extensive adjustments were received from the defenders two days ago and further advice now has to be obtained from pursuer's expert witness." (2) "On behalf of the pursuer for interim custody of the child … and for interim aliment for said child at the rate of … in respect of (1) the averments contained in articles 4 and 5 of the condescendence and (2) [where appropriate] the other factors narrated in paper apart 'A' annexed hereto."

APPENDIX I

Column 1	*Column 2*
Dispensation with service or intimation (or further service any document).	Reason for dispensation to be stated. Any previous executions of service or intimation to be lodged with this motion.
Second sist for legal aid.	Reason for application to be stated.
[1]Late documents (except late closed records).	Reason for the delay on lodging the document to be stated.
Commission to take evidence.	Reason for the taking of the evidence on commission to be stated. Where appropriate any supporting documents such as medical or birth certificates to be lodged.

[1] As amended by Practice Note No. 5 of 1991.

Column 1	*Column 2*
Application for authority to print a record on minute and answers or on petition and answers (as adjusted where appropriate) which is not made of consent.	Adjustments should be shown on principal documents to enable clerk of court to decide whether the expense of printing a record is necessary.
Continuation of adjustment period or restoration of cause to adjustment roll.	Reason for further continuation of adjustment or resoration to the roll to be stated. Any adjustments made to date should be shown on either an adjusted copy of the open record or, in the case of minute and answers, on the principal documents.
Lost step in process.	Explanation of the likely fate of the lost step of process and efforts made to try and trace same to be stated.
To allow a parole consistorial proof (other than nullity).	Reason why affidavit procedure inappropriate to be stated.
To discharge diet of proof or jury trial.	Reason for discharge to be stated, with provision for expenses.
Recall of arrestment/inhibition (by party who has arrested/inhibited).	Reason for recall to be stated. (As a party is entitled to recall any diligence no reason is really necessary other than why it requires to be done by motion as opposed to extrajudicially.)
Prorogation of time for lodging documents outwith time ordered by interlocutor or imposed by Rule of Court.	Reason why time limit cannot be complied with to be stated.
Prorogation of time for finding caution.	Reason why time limit cannot be complied with to be stated.
First order in judicial review (not accompanied by a motion for an interim order therein).	(As the only matter in contention at this stage is the date of the first hearing—which can be arranged between keeper and clerk, as is indeed the practice—there would seem to be no necessity for agents to supply further information.)

Column 1	*Column 2*
Interim custody and aliment (and variation thereof).	Up to date information on custody arrangements and the financial circumstances of the parties to be submitted along with the motion. Where information regarding the financial position of the other party is not available or cannot be obtained an appropriate explanation should be made in the motion sheet and the most recent information should be produced. (To enable the court to exercise its discretion in respect of any award of aliment the motion should include the phrase "or such other lesser sum as to the court shall seem proper".)
Interim access (and variation thereof).	Details of the arrangements for access should be provided with the motion sheet.
Assessment of liability for expenses under s. 2 (6) (e) of Legal Aid (Scotland) Act 1967.	Motion to be accompanied by statement of parties' income and expenditure (either wage certificates or a certificate of earnings) and a statement of estimated expenses.
Recall of arrestment/inhibition (by party other than party who arrested/inhibited).	Copy letter of intimation confirming that the other party has received intimation of the motion to be produced, with provision for expenses.
To open "confidential" envelope recovered under specification.	Reason as to why contents are relevant to be stated. Copy letter of intimation to havers to be produced.
Appointment ad interim of curator/factor after service of petition.	Reason for application to be stated.
Appointment of provisional/official liquidator.	Statement of assets of the company to be included.
Of new for appointment of curator/factor.	Reason why caution not found timeously to be included.
For award of sequestration	Name of proposed interim trustee to be included.
For appointment of a curator ad litem.	Reason for the appointment to be included. Where necessary, relevant medical certificate to be produced.
[1]Late closed records	Reasons for delay to be stated.

NOTE.

The [fifth last to second last] items in this appendix could well be added to appendix I were it not for the fact that the interlocutors would still require the signature of the judge.

[1] As inserted by Practice Note No. 5 of 1991.

27TH MARCH 1987: PUBLICATION OF ADJUSTMENT ROLLS

As from the commencement of the summer session of the court the practice whereby causes due to call in the adjustment roll and continued adjustment roll are published in the rolls of court on the preceding Friday and Monday will cease, and the following practice will be introduced in place thereof:— **C5.18**

1. A list of causes calling in the adjustment roll on any Wednesday will be published on that day with a note of the date to which the adjustment of record has been continued prefixed thereto.
2. A list of causes due to call in the continued adjustment roll on any Wednesday will be published on the preceding Friday.

To facilitate identification of causes in each of the aforementioned lists the names of the solicitors for parties will be shown.

NO. 1 OF 1987: BANKRUPTCY PROCEDURE

With effect from Monday, 20th July 1987, a new procedure will commence in accordance with s. 12(2) of the Bankruptcy (Scotland) Act 1985 for the citation of debtors in sequestration proceedings at the instance of a creditor or a trustee acting under a trust deed. The procedure for ordering a respondent to enter appearance in a sequestration process will no longer apply and the court will now fix a date for the debtor to appear when issuing the first deliverance in the sequestration. C5.19

After presentation of the petition, the court on granting a first deliverance citing the debtor shall fix a hearing for a date more than 14 days from the date of the first deliverance. Any request for an earlier diet should be made within 24 hours of the presentation of the petition.

One day a week will be fixed for the hearing of orders for sequestration (not the first deliverance which can be dealt with on any date) and that will be on a Thursday of each week. Counsel will be required to appear at that hearing to move for the sequestration order in anticipation of an appearance by a debtor. The new procedure will also require the petitioner's counsel to make a motion at the bar for sequestration as no motion will now be enrolled in the motion sheet for an award of sequestration.

16th July 1987

NOTICE: 3RD DECEMBER 1987: OPINIONS

Following representations from interested individuals and bodies a working group examined and reported on the proposal that judges' opinions should be prepared and published to a common style. One of the recommendations, since approved by the Lord President, was that the names of local correspondents be included on the backing of the opinion and thereafter published with the report of the case. This information is only available if Edinburgh solicitors include the details on the backing of the record. Practitioners are requested to provide these details with immediate effect, as agreed at the recent meeting of the Joint Committee of Legal Societies in Edinburgh and Midlothian. C5.20

NOTICE: 11TH DECEMBER 1987: SOLICITORS' REFERENCES ON PRINCIPAL WRIT

With a view to improving communication between court staff and solicitors in a cause, solicitors are requested to provide their reference on the backing of their principal writ. It would also be of considerable assistance in this regard if the respective references of solicitors were shown on any closed record lodged in process. **C5.21**

NO. 4 OF 1987: NAMES OF COUNSEL IN THE ROLLS

1. From 5th January 1988, where particulars of any cause set down for hearing are published in the rolls of court, the name(s) of counsel in the cause will not be shown. **C5.22**

2. With regard to the motion roll, notwithstanding the provision in Rule of Court 93(b), the solicitor or his representative shall, when enrolling a motion in any cause, hand to the clerk a slip containing the names of the parties and the title of his firm abbreviated to the first two names thereof, where appropriate.

3. In consequence of the foregoing, and in order to facilitate communication between counsel in a cause solicitors, when instructing counsel for any proof, jury trials or debate, should provide him/her where possible with the name of counsel for the other party or parties.

11th December 1987

NO. 2 OF 1988: COPIES OF PETITIONS FOR ADVOCATES' LIBRARY

Solicitors are reminded that, in addition to the provisions of Rule of Court 200, a copy of any petition presented to the Outer House should be lodged, at the same time as the principal petition, for the use of the Advocates' Library. **C5.23**

2nd March 1988

NO. 4 OF 1988: FEE FUND DUES

From 1st July 1988, a Kalamazoo System of receipting/debiting will be introduced in all offices of the Court of Session and High Court of Justiciary. Solicitors will be issued with an individual receipt/debit slip for every first paper or document lodged, or for enrolment or opposition to a motion by which a party, other than the originating party, first makes appearance in a cause or proceeding. C5.24

Paragraph B11 makes provision for charging to each party of a fee in respect of the lodging of a closed record. In addition to the receipt/debit slip issued to the party lodging the closed record, a receipt/debit slip will also be issued to each other party to the cause. This will be deposited in the appropriate solicitors' box outside the General Department. Where no box is available it will be mailed directly to the party concerned or their representative.

The credit system introduced on 1st April 1976 and detailed in Practice Note No. 4 of 1976, will continue to operate as before. Please note that payments falling to be made in the office of the Extractor, and in the Teinds and Justiciary offices will continue to be excluded from the credit scheme.

30th June 1988

NOTICE: 1ST JULY 1988

Further to Practice Note No. 4 of 1988 a list of standard abbreviations for use with the Kalamazoo System has been devised. These abbreviations will be contained on the receipt/debit slip issued and also on the principal credit account rendered for payment by the cashier each month. **C5.25**

A/C EXPS	Accounts of Expenses
ANS	Answers
CAV	Caveat
CCI	Certified Copy Interlocutor
CERT FEE	Certification Fee
C/R	Closed Record
DEFS	Defences
EXT	Extract Abbreviate
FIAT	Fiat
FIRST APP	First Appearance into process, other than by originating party
HOL	Certification of proceedings for Appeal to House of Lords
J/M	Joint Minute
J/P	Jury Precept
LOR	Letter of Request
LVA	Lands Valuation Appeal
MAD	Minute after Decree
M/E	Minute of Election
NOTE	Note
OBJ	Objections
OHF	Out of hours fee
OP	Opinion
PH	Photocopying
PROT	Protestation
R/M	Reclaiming Motion
SCA	Sheriff Court Appeal
SP/C	Special Case
ST/C	Stated Case
S/S	Signet and Summons
TEIND	Teind

NOTICE: 7TH MARCH 1990

Agents are reminded of the importance of notifying the keeper's office of any motion likely to take longer than 20 minutes. There have been a number of recent instances where either no prior notification has been given to this office or the estimate given is so wildly at variance with the eventual duration as to imply that no thought was given to the original estimate. On a number of occasions this has caused unacceptable delays in the commencement of proofs where, had proper notification been given, the matter could have been dealt with by another judge at a later stage in the morning. **C5.26**

NO. 2 OF 1990: EX TEMPORE JUDGMENTS

For the avoidance of doubt it is confirmed that where the court issues an ex tempore judgment the interlocutor resulting therefrom will be signed and dated on the day that judgment is delivered and not at the date of the issue of the opinion. The reclaiming days will commence on the date of issue of the interlocutor and not on the date of issue of the opinion. **C5.27**

31st May 1990

NO. 3 OF 1991: PROCEDURE ROLL

[*Revoked by P.N. No. 2 of 2004*] **C5.28**

NO. 4 OF 1991: ADVANCE COPIES OF OPINIONS

Practitioners are reminded that the only purpose of the informal practice under which advance copies of opinions are provided to them, is to allow them to prepare, in consultation with counsel, motions for expenses, leave to reclaim, etc., with a view to minimising the court time required for the advising of the opinion. **C5.29**

It is a condition of this practice that neither the opinion itself nor any indication of the contents thereof should be revealed to any other person, including any party to the action involved, in advance of the date of the advising.

There have been a number of instances where this requirement of confidentiality has been breached. Any further breaches may lead to this practice being withdrawn and a return to the system by which opinions were issued only on the day on which they were to be advised.

1st May 1991

NO. 5 OF 1991: LATE CLOSED RECORDS

1. As a result of two recent surveys, the court is concerned at the high incidence of motions to allow closed records to be received late, and in particular, at the lengthy delays in lodging many of these records. **C5.30**

2. Consequently, notwithstanding the terms of the Practice Note of 10th December 1986, and as from 14th May 1991, all motions to allow a closed record to be received late shall be dealt with by a judge who, if he is not satisfied with the explanation given for the lateness of the record, shall direct that the motion be put out starred.

3. The terms of said Practice Note are amended as follows:

(a) the words "(except late closed records)" are added to the third item in Column 1 of Appendix I; and

(b) the words "late closed records—reasons for delay to be stated" are added as a new item in Appendix II.

4. Practitioners are reminded that the court has a discretion in regard to the expenses of any appearance necessary to dispose of such motions.

9th May 1991

NO. 7 OF 1991: RECLAIMING MOTIONS

[*Revoked by P.N. No. 1 of 2010.*] **C5.31**

NO. 1 OF 1992: JUDICIAL REVIEW OF DECISION OF ADJUDICATOR APPOINTED UNDER SECTION 12 OF THE IMMIGRATION ACT 1971

1. Practitioners are advised that, where a decision of an adjudicator appointed under section 12 of the Immigration Act 1971 is subject to an application for judicial review in terms of Rule of Court 260B, the adjudicator should not be called as a respondent in the petition but he should receive intimation thereof as a person who may have an interest. **C5.32**

2. In any such petition, the Home Secretary should be called as respondent.

9th January 1992

NO. 2 OF 1992: SHORT NOTICE INNER HOUSE DIETS

From time to time tentative offers are made by the Keeper of the Rolls of diets in the Inner House of which it has been agreed that short notice may be given. It should be understood, however, that no such offer is to be taken as being confirmed as a fixed diet until written notice of the diet has been issued by the Keeper. **C5.33**

22nd July 1992

NOTICE: 6TH AUGUST 1992: TELEVISION IN THE COURTS

The Lord President has issued the following directions about the practice which will be followed in regard to requests by the broadcasting authorities for permission to televise proceedings in the Court of Session and the High Court of Justiciary. **C5.34**

(a) The rule hitherto has been that television cameras are not allowed within the precincts of the court. While the absolute nature of the rule makes it easy to apply, it is an impediment to the making of programmes of an educational or documentary nature and to the use of television in other cases where there would be no risk to the administration of justice.

(b) In future the criterion will be whether the presence of television cameras in the court would be without risk to the administration of justice.

(c) In view of the risks to the administration of justice the televising of current proceedings in criminal cases at first instance will not be permitted under any circumstances.

(d) Civil proofs at first instance do not normally involve juries, but the risks inherent in the televising of current proceedings while witnesses are giving their evidence justify the same practice here as in the case of criminal trials.

(e) Subject to satisfactory arrangements about the placing of cameras and to there being no additional lighting, which would make conditions in the court room intolerable, the televising of current proceedings at the appellate level in both civil and criminal cases may be undertaken with the approval of the presiding Judge and subject to such conditions as he may impose.

(f) Subject to the same conditions, ceremonies held in a court room may also be televised for the purpose of news broadcasting.

(g) The taking of television pictures, without sound, of Judges on the Bench—as a replacement for the still photographs currently in use—will be permitted with the consent of the Judge concerned.

(h) Requests from television companies for permission to film proceedings, including proceedings at first instance, for the purpose of showing educational or documentary programmes at a later date will be favourably considered. But such filming may be done only with the consent of all parties involved in the proceedings, and it will be subject to approval by the presiding Judge of the final product before it is televised.

NOTICE [illegible] 1992: TELEVISION IN THE COURTS

The Lord President has issued the following directions about the practice which will be followed in regard to requests by the broadcasting authorities for permission to televise proceedings in the Court of Session and the High Court of Justiciary. D.13

(a) The rule hitherto has been that television cameras are not allowed within the precincts of the court. While the rule is a matter [illegible] when the rules [illegible] apply, it is an impediment to the making of programmes of an educational or documentary nature and to the use of television in other cases where there would be no risk to the administration of justice.

(b) In future the criterion will be whether the presence of television cameras in the court would be without risk to the administration of justice.

(c) In view of the risks to the administration of justice the televising of current proceedings in criminal cases at first instance will not be permitted under any circumstances.

(d) Civil proofs at first instance do not normally involve juries, but the risks inherent in the televising of current proceedings while witnesses are giving their evidence justify the same practice here as in the case of criminal trials.

(e) Subject to satisfactory arrangements about the placing of cameras and to there being no additional lighting which would make conditions in the court room intolerable, the televising of current proceedings at the appellate level in both civil and criminal cases may be undertaken with the approval of the presiding judge and subject to such conditions as he may impose.

(f) Subject to the same conditions, proceedings held in a ceremonial [illegible] may also be televised for the purposes of news broadcasting.

(g) The televising of [illegible] ceremonies [illegible] of the Bench [illegible] may be permitted with the consent of the judges concerned.

(h) Requests from television companies for permission to film proceedings, including proceedings at first instance, for the purpose of showing an educational or documentary programme at a later date will be sympathetically considered, but such filming may be done only with the consent of all parties involved in the proceedings, and it will be subject to approval by the presiding judge of the final product before it is televised.

NO. 3 OF 1992: FORM OF ADDRESS OF FEMALE JUDGES

The fact that a woman will shortly for the first time be sitting as a temporary judge in the Court of Session makes it necessary for the Lord President to give guidance as to the way in which woman judges should be addressed in this court. **C5.35**

The office which she will hold will be that of a Temporary Lord Ordinary, since that is the term in the statute: Court of Session Act 1988, section 2(5). All interlocutors issued by a woman temporary judge will therefore refer to her as "The Temporary Lord Ordinary". She should, however, be addressed as "my Lady" or "your Ladyship" when she is sitting on the bench.

The same form of address should be followed when she is sitting as a temporary judge in the High Court, although by statute she will be sitting as a Temporary Lord Commissioner of Justiciary: Criminal Procedure (Scotland) Act 1975, section 113(1).

12th November 1992

NO. 4 OF 1992: LIQUIDATIONS—EARLY DISSOLUTION

1. An application for early dissolution under section 204 of the Insolvency Act 1986 shall be made by letter addressed to the Deputy Principal Clerk of Session. **C5.36**

2. On receipt of an application, the Deputy Principal Clerk of Session shall transmit the process to the Auditor of Court who shall obtain from the liquidator sufficient information to enable him to report to the court on whether or not in his opinion:

(a) the company may be dissolved,
(b) the liquidator be exonerated and discharged, and
(c) the liquidator be allowed to retain any remaining funds as remuneration.

3. A report lodged in terms of paragraph 2 above shall be placed before the court in chambers and an order pronounced in terms of the report, or otherwise as the court shall think fit.

3rd December 1992

NO. 6 OF 1992: SHORT NOTICE INNER HOUSE DIETS

Practitioners are advised that the Keeper of the Rolls may now issue peremptory diets in certain sheriff court and statutory appeals where the hearing has been assessed as being of not more than two days' duration. A minimum of two working days' notice of such diets will be given. **C5.37**

A notice will be published periodically in the Rolls of Court advising practitioners of the cases which may be called in under this procedure. The fact that a later diet has already been allocated in any such case will not preclude the issue of a short notice diet.

23rd December 1992

NO. 2 OF 1993: BANKRUPTCY—SEQUESTRATION OF ESTATE OF DEBTORS

1. The Practice Note of 27th March 1986 dealing with certain bankruptcy matters is hereby revoked. **C5.38**

2. In order to satisfy the court that the provision of section 5(6) of the Bankruptcy (Scotland) Act 1985 as amended by section 3(5) of the Bankruptcy (Scotland) Act 1993 (copy of petition for sequestration to be sent to Accountant of Court) has been complied with, a solicitor will require to append to the execution copy of a petition for sequestration a certificate giving notice to the court of the date on which a copy of the petition was sent to the Accountant in Bankruptcy. Such a certificate must be signed by the solicitor concerned.

16th September 1993

NO. 3 OF 1993: OFFICE OF THE AUDITOR OF THE COURT OF SESSION: CONSOLIDATED GUIDANCE NOTES FOR TAXATION OF ACCOUNTS

General

C5.39

1.1 These Guidance Notes are issued with a view to facilitating the conduct of taxations and minimising the necessity of holding continued diets.

1.2 These Guidance Notes will apply to judicial accounts lodged for taxation on or after 4th October 1993.

1.3 The Auditor will not delay consideration of an account to await subsequent production of documentation or information which is required for the taxation of an account.

Lodging of accounts of expenses

2.1 [*Revoked by*Practice Note No. 1 of 2008*(effective 1st April 2008)*.]

2.2 The account lodged for taxation shall have prefixed to it copies of every interlocutor which contains a remit to the Auditor, so far as relevant to any items contained in the account.

2.3 When an account of expenses is lodged for taxation it shall be accompanied by a note stating (1) the name and current address of the paying party, or his solicitor and the latter's file reference (2) the date on which a copy of the account was intimated to the paying party and (3) the estimated duration of the taxation when it is considered that more than half an hour will be required.

Fixing diet of taxation—contra-account

3.1 On receipt of the process and the account the Auditor will assign a diet of taxation for the earliest available date.

3.2 If the paying party has an outstanding award of expenses the account for these should be lodged forthwith to be dealt with at the same diet.

Points of objection

4.1 The paying party shall not later than three working days prior to the diet of taxation intimate to the Auditor, and the receiving party, specific points of objection, setting out the item objected to and stating concisely the nature and ground of objection in each case.

4.2 At the diet of taxation it will be expected that only those items so specified will be raised.

Papers and vouchers to be available at diet

5. There will be available at the diet of taxation the following:

(a) all precognitions and reports charged for in the account, notes by counsel, documents showing adjustments, letters of instruction to counsel and experts, all solicitors' correspondence, attendance notes, and other papers necessary, to support the entries in the account;

(b) fee notes detailing the work done by counsel; and

(c) receipts and detailed vouchers (unless previously exhibited to, and agreed with each paying party) for all sums stated to have been paid giving full details of the services rendered and the time expended and unit rate of charge.

Numbering of vouchers

6. To facilitate the progress of the taxation the supporting documentation is to be arranged and presented in chronological order and appropriately numbered to correspond to the relevant item in the account.

Schedule of witnesses' expenses

7. The fees and expenses charged for witnesses are to be set out in a separate schedule to the account in the form prescribed by paragraph 11 of Chapter II of the Table of Fees of Solicitors in the Court of Session, and the total thereof stated in the body of the account in a lump sum.

Representation at diet

8.1 The Auditor from time to time receives intimation, frequently just prior to the diet of taxation, that the solicitors for the paying party are without instructions to appear at the diet.

8.2 As a cause in which expenses have been awarded is still before the court until the Auditor's report on the taxed account has been lodged, the solicitors who acted for the paying party have a responsibility to inform their client immediately on receiving notification of the diet of taxation, which is peremptory, of the date, time and place of it, so that the client can intimate timeously any points of objection and thereafter attend personally, or be represented, at the diet.

8.3 The Auditor will proceed with the taxation of an account on the basis that such notification has been given to the client timeously.

Taxation at an agreed amount

9. In the event of parties reaching agreement as to the amount of expenses for which the paying party is to be found liable and the receiving party wishing an Auditor's report thereon, the Auditor requires to have consent in writing of the paying party specifying (1) the agreed amount of expenses and (2) to what extent the fee fund dues, which are calculated on the amount of the account lodged for taxation, are to be added to the agreed amount.

Value added tax

10. Where applicable the certificate required by Practice Note dated 14th April 1973 is to be available at the diet of taxation.

30th September 1993

NO. 1 OF 1994: NOTE OF OBJECTIONS TO AUDITOR'S REPORT

As from this date, practitioners are advised that, when attending at the office of the Keeper of the Rolls to fix a diet for a hearing on a note of objections to a report by the Auditor of Court, they will require to indicate whether or not the diet should be assigned to a particular judge and, if so, the reason for it. **C5.40**

10th March 1994

NO. 2 OF 1994: JUDICIAL FACTORS—CAUTION

1. Practitioners are reminded that a judicial factor (*a*) is an officer of court and (*b*) requires to obtain a certified copy interlocutor of his/her appointment *without delay*. **C5.41**

2. As a certified copy interlocutor is not issued until the judicial factor finds caution, the practitioner before presenting a petition for appointment should reach agreement with the nominees as to whose responsibility it will be to arrange caution.

3. If such responsibility lies with the nominee then the practitioner should advise the nominee of his/her appointment within 24 hours thereof and the nominee should proceed to find caution without delay.

4. If such responsibility lies with the practitioner then the practitioner should proceed to find caution without delay.

5. The foregoing is of particular importance where such an appointment is made *ad interim*.

26th May 1994

NO. 3 OF 1994: REVOCATION OF PREVIOUS PRACTICE NOTES

1. The practice notes listed in the Schedule to this Practice Note are hereby revoked. C5.42

2. This practice note comes into force on the day that the new Rules of the Court of Session in the Act of Sederunt (Rules of the Court of Session) 1994 [SI 1994/ 1443] come into force, that is to say, on 5th September 1994.

28th June 1994

Schedule

Practice Notes Revoked by Paragraph 1 of this Practice Note

28th January 1955	(Jury trials)
11th January 1957	(Motions)
7th May 1959	(Appeals to the House of Lords)
16th November 1961	(Walling)
20th March 1962	(Motions to ordain party to lodge account of expenses)
26th October 1962	(Lodging copies of closed record)
28th June 1963	(Lodging of issues and counter-issues)
26th November 1963	(Late lodging of closed record)
15th July 1964	(Copies of productions for use of the court)
10th March 1966	(Up to date marriage certificate in certain consistorial actions)
1st June 1967	(By Order (Adjustment) Roll)
18th July 1968	(Extract decree of divorce)
16th December 1968	(Adjustment Roll)
13th November 1969	(Motions relating to interim custody and aliment; appeals and remits from inferior courts; remits to reporters in consistorial causes)
3rd December 1969	(Hearings for petitions under the Trusts (Scotland) Act 1961)
16th January 1970	(Modification of expenses against assisted persons)
20th February 1970	(By Order (Adjustment) Roll)
31st March 1970	(Vacation Court)
14th May 1970	(Bond of caution)
2nd March 1972	(Shorthand writer to record objections)
5th May 1972	(Procedure Roll)
4th January 1973	(Consistorial causes)
23rd November 1973	(By Order (Adjustment) Roll)
9th July 1974	(Fees and expenses of reporters in matters affecting children)
21st November 1974	(Fixing undefended proofs)
29th May 1975	(Proof forms)
29th May 1975	(Diets of proof and hearing)
No. 1 of 1976	(Fixing proofs in consistorial actions)
No. 5 of 1976	(Motion roll)

No. 6 of 1976	Defended consistorial causes - 4 January 1973
No. 1 of 1977	(Diets of undefended proof in consistorial actions)
No. 2 of 1977	(Applications for undefended proofs in consistorial actions)
3rd January 1980	(Inclusive fees in undefended divorce actions)
9th July 1980	Extracts Department Regulations
30th October 1980	Remits to local authorities in consistorial causes
26th March 1981	(Amendment of pleadings in reclaiming motions)
10th February 1983	(Curator ad litem in consistorial actions)
15th September 1983	(Return of medical records to Health Boards)
21st February 1986	(Applications for fiats)
6th November 1986	Applications for leave to appeal from Employment Appeal Tribunal
No. 2 of 1987	Fixing and Allocation of Diets of Proof etc.
No. 3 of 1987	Fixing and allocation of diets of procedure roll hearings
No. 1 of 1988	Children: supervision of access arrangements by social work department
No. 3 of 1988	Fee fund dues
Notice 22nd September 1988	(Average waiting times for hearings)
No. 7 of 1988	Registration and enforcement of money judgments under s.4 of the Civil Jurisdiction and Judgments Act 1982
No. 1 of 1989	Enrolment of motions
No. 2 of 1989	Appendix in reclaiming motions and appeals from sheriff court
No. 1 of 1990	Fixing and Allocation of Diets - Form 64
Notice 22nd March 1990	Commissions to take evidence and/or recover documents
No. 6 of 1991	Warrants for diligence on the dependence of consistorial causes
No. 8 of 1991	Transaction of business by post or facsimile
No. 5 of 1992	Intimation on the walls of court
No. 1 of 1993	Optional prodecure - List of witnesses - Rule of Court 188L

NO. 4 OF 1994: TRANSACTION OF BUSINESS BY POST OR FACSIMILE

Lodging documents by post

C5.43

1. A step of process or a production may be lodged by post.

Fees

2.—(1) Where any item of business transacted by post requires payment of a fee, a cheque for the appropriate fee must be enclosed with the item, unless the person seeking to transact that item of business is an agent who holds a Court of Session account.

(2) No item of business which requires payment of a fee may be transacted by facsimile unless the person seeking to transact that item of business is an agent who holds a Court of Session account.

Signeting

3.—(1) A summons accompanied by the process, or an application for letters of arrestment or inhibition accompanied by relevant supporting documents, may be lodged for signeting by post.

(2) If the summons or letters are in order—

(a) the summons, or
(b) the letters of arrestment or inhibition and the relevant supporting documents,

duly signeted will be returned by post to the sender.

(3) If there is a defect of a kind which cannot be remedied by a telephone call from the Signet Officer—

(a) the summons and process, or
(b) the application for letters of arrestment or inhibition and the relevant supporting documents,

will be returned by post to the sender with a letter stating the reasons for their return.

Calling of summons

4.—(1) Where a summons is lodged for calling by post, there shall be enclosed with the summons (which shall have the certificate of service attached) the calling slip required by R.C.S. 1994, r. 13.13(4).

(2) If the summons is accepted for calling, the clerk of session will advise the agent by letter of the calling date.

(3) If there is a defect of a kind which may be dealt with by telephone, the clerk of session will telephone the agent for the pursuer. If the defect cannot be remedied by telephone the summons will be returned to the agent by post with a letter stating the reasons.

Entering appearance by post or facsimile

5.—(1) Appearance in an action under R.C.S. 1994, r. 17.1(1) may be made by post or facsimile.

(2) Where appearance is entered on behalf of a defender to an action by post or by facsimile, details of the cause reference number, parties to the action, date of calling and the names of counsel and agent(s) representing the defender (and

in multi-defender cases which defender they represent) must be received in the General Department not later than 4pm on the last day for entering appearance.

Petitions and notes—warrant for intimation and service

6.—(1) Where a petition or note is lodged by post, it shall be accompanied by any motion, which is required under R.C.S. 1994 to be enrolled, in accordance with R.C.S. 1994, r. 23.2 (enrolment of motions).

(2) Where an interlocutor pronounced following the procedure in subparagraph (1) above contains a warrant for intimation and service of the petition or note, a copy of the interlocutor will be transmitted by post to the agent who lodged the petition or note.

Walling of petitions and notes

7. Where a petition or note requires to be intimated on the walls of court, a copy of the first page of the petition or note may be transmitted by post or by facsimile to the Petition Department which will arrange for the petition or note to be walled.

Lodging of steps of process and productions by post

8.—(1) Productions lodged in process shall be numbered as sub-numbers of the number of process assigned to the inventory of productions (e.g. in an inventory of productions no. 15 of process, production 1 will be no. 15/1 of process; production 2 will be no. 15/2 of process; etc.).

(2) A step of process or inventory of productions sent by post, must—

- (a) be received in the Office of Court not later than the last day for lodging it; and
- (b) if intimated, be marked accordingly.

(3) When a solicitor proposes to lodge an inventory of productions and accompanying productions by post, he must—

- (a) contact the appropriate section of the General Department or the Petition Department, as the case may be, to ascertain from the clerk of session the relevant number of process; and
- (b) write the relevant number of process and the cause reference number on the inventory of productions and each production.

(4) Where a motion is required to be enrolled in respect of the lodgment of any document by post, the motion shall be sent with the document in accordance with paragraph 9 below.

Enrolment of motions by post or facsimile transmission

9.—(1) A motion or notice of opposition to a motion enrolled by post or facsimile transmission shall be accompanied by—

- (a) any paper apart required under paragraph 3 of Practice Note 10 December 1986 (Hearing of Motions); and
- (b) any relevant document or step of process which may be transmitted with it in terms of this Practice Note or Direction No. 3 of 1994 (productions which may be sent by facsimile transmission).

(2) A motion or notice of opposition to a motion may be transmitted at any time of the day but must be received in the Office of Court at such time as shall comply with the latest times for enrolment and opposition set out in the table to Direction No. 4 of 1994 (Motions).

Cause reference numbers

10. Practitioners should ascertain from the General or Petition Department, as the case may be, the cause reference number of existing cases before enrolling a motion or lodging a document. The cause reference number is shown at the top of the summons returned for service in terms of paragraph 3(2) above or the copy interlocutor transmitted in terms of paragraph 6(2) above and should be noted for future use.

Transactions by facsimile transmission

11.—(1) Practitioners who intend to conduct business by facsimile transmission are reminded that fax machines can receive messages outwith the hours during which business is normally conducted. It follows, therefore, that there may be advantage in transmitting a message in the evening for the following day rather than waiting until the following day when the line may be busier.

(2) Practitioners who intend to conduct business by facsimile transmission should ensure that appropriate arrangements are made to deal expeditiously with fax transmissions from the Court of Session (e.g. returned motions).

(3) It is unnecessary to send a hard copy of a fax message sent in terms of this Practice Note.

(4) The following are the fax numbers to be used for transacting business under this Practice Note:

(a) General Department 031-225 5496; and
(b) Petition Department 031-225 7233.

Date of commencement of this Practice Note

12. This Practice Note shall come into force on 5th September 1994.

28th June 1994

NO. 5 OF 1994: FIXING AND ALLOCATION OF PROOFS ETC.

1. Copies of Form 6.2 (form for information for fixing diets in Outer House) and Form 6.3 (form for information for fixing diets in Inner House) to be sent to the Keeper of the Rolls under R.C.S. 1994, r. 6.2(6) and r. 6.3(2) respectively may be obtained from the Keeper's Office. **C5.44**

2.—(1) Where there is an estimate that the length of a proof, jury trial or hearing will be not more than four days, the Keeper of the Rolls will normally allocate a diet of the length sought.

(2) Where there is an estimate that the length of a proof, jury trial or hearing will be more than four days or there is substantial variation in the estimates given by the parties, the Keeper of the Rolls will communicate with parties with a view to ascertaining a better estimate and fixing a diet.

3. This Practice Note comes into force on 5th September 1994.

28th June 1994

NOTE ON [illegible] LISTING AND ALLOCATION OF PROOF [illegible]

2. [illegible] of Form [illegible] containing information for fixing [illegible] and Form [illegible] information for fixing [illegible] the [illegible] Keeper of the Rolls under R.S.C. [illegible] may be obtained from the [illegible].

4.—(1) Where [illegible] the length of [illegible] hearing will be more than [illegible] the Keeper of the Rolls [illegible] third of the length [illegible].

(2) Where [illegible] the Keeper of the Rolls will communicate with the parties with a view to [illegible].

5. This Practice Note [illegible] on and from [illegible].

[illegible] June, [illegible]

NO. 6 OF 1994: HEARING OF MOTIONS

1. For paragraph 1 of the Practice Note of 10th December 1986 (Hearing of Motions) there shall be substituted the following paragraph: **C5.45**

> "1. All unopposed motions enrolled for hearing in the Outer House, other than those referred to in paragraph 9, shall *not*, in the first instance, require the appearance of counsel."

2. This Practice Note comes into force on 5th September 1994.

28th June 1994

NO. 7 OF 1994: INTIMATION ON THE WALLS OF COURT

1.—(1) The information required for intimation of the presentation of a petition, note or other application on the walls of court must include (*a*) the nature of the application, (*b*) the name and address of the applicant, (*c*) the general purpose of the application and (*d*) the name of the solicitor for the petitioner, or noter or other applicant. **C5.46**

(2) If the above information appears on the first page of the petition, note or other application, a copy of that page will be sufficient. If not, a separate typed slip must be prepared.

2. In accordance with paragraph 7 of the Practice Note No. 4 of 1994 (transaction of business by post or facsimile) a copy of the first page of the petition, note or other application may be sent by post or facsimile transmission to the Petition Department. Where a separate typed slip is required, it may also be sent by such means.

3. On the day on which an interlocutor is pronounced ordering intimation on the walls of court of the petition, note or other application, as the case may be, a clerk of session in the Petition Department will be responsible for the walling of the petition, note or other application on the notice board at the entrance to the box corridor from the reception area at door 11.

4. A walling certificate shall not be required to be attached to the execution copy of a petition, note or other application or any certificate or intimation.

5. This Practice Note comes into force on 5th September 1994.

28th June 1994

NO. 8 OF 1994: EXCHANGE OF LISTS OF WITNESSES

1. Subject to the provisions in R.C.S. 1994, Chapter 43, Part V (optional procedure in certain actions of damages), Chapter 47 (commercial actions) and Chapter 49 (family actions),[1] not later than 28 days before the diet fixed for a proof or jury trial, each party shall— **C5.47**

(a) give written intimation to every other party of a list containing the name, occupation (if known) and address of each person whom he intends to call as a witness; and

(b) lodge a copy of that list in process.

2. A party who seeks to call as a witness a person not on his list intimated under paragraph (1) may do so subject to such conditions, if any, as the court thinks fit.

3. This Practice Note comes into force on 5th September 1994.

28th June 1994

---

[1] As amended by Practice Note No.1 of 2021

NO. 9 OF 1994: VALUE ADDED TAX IN ACCOUNTS FOR EXPENSES

1. For the first paragraph of the preamble to the Practice Note 14th April 1973 (Office of Auditor of Court of Session: Value added tax, etc.), there shall be substituted the following paragraph:— **C5.48**

"R.C.S. 1994, r. 42.12(1) (Value added tax) authorises solicitors to make an addition to fees, where appropriate, of such amount as is equal to the amount of value added tax."

2. This Practice Note comes into force on 5th September 1994.

28th June 1994

NO. 10 OF 1994: REVOCATIONS

The following Practice Notes are hereby revoked with effect from 5th September 1994: **C5.49**

No. 3 of 1976 (signeting of summonses)

27th March 1986 (procedure for minutes of amendment).

12th August 1994

NO. 11 OF 1994: PETITIONS FOR THE APPOINTMENT OF TUTOR DATIVE

As from this date, a petition for the appointment of a tutor dative will require to seek service in common form on the Mental Welfare Commission for Scotland, 25 Drumsheugh Gardens, Edinburgh EH3 7RB. **C5.50**

18th August 1994

NOTICE: 18TH AUGUST 1994

Agents are asked to note, pending the introduction of the Rules of the Court of Session 1994, on 5th September 1994, that with effect from Monday 22nd August 1994, all processes in relation to appeals from inferior courts shall in the first instance be lodged in the Signet Office, within the General Department, and not the Petition Department as has been the practice previously. **C5.51**

Agents are also asked to note that with effect from Monday 22nd August 1994, all processes at the instance of the Royal Bank of Scotland and the Bank of Scotland shall be transferred to Section P-Z of the General Department and shall cease to be held on Section A-C.

NO. 12 OF 1994: COMMERCIAL ACTIONS

[Revoked by P.N. No. 6 of 2004.] **C5.52**

NO. 1 OF 1995: EARLY DISPOSAL OF RECLAIMING MOTIONS AND APPEALS

[Revoked by P.N. No. 1 of 2010.] **C5.53**

NO. 2 OF 1995: COURT OF SESSION ETC. FEES AMENDMENT ORDER 1994

The Court of Session etc. Fees Amendment Order 1994 which comes into effect on 1st February 1995 introduces at items B14, B15, B16, B17, B18, C16, C17, C18 and C19, fees in respect of certain "hearings". **C5.54**

Solicitors who currently hold a Supreme Courts' account will have the fees invoiced to them at the end of the hearing under the existing procedure for these accounts.

For solicitors who do not have a Supreme Courts' account, an account will be opened in their name for the purposes of levying hearing fees. They will be invoiced each month for the fees incurred in all actions where a hearing has taken place during the preceding month. Payment will be required within 14 days of receipt of the invoice.

In order that solicitors can monitor the fee which is charged, a copy of the Court calculation will be transmitted to solicitors at the conclusion of each hearing along with the requisite debit slip when the fee is debited to their account.

Party litigants who incur a fee for a hearing will require to pay the appropriate fee to the Clerk of Court, in the case of a hearing of up to one day's duration, at the end of the hearing. In the case of hearings lasting more than one day they will require to pay the fee at the end of each day of the hearing. The exact amount payable should be ascertained from the Clerk of Court. Details of the appropriate fees can be obtained from the Offices of Court.

31st January 1995

NO. 3 OF 1995: APPLICATIONS FOR ADDITIONAL FEE REMITTED TO THE AUDITOR

Where an application for an additional fee has been remitted to the Auditor in terms of R.C.S. 1994, r.42.14(2)(b), there shall be lodged with the account of expenses a full statement of reasons in support of the particular factors which are considered justify the allowance of an additional fee. **C5.55**

A copy of the statement must accompany the intimation copy account of expenses under R.C.S. 1994, r.42.1(2)(b).

31st January 1995

P.N. NO. 1 OF 1996: NOTICE (SIC): CONSIGNATION

With effect from June 3, 1995 the present practice of lodging funds on consignation receipt shall cease. All moneys consigned under orders of court, or otherwise, in the name of the Accountant of Court shall be placed on special deposit account, which will be held solely by The Royal Bank of Scotland plc, North Bridge branch, Edinburgh. Special deposit accounts will continue to afford to the court maximum flexibility in the partial release of funds but attract a higher rate of interest than that previously earned by consignation receipt. **C5.56**

Moneys may be lodged (a) at the branch concerned, (b) at any bank or branch and transferred through the bank's credit transfer system, or, in exceptional circumstances (c) with the Accountant of Court (registration department).

Funds currently consigned on receipt will be transferred into special deposit accounts by the Accountant of Court as soon as is reasonably practicable. No action by a solicitor will be required.

30th May 1996

P.N. NO. 2 OF 1996: NOTICE (SIC): DAILY CALL OVER OF CASES

1. With effect from June 18, 1996 a representative from each agent will be required to attend jointly the office of the Keeper of the Rolls between 10 am-10.20 am each day in relation to those cases awaiting allocation to court that day as proofs or procedure rolls. **C5.57**

2. The keeper, or a member of his staff, will require to be informed of those cases in which discussions with a view to settlement are current or imminent.

3. The keeper, or a member of his staff, may require agents or their representatives, to re-attend at intervals throughout the day.

13th June 1996

P.N. NO. 3 OF 1996: NOTICE (SIC): HEARINGS FOR JUDICIAL REVIEW

With effect from Friday 5th July 1996 when fixing diets of hearing for judicial review etc, a full copy of the petition will be required by the Keeper's office. **C5.58**

4th July 1996

NO. 4 OF 1996: STARRED MOTIONS

1. With effect from 24th September 1996 any motion enrolled which is expected to be starred and to require 10 minutes or more duration on the motion roll will require to have the relevant duration marked on the motion slip. **C5.59**

2. Any agent or party who opposes a previously enrolled motion will require to mark upon the opposition slip the expected duration of hearing upon the motion roll.

3. A Lord Ordinary who has been allocated substantive business (for example a proof) may be allocated, in normal circumstances, no more than three opposed motions, each estimated to require no more than 10 minutes. Allowance will be made for such other number of starred motions or other interlocutory work as can be accommodated within the time available up to 10.30 am.

4. All other starred motions, and those motions which are likely to take more than 10 minutes, will: (a) be allocated to a judge assigned to that category of business; (b) be published for disposal in groups allocated to a specific period of one half hour between the hours of 10.00 am and 1.00 pm and those remaining thereafter, published for disposal not before 2.00 pm; (c) be considered in the order printed upon the roll unless the court otherwise allows.

15th August 1996

NO. 5 OF 1996: COUNSEL'S FEES FOR SETTLED OR DISCHARGED CASES

Rule 42.10(1) of R.C.S. 1994, in regard to fees of solicitors, states that only such expenses as are reasonable for conducting the cause in a proper manner shall be allowed. In the light of Lord Osborne's observations in *Gorrie's Executrix v. Ciba Geigy Ltd* , 26th June 1996, the question has arisen whether a solicitor is nevertheless entitled to include in his account the fee charged by counsel, in accordance with paragraph 5.12 of the *Guide to the Professional Conduct of Advocates*, where he has been instructed for a case which has subsequently settled or the diet in which has been discharged. **C5.60**

The solicitor should continue to include this fee in his account for consideration at taxation by the Auditor where it was reasonable for the solicitor, in order to conduct the cause in a proper manner, to instruct counsel in order to retain his services for the proof or other hearing in the case. It will then be for the Auditor to consider, having regard to the factors mentioned in paragraph 5.12 of the Guide, whether the fee charged by counsel is appropriate to the circumstances.

26th September 1996

NO. 6 OF 1996: NOTES OF ARGUMENT

[*Revoked by P.N. No. 2 of 2004*] **C5.61**

1914

NO. 7 OF 1996: OPPOSITION TO MOTIONS

For an experimental period, where a party seeks to oppose a motion he shall, at the same time, notwithstanding the terms of Rule of Court 23.4, include therein, and in the intimation thereof, a brief statement of the extent and basis of said opposition. C5.62

To facilitate this, a party enrolling a motion on or after 25th November 1996 should, notwithstanding the terms of Rule of Court 23.3(3) and subject to the exceptions contained therein, intimate the motion so that the intimation reaches the other party not later than 12.30 pm two days before its enrolment.

Further, where a motion for recovery of documents under a specification is opposed, the Court will expect Counsel for parties to have discussed the call or calls in question with a view to resolving the matters in issue before appearing in Court. Counsel should be in a position to tell the Court that this has taken place.

5th November 1996

NOTICE (SIC): RECLAIMING MOTIONS—MERITS/EXPENSES

1. It has become apparent that practitioners are unsure about the proper time limits for enrolling a reclaiming motion against an interlocutor disposing of the whole merits of the cause. **C5.63**

2. In the recent (as yet unreported) case of *Dingley v. Chief Constable, Strathdyde Police* , 6th December 1996 [1996 G.W.D. 2-49], the court, under reference to rules 38.3, 38.8(1) and 38.8(2) of the Rules of the Court of Session, indicated that, where there is an interlocutor disposing of the merits but continuing the cause on the question of expenses, a party *must* reclaim that interlocutor within the period of 21 days set down in rule 38.3(2), even though that interlocutor is followed by an interlocutor at a later date disposing of the question of expenses.

6th February 1997

NOTICE (SIC): RECORDING OF PROCEEDINGS

[*Revoked by P.N. No. 4 of 2004*] **C5.64**

P.N. NO. 1 OF 1997: ROYAL ARMS IN SCOTLAND

The attention of practitioners is drawn to the fact that it is permissible for them to reproduce a facsimile of the Royal Arms in Scotland on a principal petition or principal summons. **C5.65**

5th June 1997

NOTICE (SIC): GENERAL DEPARTMENT SECTIONS

With effect from Monday 9 June 1997 there will be a slight alteration to the alphabetical divisions between the sections in the General Department. The three sections will be: A—F; G—Mac; Mad—Z. **C5.66**

(undated)

NO. 2 OF 1997: FLAT, BOXED PROCESS

For an experimental period commencing on 23 September 1997 Rules of Court (sic) 4.1, 4.3, 4.4 and 4.5 will not apply. C5.67

In lieu thereof the following will apply:—

(1) **Form, size etc. of documents forming the process [in lieu of Rule 4.1]**

(a) In an action or petition the principal writ or other writ bringing a cause before the court shall be in the appropriate or prescribed form; it and all steps of process, except motion sheets, shall be completed in writing, transcript or print on durable quality paper of A4 size and shall be backed and securely fastened with a two-piece filing clip.

(b) Motion sheets shall be in A4 size and consist of a backing sheet and two-piece filing clip.

(2) **Steps of process [in lieu of Rule 4.4]**

(a) The process shall include the following steps enumerated thus:—

(1) the principal writ;
(2) certified copy principal writ;
(3) the interlocutor sheets;
(4) a motion sheet;
(5) a minute of proceedings;
(6) (number reserved for pursuer's productions)
(7) (number reserved for defender's productions)
Ø an inventory of process

(b) A step of process referred to in paragraph 2(a) above other than the principal writ, certified copy writ and motion sheet writ shall contain at least 2 pages.

(c) A step of process shall be assigned a number corresponding to (a) above where appropriate or another number consecutive thereto and said number shall be marked on the backing along with the cause reference number and recorded in the inventory of process.

(3) **Lodging of process [in lieu of Rule 4.3]**

(a) A process shall be lodged in every cause commenced by summons or petition when—

(i) in the case of a summons, the summons is presented for signetting; and

(ii) in the case of a petition, the petition is presented to the Petition Department.

(b)

(i) Subject to (b)(ii) below, a black process box shall be lodged by the agent for the pursuer or petitioner

— along with the Open Record prescribed by rule of court 22.1 in a cause commenced by summons or

— within 3 days of answers having been intimated in a cause commenced by petition.

(ii) A red process box shall be lodged by the agent for the pursuer

— within 3 days of defenses having been intimated in a Commercial Action or

— along with the Open Record prescribed by rule of court 22.1 in any cause relating to Intellectual Property.

(c) A process box shall conform to the following specification:

(i) of durable plastic with secure fastener;

(ii) depth 245 mm x width 60 mm x height 330 mm
(iii) with space for names of parties and a finger hole on its spine.

(4) **Productions [in lieu of Rule 4.5]**

(a) On each occasion a production is lodged in process:

(i) an inventory of productions shall be lodged in process; and

(ii) a copy of the inventory of productions shall be sent to every other party.

(b) A production shall be:

(i) marked with a number of process with the cause reference number assigned to the principal writ; and

(ii) if consisting of more than one sheet, securely fastened together.

(c) Productions should be numbered as follows:

(i) where there is only one pursuer, all pursuer's productions will be assigned number 6 of process and will be numbered consecutively thereafter e.g. 6/1—6/x;

(ii) where there is only one defender, all defender's productions will be assigned number 7 and will be numbered consecutively thereafter e.g. 7/1—7/x;

(iii) where there are further pursuers/defenders another number of process will be assigned to each and productions should be enumerated as at (i) and (ii) above.

10th July 1997

NOTICE (SIC): ISSUING OF JUDGMENTS

Practitioners may wish to note that, in future, unless a judge orders otherwise, all judgments of the Court of Session will be issued in what is currently referred to as "vacation style" i.e. without the necessity of the attendance of counsel or solicitor. **C5.68**

As at present, clerks will give agents notice of the date an opinion will be issued. Where possible, this notice will be given at least 2 days prior to the date of the opinion. Opinions may be collected on or after the date of issue, from the Opinions desk, within opening hours, upon payment of the prescribed fee.

Where the opinion does not address the matter of expenses a motion therefor should be enrolled as soon as practicably possible. Unless opposed, or starred by the court, motions for expenses will be dealt with by the appropriate judge in chambers.

The names of cases in which opinion have been issued will continue to be published in the rolls of court.

4th September 1997

NO. 3 OF 1997: SCHEDULE OF DAMAGES ETC.

On or after 6 October 1997, in all cases to which the Social Security (Recovery of Benefits) Act 1997 applies, parties seeking decree (except where that decree is sought of consent, for instance, as the result of a Joint Minute) should lodge in process a schedule of damages stating the amount of any compensation which is claimed in respect of the relevant period under any of the headings in Column 1 of Schedule 2 of the Act. **C5.69**

For the avoidance of doubt it should be noted that this requirement will apply not only to final decrees after proof or jury trial but to decrees in absence, decrees by default, summary decrees, interim decrees and decrees for provisional damages.

Issues in cases where the jury trial will take place on or after 6 October 1997 should be drafted in such a way as to ensure that the provisions of the Act can be applied to the jury's verdict.

24th September 1997

NO. 4 OF 1997: NOTES OF ARGUMENT

[*Revoked by P.N. No. 2 of 2004*] **C5.70**

1932

NO. 1 OF 1999: LIMITATION ACTIONS

In any limitation action raised in pursuance of the Merchant Shipping (Oil Pollution) Act 1971:— **C5.71**

(1) any order for advertisement for condescendence and claims to be lodged and the time limit for lodging them shall be as directed by the court;

(2) any order for the lodging of objections to said condescendence and claims, and the time limit for lodging them shall be as directed by the court;

(3) any order for adjustment to the condescendence and claims and objections thereto, shall be applied for by motion, and shall be for such period as may be directed by the court;

(4) within two weeks of the lodging of objections, or after the expiry of any period of adjustment, the condescendence and claim, and objections thereto, shall be put out by order to determine further procedure;

(5) where the condescendence and claim are based upon any existing payment action in this court no further steps in that action shall be taken. All steps of process in that payment action, the pleadings, productions, minute of proceedings, opinions and interlocutors all as at the date of lodging the condescendence and claim in the limitation action shall become steps of process etc. in the limitation action.

15th May 1999

NOTICE (SIC): OPINIONS

The present system for issuing opinions in the Court of Session is being modified. **C5.72**

The opinions will continue to be issued formally at 10am on the day of advising and will be available for collection by the media at that time. The court will, however, send an advance copy by email to the parties' Edinburgh agents' central mail box before 9.30am on the day of issue. This copy will be provided on a confidential basis so that agents will be in a position to inform their clients of the decision when it is formally issued at 10am.

If, in a particular case, it is more convenient for an agent to receive the opinion in hard copy, the agent should inform the opinions desk in advance and arrangements will be made for the hard copy to be available, on the same confidential basis, at 9.30am in the petition department.

No change is being made to the system for issuing opinions in the High Court.

If you do not receive the emailed opinion please contact *supremecourts@scotcourts.gov.uk*, or telephone 0131 240 6772.

28th May 2001

NO. 1 OF 2001: ALLOCATION OF DIETS IN THE OUTER HOUSE

As recommended in Lord Cullen's Review of Business in the Outer House, the Keeper of the Rolls consults a senior Lord Ordinary before making the weekly allocation of cases to the judges sitting in the Outer House. **C5.73**

In order to further improve this arrangement, practitioners are invited to inform the Keeper of the Rolls, in writing no later than 12 noon on the Friday of the week preceding the diet, of any factors they consider may have a bearing on setting the priority of their case.

Any information received will be placed with the papers considered by a senior Lord Ordinary.

31st July 2001

NO.2 OF 2001: ENTERING APPEARANCE BY EMAIL

(1) For an experimental period appearance in an action under the Rules of the Court of Session 1994, rule 17.1(1) may be made electronic by email. **C5.74**

(2) Where appearance is entered on behalf of a defender to an action by email, details of the cause reference number, parties to the action, date of calling and the names of counsel and agent(s) representing the defender (and in multi-defender cases which defender they represent) must be sent to the following email address: *supreme.courts@scotcourts.gov.uk* not later than 4pm on the last day for entering appearance.

(3) Appearance in an action may still be made by post, facsimile or attendance at the public counter.

(4) This practice note shall come into force with immediate effect.

31st July 2001

NO. 1 OF 2002: EXEMPTIONS FROM PAYMENT OF FEES

The following guidance note has been issued by the depute in charge in relation to applications for exemption from payment of court fees in the Court of Session: **C5.75**

Background

The Court of Session etc Fees Amendment Order 2002 (S.S.I. 2002 No.270) came into force on 1st July 2002. It extended the fee exemption provision previously available only for simplified divorce applications, to all fees regulated by the order with the exception of those for commissary and criminal complaints. To adequately monitor and police the use of exemption claims the former fee exemption certificate has been adjusted for use from 1 July 2002. In addition, a fee exemption slip has been produced which is used to certify the continuing need for fee exemption for example on enrolling a motion. Copies of these forms can be accessed on the Scottish Court Service web site (*www.scot courts.gov.uk*) under "New Rules". The order does not prescribe that fee exemption applies retrospectively. Parties can only be treated as "fee exempt" on receipt by the court of a fee exemption certificate.

The procedures to be followed in the Court of Session

1. Summons and petition proceedings

(a) An action is lodged for signet/first order accompanied by a fee exemption certificate. The form may be signed by the applicant personally or by a solicitor on their behalf. We cannot accept a faxed exemption certificate. Verification or proof of eligibility will periodically be sought by this office to comply with audit requirements.

(b) The same procedure requires to be followed on the lodgment of defences, answers to a petition etc (ie the lodgment of a document by which a party enters a process).

(c) The exemption certificate is lodged as a part of process and marked as such in the inventory.

(d) Our computerised records will reflect the fact that a party is "fee exempt". The process requires to be marked (FE) by the solicitors (or runners) to reflect this.

(e) A white sticker will be attached to the front of the process indicating the presence of a fee exemption certificate, showing which party is exempt and the nature of their exemption. This quickly identifies such cases to all those who come into contact with the process.

It may be that entitlement to exemption arises part way through proceedings. On receipt of an exemption certificate the court will carry out the procedures set out above.

The detailed exemption form need only be lodged at the outset of the proceedings or entitlement unless there has been a change of circumstances, in which case a fresh application should be lodged. The benefits office and/or legal aid reference numbers must be completed as appropriate.

The marking on parts of process (FE) is an administrative step, which will greatly assist the processing of business, but has no legal significance. (AP) is marked on a process when a legal aid certificate is lodged in process. This is in compliance with rule 3 of the Act of Sederunt (Legal Aid Rules) 1987 and of course carries with it special significance in relation to awards of expenses. It may be that parties will be described as (FE) (AP) but the two are not mutually exclusive. A party may be (FE) but not be in receipt of legal aid.

2. Enrolling and opposing motions

In every case where fee exemption continues to be claimed, parties enrolling (or opposing) a motion will require to lodge an exemption slip which certifies that there has been no change in circumstances detailed in the original exemption form. This can be signed by the applicant personally or by a solicitor on their behalf. This document may be faxed to the court along with a motion or opposition.

3. Lodging of closed records, court time and the allowance of proofs etc

There are a number of occasions when fees are payable by all parties to an action such as those for lodging closed records, fees arising out of court time and the allowance of proof etc. It will not be necessary for parties to provide a continuing exemption slip for these fees in isolation. However, in relation to closed records, these are accompanied by a motion in terms of RCS, rule 22.3 (5), seeking the allowance of a mode of proof or appointment to the by order (adjustment) roll. Therefore an exemption slip will be sought for the accompanying motion in accordance with para 2 above.

4. Change in circumstances

If circumstances prevail which result in the entitlement to exemption no longer applying, the court must be notified in writing at the earliest possible opportunity. The letter will be recorded in the inventory, and the process marked accordingly. The onus is on the party seeking exemption or the solicitor on their behalf, to inform the court of any material change of circumstances affecting eligibility.

NO. 2 OF 2002: PETITIONS RELATING TO THE DISTRIBUTION OF ESTATES OF DECEASED LLOYD'S NAMES

[Revoked by P.N. No. 1 of 2006] **C5.76**

NO. 2 OF 2003: PERSONAL INJURIES ACTIONS

The following notes are designed to explain how the Courts will approach the application and interpretation of the new rules for personal injuries actions. For the most part, they are arranged by reference to the rules in the Act of Sederunt. Practitioners may find it helpful to refer to the Report of Working Party chaired by Lord Coulsfield, issued in 1998 and to the Supplementary Report issued in 2002, both of which are available on the Scottish Courts Website *www.scotcourts.gov.uk.* C5.77

Rule 43.1 Application and interpretation

Personal injuries actions are defined as actions of damages for or arising from personal injuries or the death of a person from personal injuries and personal injuries are defined as including any disease or impairment, physical or mental. It is not intended that actions of defamation or any actions which are not, in ordinary parlance, concerned with personal injuries should be covered by these rules. Any such actions are likely to be transferred to the ordinary roll if they are raised under Chapter 43.

Rule 43.2 Summons and pleadings

The question of pleadings was discussed in the original Working Party Report and in the Supplementary Report on pleadings. In the original report it was pointed out that, in the past, it had proved difficult to restrict pleadings even though it had for very many years been the rule that pleadings should be short and simple. It was therefore emphasised that for the purposes of these rules pleadings should be kept to a basic minimum. The Working Party stated:

> "The discussions in the Working Party tended to the conclusion that, realistically speaking, what it is required in most cases in relation to liability is the briefest description of the events on which the claim is based, together with a brief indication of the ground of fault alleged and a specific reference to any statutory provision which may be founded upon."

In the Supplementary Report, it was stated that the Committee remained of the view that the approach of the Working Party was correct, notwithstanding some observations which had been made upon it. The Committee stated:

> "Essentially, therefore, we agree that what is necessary is a method of pleading which encourages brevity and simplicity and discourages technicality and artificiality."

Rule 43.4 Specification and recovery of documents

Specifications for recovery of medical records should not be intimated to the Lord Advocate. The specification should be sent directly to haver.

The question has been raised as to the action to be taken if documents are not returned after the pursuer has finished with them. Any such situation is dealt with under the existing rules applicable to ordinary procedure, namely that application may be made to the Court for an order requiring the pursuer to return the documents.

Rule 43.5 Applications to dispense with timetable

(a) Motions

In general, the rules as to motions are those which apply in ordinary actions. Certain motions will be placed before a judge and may be granted, in accordance with existing practice, if sufficient information is before the judge in writing. It should, however, be noted that motions for sist, for removal of the case to the ordinary roll and for the alteration of a timetable will not be granted, even if made of consent, unless information to justify them, in accordance with the terms of the rules, is before the judge. Such motions will be starred if there is objection to them or if there is insufficient material placed before the judge to satisfy the requirements of the rules.

(b) Dispensing with the timetable

It should be noted that a motion to dispense with the timetable is to be made within 28 days. This rule is intended to be strictly observed. Further, it should be noted that it is not to be granted unless there are exceptional reasons, and that an interlocutor granting or refusing a motion under this rule may be reclaimed against only with leave of the Court within fourteen days. It should be understood that if a case is regarded as suitable for the procedure under this Chapter (that is, if a motion for removal to the ordinary roll is not made or not granted) a motion to extend a period of time under the timetable (Rule 43.8) is most unlikely to be granted.

(c) Sist

It should be noted that the timetable is set from the lodging of defences. Wherever possible, an application for sist should be made before or at the lodging of defences in order to avoid the issue of a timetable which may later require to be changed. It is provided in the rules that a sist will be for a fixed period, and the Court will take account of all the circumstances of the case in fixing the period and, whenever possible, will avoid any delay to any timetable which may have been issued.

The Court will expect parties to consider at the earliest possible stage whether they may require to make an application to the Scottish Legal Aid Board, such as in respect of sanction for an expert witness or for work of an unusual nature. Delay in making an application for legal aid or in applying for a sist, may lead to the motion being refused. Generally, the Court will expect parties to adhere to guidance issued by the Scottish Legal Aid Board.

Rule 43.6 Allocation of diets and timetable

(a) Timetable

This rule provides for the issue of a timetable. The rules do not set out specific periods to be entered in the timetable for most purposes. The periods which will be followed, so far as possible, will from time to time be prescribed by the Lord President. The table in the Appendix to this Note incorporates the periods which, as at the date of issuing of this Practice Note, it is envisaged will be so prescribed.

A party who is concerned that a step of procedure has not been complied with timeously, or that a party is not complying with the spirit of the procedures, and that failure is threatening to cause delay to or prejudice the settlement of the action, should:

- if the matter relates to a stage in the timetable, approach the Keeper of the Rolls with a view to having the case put out By Order; or
- if the matter is outwith the control of the timetable, enrol a motion to bring it before the court.

(b) Third Party Notices

The timetable provides a limited period for the service of third party notices. Parties should be aware that this period, like other periods in the timetable, will be strictly insisted on. If timeous application is not made, any question of third party involvement may require to be raised in a separate action.

(c) Productions

Where any productions are sought to be lodged late, permission will be granted only by the Court and subject to such order, in particular as to expenses, as the Court may consider appropriate.

(d) Order for further procedure

Rule 43.6(5) deals with the making of an order for further procedure after the lodging of a record. It should be stressed, consistently with what has been already said in regard to written pleadings, that it is anticipated that an order for inquiry will be made at this stage. If the defender does not agree with the pursuer's motion, he should oppose it. If a party seeks a debate then full notice of the grounds will require to be given in writing. In particular, if the specification of the pursuers' case is criticised, details of the averments which ought to be made and which have not been made should be included in the grounds for the motion so that the pursuer may have an opportunity to consider whether to meet any such objections in advance of the hearing of the motion. A motion for Procedure Roll will not be granted lightly. Normally any question of specification will be dealt with on the motion roll hearing.

Where a party enrols for jury trial, where practicable the diet assigned in the original timetable will, where practicable, be adhered to. A party opposing such a motion will be expected to specify fully, in the notice of opposition, the grounds on which the motion is opposed.

A party seeking inquiry who estimates that the allocation of four days is not appropriate should communicate with the Keeper with a view to the making of any necessary additional arrangements.

Rule 43.7 By Order hearings

Where under the rules any matter is put out to be heard By Order, the hearing is to take place and parties are to be represented even if, for example, any document not timeously lodged or any step not timeously taken has been lodged or taken prior the hearing. The object of this requirement is to enable the Court to insist upon, and consider, any explanation for failure to act timeously.

Rule 43.8 Motions for variation of timetable

Reference has been made earlier with regard to motions to dispense with the timetable (R.43.5(2)). Rule 43.8(1) deals with motions to vary the timetable. Variation may be by either extension or acceleration. Such motions should be made as soon as the timetable has been issued. Motions for extension are most unlikely to be granted. However, the Court would look with considerable sympathy on any application for acceleration of the timetable where the pursuer has a life expectancy which does not exceed the duration of the timetable that has been issued by the Keeper.

A motion to vary the timetable should give full details of the grounds on which the motion is based and where relevant be accompanied by supporting medical evidence. Any party opposing such an application will be required to demonstrate that their opposition is well founded. When hearing the motion the judge will give such directions as he or she considers appropriate.

Rule 43.9 Statements of valuation of claim

The statements of valuation required by this rule are not binding upon the parties who make them. It is, however, intended that these statements should reflect a real assessment of the value of the claim and accordingly it will be open to either party to found upon the making of its own statement of valuation or upon that of the other party.

Parties' attention is drawn to the terms of rule 43.9(7), which provides for either the dismissal of the action or an award of expenses where a statement of valuation is not lodged timeously.

Rule 43.10 Pre-trial meetings

The object of the rule is to ensure that a pre-trial meeting takes place in accordance with the recommendations of the Working Party. The Working Party stressed that in order to be of value the meeting must be a real meeting, that is a meeting conducted by the legal advisers who are in charge of the conduct of the case, along with each of the parties or someone who has the complete authority to act on behalf of a party at the time. The Working Party stopped short of laying down formal requirements for the meeting since to do so would possibly interfere with the professional requirements of the parties' advisers. Accordingly the Working Party was prepared to contemplate that meetings might be carried out, for example, by video conferencing. It should however be understood that it is the obligation of each party to take all such steps as are necessary to comply with the letter and the spirit of the rule. Similarly, the obligation to sign a minute of the meeting is placed upon counsel or solicitor-advocate acting in the case. It has to be clearly understood that in signing such a minute the signatory is accepting responsibility to the Court for the conduct of the meeting and the recording of what took place at it.

Electronic Communication

It is already the case that under Practice Note 2 of 2001 parties may enter appearance by e-mail. Generally parties are encouraged to supply the necessary references and addresses when entering appearance to make it practicable to utilise electronic communication to the maximum practicable effect

14 March 2003

APPENDIX

Stage in proceedings	*Date*
Motion for 3rd party notices, additional defenders to be lodged by	(defences +28 days)
Commission under rule 43,4 to be executed by	(defences +28 days)
Motion to withdraw from this procedure and appoint to Ordinary Roll to be lodged by	(defences +28 days)
Pursuers valuation to be lodged by	(defences + 8 weeks)
Adjustment period ends on	(defences + 8 weeks)
Record to be lodged and motion enrolled for proof or jury trial by	(defences + 10 weeks)
Defenders valuation to be lodged by	(defences + 16 weeks)

Stage in proceedings	*Date*
Productions/ lists of witnesses to b lodged by	(proof - 8 weeks)
Pre-trial minute to be lodged by to be lodged by	(proof-21 days)
Diet of proof/jury trial	Defences + 12 months[1]

[1] This date may be adjusted to reflect periods of Vacation and loading at the discretion of the Keeper of the Roll with the approval of the Lord President.

NO. 3 OF 2003: ACCELERATED DIETS IN PERSONAL INJURIES ACTIONS ON THE ORDINARY ROLL

As from 1st April 2003 new procedures for the disposal of personal injuries actions will come into force (SSI 2002/570). Under Rule 43.8 a party may apply to the court for a variation of the timetable and an accelerated diet of proof or jury trial. **C5.78**

Practitioners are reminded that in any personal injuries actions which have been raised under the existing procedures or transferred to the ordinary roll, it is possible for a party to seek an early or accelerated diet of proof or jury trial, where there is good reason for doing so. The Keeper intends to review diets of proof and jury trial which have been fixed for dates later than 31 October 2003, with a view to identifying any cases in which the diets ought to be accelerated by the Court on its own initiative. Applications by parties for an early or accelerated diet should be made to the Keeper of the Rolls and intimated to the other parties.

When he deems it appropriate, the Keeper of the Rolls will consult with parties before dealing with such applications. In the event of any continuing issue as to whether an application for an accelerated diet should be granted, the case will be put out By Order for the determination of further procedure. If an accelerated diet is fixed for a date to which any party objects, it is open to that party to enrol a motion seeking to have the diet discharged and a further diet fixed.

14th March 2003

NO. 1 OF 2004: AFFIDAVITS IN FAMILY ACTIONS

[Replaced by Practice Note No.1 of 2018.] **C5.79**

NO.2 OF 2004: PROCEDURE ROLL

1. The following practice notes are hereby revoked: **C5.80**

26th April 1991 (No.3 of 1991)	Procedure Roll
30th October (No.6 of 1996)	Notes of Argument
12th December 1997 (No.4 of 1997)	Notes of Argument.

2. Practitioners are reminded that the court expects that, on the closing of the record, discussions will take place between parties about the future procedure in the cause with particular regard to the resolution of points at issue without recourse to a hearing on the Procedure Roll.

3. The court may, in determining any question of expenses arising out of a hearing on the Procedure Roll, take into account the extent to which parties have complied with paragraph 2 above.

6th August 2004

NO.3 OF 2004: PLEAS-IN-LAW IN PERSONAL INJURIES ACTIONS

1. Summonses, defences, and all other pleadings in personal injuries actions to which Chapter 43 of the Rules of Court applies should not contain pleas-in-law. Pleadings not complying with this Practice Note will not be accepted by the General Department. Defenders who wish to include in their pleadings an outline of their propositions in law should do so be inserting a brief summary of those propositions in the last answer of the defences. **C5.81**

2. For the avoidance of doubt, those defences containing pleas-in-law which have already been accepted by the General Department prior to the issue of this Practice Note will be permitted to continue in that form.

3rd September 2004

NO.4 OF 2004: REVOCATION

The following Practice Note is hereby revoked with effect from 12th November 2004: **C5.82**

6th March 1997 (recording of proceedings).

12th November 2004

NO.5 OF 2004: FORM OF OPINIONS AND NEUTRAL CITATION

Form of opinions C5.83

With effect from 1 January 2005 all opinions in the Court of Session will be issued with single spacing, paragraph numbering but no page numbers. In courts consisting of more than one judge the paragraph numbering will continue sequentially through each opinion and will not start again at the beginning of the second or any subsequent opinion. Indented paragraphs will not be given a number.

Neutral citation of cases

With effect from 1 January 2005 a form of neutral citation will be introduced in the Court of Session. A unique number will be given by the Deputy Principal Clerk of Session to opinions issued by the Court of Session. Opinions will be numbered in the following way:

Court of Session, Outer House: [2005] CSOH 1 (2, 3 etc.)
Court of Session, Inner House: [2005] CSIH 1 (2, 3 etc.)

Under these new arrangements any particular paragraph of the case to be referred to will be cited in square brackets at the end of the neutral citation as follows:

Smith v Brown [2005] CSOH 1.

The neutral citation will be the official number attributed to the opinion by the court and must always be used on at least the first occasion when the case is cited and referred to in any later opinion. Once the case is reported the neutral citation will appear in front of the citation from the law report series.

Citation of cases in court

It is permissible to cite a case reported in a series of reports by means of a copy of a reproduction of the opinion in electronic form that has been authorised by the publisher of the relevant series, provided that the report is presented to the court in an easily legible form and that the advocate presenting the report is satisfied that it has been reproduced in an accurate form from the data source. In any case of doubt the court will rely on the printed text of the report unless the editor of the report has certified that the electronic version is more accurate because it corrects an error in an earlier printed text of the report. For the avoidance of doubt, the Court of Session requires that where a case has been reported in Session Cases it must be cited from that source. Other series of reports may only be used when a case is not reported in Session Cases.

16th November 2004

NO.6 OF 2004: COMMERCIAL ACTIONS

Application and interpretation of Chapter 47: R.C.S. 1994, r. 47.1 C5.84

1. The actions to which the rules apply are intended to comprise all actions arising out of or concerned with any relationship of a commercial or business nature, whether contractual or not, and to include, but not to be limited to—

the construction of a commercial or mercantile document,
the sale or hire purchase of goods,
the export or import of merchandise,
the carriage of goods by land, air or sea,
insurance,
banking,
the provision of financial services,
mercantile agency,
mercantile usage or a custom of trade,
a building, engineering or construction contract,
a commercial lease.

Some Admiralty actions in personam, such as actions relating to or arising out of bills of lading, may also be suitable for treatment of commercial actions if they do not require the special facilities of Admiralty procedure in relation to defenders whose names are not known.

Commercial judge: R.C.S. 1994, r. 47.2

2. The commercial judge may hear and determine a commercial action when the court is in session or in vacation: rule 10.7.

Election of procedure: R.C.S. 1994, r. 47.3

3.—(1) The initial pleadings in a commercial action are expected to be in an abbreviated form: the purpose of the pleadings is to give notice of the essential elements of the case to the court and the other parties to the action. Compliance with the requirements of paragraph 11 of the practice note will enable the essential elements of the case to be presented in the pleadings in succinct form. Where damages are sought, a summary statement of the claim or a statement in the form of an account will normally be sufficient. Where it is sought to obtain from the court a decision only on the construction of a document, it is permissible for the summons to contain an appropriate conclusion without a condescendence or pleas-in-law. The conclusion in such a case should specify the document, the construction of which is in dispute and conclude for the construction contended for.

(2) Rule 47.3(3) is intended to require a party to produce with its summons the "core" or essential documents to establish the contract or transaction with which the cause is concerned. Under rule 27.1(1)(a) documents founded on or adopted as incorporated in a summons must be lodged at the time the summons is lodged for calling.

(3) When the summons is lodged for signetting, a commercial action registration form (Form CA 1), copies of which are available from the General Department, must be completed, lodged in process and a copy served with the summons.

Disapplication of certain rules: R.C.S. 1994, r. 47.4

4. The ordinary rules of the Rules of the Court of Session 1994 apply to a commercial action to which Chapter 47 applies except insofar as specifically excluded under rule 47.4 or which are excluded by implication because of a provision in Chapter 47.

Procedure in commercial actions: R.C.S. 1994 r. 47.5

5. The procedure in, and progress of, a commercial action is under the direct control of the commercial judge. He will take a proactive approach.

Defences: R.C.S. 1994 r. 47.6

6.(1) In the first instance detailed averments are not required in the defences any more than in the summons and it is not necessary that each allegation should be admitted or denied provided that the extent of the dispute is reasonably well identified. One of the objectives of the procedure is to make the extent of written pleadings subject to the control of the court. Compliance with the requirements of paragraph 11 of this practice note will enable the essential elements of the defence to be presented in the defences in succinct form.

(2) Under rule 27(1)(1)(b), documents founded on or adopted as incorporated in defence must be lodged at the time the defences are lodged.

(3) Defences must be lodged within 7 days after the summons is lodged for calling: rule 18.1(1).

(4) The defenders must complete a commercial action registration form (Form CA 1) and lodge it in process, or complete the process copy, with the information required.

Counterclaims and Third Party Notices: R.C.S. 1994, r. 47.7.

7. No counterclaim or the bringing in of a third party may be pursued without an order from the commercial judge.

Commercial Roll: R.C.S. 1994, r. 47.8

8. In the Outer House, an action, and all proceedings in it, in which an election has been made to adopt the procedure in Chapter 47 for commercial actions or which has been transferred under rule 47.10 to be dealt with as a commercial action, shall be heard and determined on the Commercial Roll.

Withdrawal of action from Commercial Roll: R.C.S. 1994, r. 47.9

9. The object of rule 47.9 is to enable cases which are unsuitable for the commercial procedure to be removed from the Commercial Roll, but it should be understood that the commercial procedure is not to be regarded as limited to cases which are straightforward or simple or as excluding cases which involve the investigation of difficult and complicated facts.

Transfer of actions to Commercial Roll: R.C.S. 1994, r. 4 7.10

10.—(1) An ordinary action which has not been brought as a commercial action under rule 47.3(1) may be transferred to the Commercial Roll as a commercial action on application by motion by any party (including the pursuer) to the commercial judge if it is an action within the meaning of a commercial action in rule 47.1(2).

(2) An interlocutor granting or refusing a motion to transfer an action to the Commercial Roll may be reclaimed against only with leave of the commercial judge within 14 days after the date of the interlocutor: rule 38.4(6).

Pre-action communication

11.—(1) Before a commercial action is commenced it is important that, save in exceptional cases, the matters in dispute should have been discussed and focused in pre-litigation communications between the prospective parties' legal advisers. This is because the commercial action procedure is intended for cases in which there is a real dispute between the parties which requires to be resolved by judicial decision, rather than other means; and because the procedure functions best if issues have been investigated and ventilated prior to the raising of the action.

(2) It is therefore expected that, before a commercial action has begun, the solicitors acting for the pursuers will have:

(i) fully set out in correspondence to the intended defender the nature of the claim and the factual and legal grounds on which it proceeds;

(ii) supplied to the intended defender copies of any documents relied upon; and

(iii) where the issue sought to be litigated is one for which expert evidence is necessary, obtained and disclosed, to the intended defender, the expert's report.

For their part, solicitors acting for the defender are expected to respond to such pre-litigation communications by setting out the defender's position in substantial terms; and by disclosing any document or expert's report upon which the defender relies. To that response the solicitors for the pursuers are expected to give a considered and reasoned reply. Both parties may wish to consider whether all or some of the dispute may be amenable to some form of alternative dispute resolution.

(3) Saving cases involving an element of urgency, actions should not be raised using the commercial procedure, until the nature and extent of the dispute between the parties has been the subject of careful discussion between the parties and/or their representatives and the action can be said to be truly necessary.

Preliminary hearing on Commercial Roll: R.C.S. 1994 R. 47.11

12.—(1) The preliminary hearing will normally be conducted on the basis that the provisions of paragraph 11 in relation to pre-action communication have been complied with. The preliminary hearing, and any continuations thereof, are not designed to give parties the opportunity to formulate their claim and response thereto.

(2) Parties should lodge, prior to the preliminary hearing, and for consideration at the preliminary hearing all correspondence and other documents which set out their respective material contentions of fact and law which show their compliance with the provisions of paragraph 11. These provisions are supplementary to the provisions of rule 47.3(3).

(3) Where it appears to the court that the need to grant any request for a continuation of a preliminary hearing is brought about by a failure to comply with the provisions of paragraph 11, this may result in the party responsible for any such failure having the expenses of the continued hearing awarded against him on an agent/client basis. Apart from that possible disposal, motions for

continuations of the preliminary hearings which are sought simply to enable information to be obtained, which could and should have been obtained, prior to the preliminary hearing, may be refused.

(4) At the preliminary hearing the parties should be in a position to lodge a document setting out in concise form the issues which they contend require judicial determination. The statement of issues should, where possible, be set out in an agreed document.

(5) In applying rule 47.11(3), the court will expect to set realistic time limits; but once established those time limits will be expected to be achieved and extension will only be granted in certain circumstances. This emphasises the importance of ensuring that parties at the preliminary hearing are in a position to explain fully what will be required. Since it is part of the administration of commercial causes that wherever possible a commercial action should at all stages be heard before the same judge, it is important to avoid repeated appearances of the action on the commercial roll. For that reason it is necessary to try to give the court accurate information in order to enable the appropriate time limits for a particular case to be established in the manner which is both realistic and does not prejudice the overall requirement that commercial actions should be dealt with expeditiously.

Procedural Hearing on Commercial Roll: R.C.S. 1994, r. 47.12

13.—(1) The procedural hearing is also an important hearing at which parties will be expected to be in a position to discuss realistically the issues involved in the action and the method of disposing of them. It should normally be expected that by the time of the procedural hearing the parties' positions will have been ascertained and identified and that all prospects for settlement have been fully discussed. In consequence it is expected that, once a case has passed beyond the stage of a procedural hearing, it will not settle.

(2) This is one of the ways in which it is sought to meet the problem of ensuring that the judge is in the position to deal realistically with the procedure which he cannot do unless he is given information on which to proceed.

(3) Rule 47.12(2) is the kernel of the procedures and it is intended to enable the court to direct what is really to happen.

Debates: R.C.S. 1994, r. 47.13

14. A debate in a commercial action is not heard on the Procedure Roll but on the Commercial Roll. The provisions of Chapter 28 of the R.C.S. 1994 (Procedure Roll), however, do apply to a debate in a commercial action.

Pre-Proof By Order Hearing

15. When a proof, or proof before answer, has been allowed, the court will normally also fix a pre-proof by order hearing to take place in advance of the proof diet. The general purpose of such a hearing is to ascertain the parties' state of preparation for the proof hearing and to review the estimated duration of that hearing.

Without prejudice to the foregoing generality, the following matters will be dealt with at the pre-proof by order hearing:

(1) Consideration of any joint minute of admissions, agreed by the parties, which should be lodged no later than two days prior to the pre-proof by order hearing.

(2) A review of the documents, or other productions which the parties at the time of the pre-proof by order hearing consider will be relied upon at the proof hearing. Any such document should be lodged no later than two days prior to the pre-proof by order hearing.

(3) The up-to-date position with regard to any expert reports which are to be relied upon by the parties will be reviewed. The parties should be in a position to advise the court of what consultation, if any, has taken place between their respective experts with a view to reaching agreement about any points held in common and what matters remain truly in dispute between them.

(4) Where a proof before answer has been allowed, parties should *produce*, for consideration, at the pre-proof by order hearing, a statement of legal arguments and lists of authorities which they may seek to rely on at the diet of proof before answer, insofar as these have not already been lodged.

Lodging of productions: R.C.S. 1994, r. 47.14

16. Before any proof or other hearing at which reference is to be made to documents, parties shall, as well as lodging their productions, prepare for the use of the court a working bundle in which the documents are arranged chronologically or in another appropriate order without multiple copies of the same document.

Hearings for further procedure: R.C.S. 1994, r. 47.15

17. The commercial judge or a party may have a commercial action put out for a hearing other than a preliminary or procedural hearing to deal with a procedural or other matter which has arisen for which provision has not been made.

Failure to comply with rule or order of commercial judge: R.C.S. 1994, r. 47.16

18. The purpose of this rule is to provide for discipline to ensure effective supervision of case management.

General

19.(1) Arrangements will be made to ensure that (save in exceptional circumstances) at all appearances of an action in the commercial roll the same judge shall preside. Parties are expected to arrange that counsel, or solicitors having rights of audience responsible for the conduct of the case, and authorised to take any necessary decision on questions both of substance and procedure, are available and appear at any calling in the commercial roll.

(2) Where any pleadings or other documents are to be adjusted, the party proposing adjustment shall do so by preparing a new copy of the document as adjusted in which the new material is indicated by underlining, sidelining, a difference in typeface, or other means.

(3) An interlocutor pronounced on the commercial roll, other than a final interlocutor, may be reclaimed against only with leave of the commercial judge within 14 days after the date of the interlocutor: rule 38.4(7).

Revocation of previous practice note

20.1. The Practice Note No.12 of 1994 (commercial actions) is hereby revoked.

29th November 2004

NO. 7 OF 2004: PROCEDURE ROLL DIETS

With effect from 1st January 2005, a party seeking the discharge of a procedure roll diet which has been allocated under rule 6.2(4) will require to make an application by motion for discharge of that diet and further (specified) procedure. **C5.85**

Accordingly, the practice of discharging such diets following a telephone call or other informal request, will cease. The intention is that this will reduce delays arising while causes remain appointed to the procedure roll without fixed or allocated diets.

16th December 2004

NO. 1 OF 2005: APPLICATIONS UNDER SECTION 103A OF THE NATIONALITY AND IMMIGRATION AND ASYLUM ACT 2002

1. This Practice Note shall come into force on 4 April 2005. **C5.86**

2. A petition on relation to which paragraph 30 of Schedule 2 to the Asylum and Immigration (Treatment of Claimants, etc.) Act 2004 has effect shall be lodged at the following address—

Asylum and Immigration Tribunal
Field House,
P.O. Box 6987,
Leicester,
LE1 6ZX.

24th March 2005

NO. 1 OF 2006: PETITIONS BY EXECUTORS OF UNDERWRITING MEMBERS OF LLOYD'S OF LONDON

1. This practice note has effect from 17th March 2006. C5.87

2. The purpose of this practice note is to provide guidance in respect of applications to which Rule 63.6A of the Rules of the Court of Session applies[1]

3. Reinsurance

It is anticipated that Rule 63.6A will only apply where the liabilities of the estate in respect of syndicates of which the deceased was a member—

(a) for years of account before and including 1992, have been reinsured (whether directly or indirectly) into the Equitas Group; and

(b) for years of account from and including 1993, have arisen from membership of syndicates in respect of which any liability will be met by the Central Funds at Lloyd's or which is otherwise reinsured or the subject of indemnity (such as by being protected by an Estate Protection Plan covered by Centrewrite Ltd. or by EXEAT insurance cover provided by Centrewrite Ltd).

4. Remit to a reporter

In accordance with the opinion of the Inner House in the Petitions of *James Crosby Chisholm (Pardoe's Executor) and Others* [2005] CSIH 82, in general it will be sufficient that the remit to a reporter on an application under rule 63.6A(2)(a) covers—

(a) identification of the insurance business underwritten by the deceased;

(b) confirmation from the documentation produced by the petitioners of the reinsurance cover taken or other indemnity;

(c) where relevant, an assessment of the current position of the Equitas Group from the most recently available reports; and

(d) where relevant, confirmation in documentary form that the Lloyd's Central Fund remains available to meet prospectively valid claims by a relevant policy holder or that there is available some other suitable reinsurance or indemnity in respect of such claims.

5. Revocation

Practice Note No. 2 of 2002 (petitions relating to the distribution of estates of deceased Lloyd's names) is hereby revoked.

10th March 2006

---

[1] Rule 63.6A was inserted by S.S.I. 2006 No. 83.

NO. 2 OF 2006: SPECIFICATIONS FOR RECOVERY OF MEDICAL RECORDS

1. This practice note has effect from 1st November 2006. **C5.88**

2. For the purpose of rule 35.2(3)(c), the court no longer considers it necessary for a copy of a specification for the recovery of medical records to be intimated to the Lord Advocate.

3. The Practice Note of 1950 in respect of the recovery of hospital records (1950 S.L.T. 87) is revoked.

19th October 2006

NO. 1 OF 2007: PERSONAL INJURIES ACTIONS: EXPERT EVIDENCE

1. Under Rule 43.6 of the Rules of the Court of Session, parties in Personal Injuries Actions are required to lodge in process any productions on which they intend to rely in accordance with the timetable issued by the Keeper of the Rolls, generally 8 weeks before the diet of proof or jury trial. **C5.89**

2. Practitioners are reminded of the principles of early disclosure of evidence underlying the procedures set out in Chapter 43 with a view to facilitating early settlement. The practice whereby parties delay disclosure of expert reports until the last minute is to be discouraged. Parties will be expected to lodge in process, within a reasonable time after receipt, all expert reports on which they intend to rely, whether in relation to liability or quantum. Failure to do so without reasonable cause may have a consequence in expenses.

16th January 2007

NO. 2 OF 2007: ANONYMISING OPINIONS PUBLISHED ON THE INTERNET

This practice note shall come into force 20th July 2007. C5.90

The purpose of this practice note is to advise on the policy of the court on the anonymising of opinions of the Court of Session that are published on the internet.

General

The general principle is that, subject to specific exceptions, judicial proceedings are heard and determined in public; there should accordingly be public access to judicial determinations including the reasons given for them. The circumstance that publication on the internet gives readier access to Opinions to a wider public does not affect that principle.

The purpose of the Court publishing Opinions on the internet is to make legal information more available to practitioners, students and members of the public who may be interested in it. Unlike the media, the Court has no separate interest in publishing information about the parties to any dispute. It follows that, where for some reason information about a named individual cannot be published, steps will be taken to conceal his identity in order to allow legal information to be published.

Contempt of Court Act 1981

Where at any stage of proceedings the Court makes an order in terms of section 4(2) of the Contempt of Court Act 1981, which prohibits publication of a report of the proceedings, the Court may not publish any Opinion which relates to those proceedings, while the section 4(2) order is in force.

Where the Court has allowed a name or other matter to be withheld from the public in court and has given directions under section 11 of the 1981 Act prohibiting publication of the name or other matter, that name or other matter will not be revealed in the Opinion published on the internet.

Children and Young Persons (Scotland) Act 1937

Where the Court has made a direction under section 46 of the Children and Young Persons (Scotland) Act 1937 that no newspaper, picture or broadcast report shall reveal the name, address or school or include any particulars calculated to lead to the identification of a person under the age of 17 concerned in proceedings, the terms of the Opinion published will omit references to the information specified in the direction.

Asylum Proceedings

The Court has noted that courts in other European jurisdictions have adopted the practice of anonymising judgments in cases involving asylum seekers. It is satisfied that the publication of the names of asylum seekers may create avoidable risks for them in the countries from which they have come.

An opinion in a case involving an asylum seeker will be anonymised before that opinion is placed on the website unless the court gives a direction to contrary effect.

Other Civil Proceedings

In addition to orders under the Contempt of Court Act 1981, an order may be made under section 57 of the Adoption (Scotland) Act 1978 requiring adoption order proceedings and certain similar proceedings to be heard and determined in private. This may also be applied, with modifications, to proceedings in relation to parental orders made under section 30 of the Human Fertilisation & Embryology Act 1990 and related proceedings. Subject to a dispensing power, there is a prohibition on the publication of matter bearing on the identification of a child concerned in a children's hearing or related proceedings under section 44 of the Children (Scotland) Act 1995 and in all these circumstances, and under any other statutory provisions to similar effect, any Opinion will be suitably amended before publication.

It may be appropriate to extend the protection of anonymity to other circumstances. Where, for example, evidence in proceedings concerning children discloses sexual abuse or other conduct the general publication of which would potentially be damaging to a child, the Court may frame the Opinion in a way which affords anonymity to that child. The Court may do the same in cases relating to adults, for example, persons suffering from a condition of an intimate nature where publication of the details would distress them.

22nd June 2007

NO. 3 OF 2007: ESTIMATES OF DURATION OF DIETS

1. This practice note has effect from 7th January 2008. **C5.91**

2. The amended provisions of rules 6.2, 6.3, and 43.6 are intended to improve the reliability of estimates of the likely duration of diets and thereby contribute to reducing the number of proofs, debates or other hearings which have to be continued because they do not conclude within the allotted time.

3. The giving of a carefully considered estimate will usually be assisted by discussion between the parties. It is therefore expected that prior to the enrolment of a motion for a diet or hearing counsel or the solicitor advocate instructed in the case or, in personal injuries actions, the solicitor for the party enrolling the motion will have discussed the likely duration with counsel or solicitor advocate or solicitor instructed for the other party or parties. Where senior counsel has been instructed, junior counsel will usually be expected to have conferred with senior prior to providing his estimate. Similarly, in any case put out By Order in terms of rule of court 6.3(5) and (6) in which senior counsel has been instructed, junior counsel instructed in the case appearing at that By Order hearing in the absence of senior counsel will normally be expected to have discussed with senior counsel their joint assessment of the likely duration in terms of rule of court 6.3(6)(b). Where counsel appearing at that By Order is not counsel instructed to conduct the hearing on the Summar Roll, the estimate which he or she gives will normally be expected to be an estimate which has been represented to him by those instructing him to be the estimate of counsel instructed in the case and, where senior and junior are instructed, their joint assessment.

4. Parties are expected to keep their estimates of duration of diets under review and, where an estimate changes, that party should inform the court by lodging a further form 6.2 as soon as practicable and in any event not later than 14 days before the relevant diet.

5. In personal injuries actions the initial allocation of a proof diet under rule 43.6(1)(a) is provisional and the adequacy of the duration of that initial allocation requires active consideration prior to the enrolment of a motion under rule 43.6(5).

11th December 2007

NO. 4 OF 2007: APPLICATIONS FOR JUDICIAL REVIEW: FIRST ORDERS

1. This practice note has effect from 7th January 2008. **C5.92**

2. By virtue of changes to the Rules of the Court of Session which come into force today, it will no longer be necessary in all cases for counsel or another person having rights of audience to be heard by the Lord Ordinary before considering the granting of a First Order. Instead, where attendance before the Lord Ordinary is required, this will be intimated to the petitioner by the Keeper of the Rolls or the Clerk of Court.

11th December 2007

NO. 1 OF 2008: INTIMATION OF COPY ACCOUNT OF EXPENSES

1. This practice note has effect from 1st April 2008. **C5.93**

2. Paragraph 2.1 of Practice Note No. 3 of 1993 (Office of the Auditor of the Court of Session: consolidated guidance notes for taxation of accounts) is revoked.

13th March 2008

NO. 2 OF 2008: UNOPPOSED MOTIONS FOR ADDITIONAL FEE: RULE 42.14

1. This practice note has effect from 14th July 2008. C5.94

2. Parties are reminded that motions for an additional fee under Rule of Court 42.14 should give sufficiently clear and detailed written reasons for the additional fee sought, with reference to the relevant sub-headings of the rule. Unopposed motions will be placed before a Lord Ordinary in chambers. Where the Lord Ordinary considers that sufficiently clear and detailed reasons have been provided, he or she may grant the motion without hearing the parties. If the Lord Ordinary wishes to be addressed on the motion, the motion will be starred and normally only the party making the motion will be required to appear.

3. A motion for an additional fee under regulation 5(4) of the Civil Legal Aid (Scotland) (Fees) Regulations 1989 should give sufficiently clear and detailed written reasons for the additional fee sought with reference to the relevant sub-headings of rule 7 of the Act of Sederunt (Civil Legal Aid Rules) 1987. A motion which is not opposed by the defender or by the Scottish Legal Aid Board shall be dealt with as noted in paragraph 2.

13th June 2008

NO. 3 OF 2008: APPLICATIONS FOR JUDICIAL REVIEW: DISCRETIONARY TRANSFERS TO THE UPPER TRIBUNAL

[*Replaced by Practice Note No.5 of 2015.*] **C5.95**

NO. 4 OF 2008: APPLICATIONS FOR JUDICIAL REVIEW: TRANSFERS TO THE UPPER TRIBUNAL

[*Replaced by Practice Note No.5 of 2015.*] **C5.96**

NO. 1 OF 2009: EARLY DISSOLUTION OF LIQUIDATIONS

1. Practice Note No 4 of 1992 ("PN 4 of 1992") is to be read subject to this Practice Note. **C5.97**

2. An application for early dissolution must be accompanied by—

(a) a statement of the company's affairs;

(b) an account of the liquidator's intromissions; and

(c) any claim in respect of the liquidator's remuneration and outlays.

3. It shall no longer be a requirement that prior to the determination of the application a report is obtained from the Auditor of Court as described in paragraph 2 of PN 4 of 1992.

4. Instead, the application shall be placed before the court in chambers directly. The court may decide to determine the application without such a report or it may decide to order such a report prior to determining the application. If the court so decides, the Deputy Principal Clerk shall transmit the process to the Auditor as described in paragraph 2 of PN 4 of 1992 and the matter shall thereafter be dealt with in accordance with that paragraph and paragraph 3 of PN 4 of 1992.

5. This Practice Note has effect in relation to applications for early dissolution made on or after 1st April 2009.

9th March 2009

NO. 2 OF 2009: AMENDMENT BY WAY OF MOTION

Practitioners are reminded that Rule of Court 24.2(2) is in the following terms: C5.98

"Where the amendment proposed is of a minor and formal nature, the party seeking to amend may enrol a motion to allow amendment in the terms set out in the motion."

If the only amendment sought is an alteration of the sum sued for, a motion in terms of Rule 24.2(2) avoids the need for a Minute of Amendment.

Ch 43: Pre-trial meetings involving defenders and/or third parties

In cases involving multiple defenders and/or third parties, practitioners representing defenders and/or third parties may find it useful to have a voluntary meeting prior to the compulsory pre-trial meeting with the pursuer's representatives.

Ch 43: Statements of valuation of claim

Rule of Court 43.9(7) gives the court power to dismiss an action, or to grant decree against the defender for an amount not exceeding the amount of the pursuer's valuation, in the event of a party's failure to lodge a statement of valuation of claim in terms of that rule. Practitioners should note that those powers may be exercised where a "statement" has been lodged with gives no, or inadequate, information, and where no reasonable explanation for that lack or inadequacy is given to the court. In complex cases where it is impractical to provide the information in accordance with the timetable, parties should consider enrolling a motion for variation of the same.

Ch 43: Specification for recovery of documents

Parties are reminded that when a specification for the recovery of documents has been granted the documents called for should be released promptly.

27th May 2009

NO. 3 OF 2009: MOTIONS ETC. INTIMATED AND ENROLLED BY EMAIL

1. This practice note has effect from 1st February 2010. C5.99

2. The purpose of this practice note is to provide guidance in respect of the procedure for intimating motions, or consent or opposition to motions, by email in accordance with Parts 2 and 4 of Chapter 23 of the Rules of the Court of Session.

3. An email address which is provided by a party or by an agent of a party for the purpose of receiving intimation of motions, or intimation of consent or opposition to motions, must be in regular use. The provision of the email address for this purpose should be made to the Deputy Principal Clerk of Session. Any declaration by an agent that they do not have suitable facilities for the purpose of transacting motion business should also be made, in writing, to the Deputy Principal Clerk of Session.

4. The Deputy Principal Clerk of Session will maintain a list of all email addresses provided for this purpose which will be published on the Scottish Court Service website. The Deputy Principal Clerk of Session will also maintain a separate list of those agents who have made a declaration that they do not have suitable facilities for the purpose of transacting motion business. That separate list will be published on the same website.

5. Where, in the case of an agent to a receiving party, the identity and separate email address of a fee earner or other person who is handling the matter for the agent is known, the enrolling party should send any intimation required under Part 2 of Chapter 23 of the Rules to that separate email address at the same time as sending it to the provided email address.

6. Where a party or an agent provides an email address for the purpose of transacting motion business, the same email address will be used for the purpose of sending interlocutors to that party or agent once a motion has been determined under the procedure contained in Part 2 of Chapter 23.

7. Where an unopposed motion is enrolled by email under rule 23.1F but the entry in the Rolls of Court in respect of that motion is starred, the motion will be allocated by the Keeper of the Rolls for a hearing before the Lord Ordinary in accordance with the procedure that applies in relation to an opposed motion.

8. Where a motion which is enrolled by email in accordance with Parts 2 and 4 of Chapter 23 refers to a document, or the court requires a document to be lodged with the motion, the document is to be attached to the motion in electronic form, using either "Word" or "pdf" format. Where such a document requires to be signed, a scanned signature will be acceptable.

9. Where any type of record or other document comprising 20 pages or fewer is attached to a motion enrolled by email in accordance with Parts 2 and 4 of Chapter 23, the necessary number of copies of that document will be printed at the court by court staff and lodged in the process of the action to which the motion relates.

10. Where any type of record or other document comprising more than 20 pages is attached to a motion enrolled by email in accordance with Parts 2 and 4 of Chapter 23, one copy of the document will be printed at the court by court staff and lodged in process. Any necessary additional copies of the document will require to be lodged by parties on the following court day.

11. Subject to paragraph 12, where a motion enrolled by email in accordance with Parts 2 and 4 of Chapter 23 refers to accompanying productions, only the inventory of productions should be sent by email. The inventory of productions will be printed at the court by court staff and lodged in process. The productions should then be lodged by the enrolling party on the following court day.

12. Where a motion is starred on the Rolls of Court, parties must lodge productions prior to the motion roll hearing where they are relevant to the hearing. For example, the relevant productions must be lodged where a motion is made to allow those productions to be lodged late.

13. Where a party enrolling a motion by email in accordance with Parts 2 and 4 of Chapter 23 claims a fee exemption, the appropriate fee exemption form shall be attached, in electronic form, to the motion. The fee exemption form will be printed at the court by court staff and lodged in process.

14. A party or an agent may amend or withdraw an email address provided for the purpose of transacting motion business by sending a notice in writing to the Deputy Principal Clerk of Session. Upon receipt of such a notice, the Deputy Principal Clerk of Session will arrange to amend the email address on the list published on the Scottish Court Service website or remove the email address from that list as soon as possible.

15. In the event of a failure of one or more electronic servers, resulting in delayed transmission or non-transmission of emails, the Court may treat a motion intimated or enrolled in writing or by facsimile transmission as though it had been intimated or enrolled in accordance with Parts 2 and 4 of Chapter 23.

5th November 2009

NO. 1 OF 2010: CAUSES IN THE INNER HOUSE

[*Revoked by P.N. No. 3 of 2011.*] C5.100

2000

NO 2 OF 2010: EXPEDITIOUS PROGRESS OF CAUSES IN THE OUTER HOUSE

1. With a view to securing the expeditious progress of causes in the Outer House, the following changes to practice take effect from 21 September 2010. **C5.101**

2. Discharge of diets and further procedure

The practice set out in Practice Note No 7 of 2004, whereby a party seeking the discharge of a procedure roll diet allocated under rule 6.2(4) requires to make an application by motion for discharge of that diet and further (specified) procedure, shall be extended to apply to:

(a) all procedure roll diets;
(b) diets of proof or jury trial;
(c) first hearings and second hearings in petitions for judicial review.

3. Where is not possible at that stage for the court to fix further procedure, the ordinary practice should be for the court to make an order for the case to be put out for a by order hearing on a date as near as possible to two months ahead.

4. Sists

The ordinary practice should be for any sist to be for a determinate period.

5. Where there has been no or insignificant activity in a cause in the period of one month following the expiry of a sist, the process will be placed before a Lord Ordinary for consideration as to whether the cause should be put out for a by order hearing.

6. Where (exceptionally) a cause is sisted for an indeterminate period the process will be placed before a Lord Ordinary every six months for consideration as to whether the cause should be put out for a by order hearing.

7. Inactive causes

Where there is no or insignificant activity in a cause for six months the process will be placed before a Lord Ordinary for consideration as to whether the cause should be put out for a by order hearing.

8. Parties are reminded that where they are concerned about undue delay in an inactive cause, it is open to them to enrol a motion for further procedure.

19 August 2010

NO 3 OF 2010: DIGITAL RECORDING OF PROCEEDINGS

1. The purpose of this practice note is to provide guidance to presiding judges, and to legal representatives and other court users, on the proper use of the equipment installed in the courtroom to support digital recording of proceedings, and (where installed) sound enhancement and hearing impaired systems. It should be noted that, where there is no requirement to record proceedings, the sound enhancement system and assistance for the hearing impaired part of the system (where installed) will still be in operation. Such recording and other systems are designed to facilitate the administration of justice by improving the quality of recording and of audibility in court. **C5.102**

2. With the exception of the Bench microphones for the digital recording and the sound enhancement / hearing impaired systems, which, through a single push button on the Bench, have a press-to-mute facility to permit private conversation between judge and clerk of court, all other microphones are live and cannot be unplugged or muted. As "evidence at a proof" and "proceedings at a jury trial" must by rules (RCS 36.11(1) and 37.5A(1) respectively) all be recorded, the use of this facility should be rare.

3. It is recognised that on occasion legal representatives wish to engage in private conversations at the Bar and wish to exclude completely the possibility of such conversations being overheard in the courtroom. It should be noted that testing has demonstrated that softly spoken conversations undertaken away from the direct vicinity of microphones are unlikely to be picked up by either of the recording or sound enhancement systems. That can be achieved by those conversing turning away from the microphones. In the event of any concern about a particular conversation being overheard, it is open to the presiding judge to interrupt the proceedings and direct the clerk to turn off the sound enhancement system. Such interruption is unlikely to be necessary.

4. Even in proceedings that do not require to be recorded, sound enhancement systems should not routinely be turned off when the court is in session since the general public and persons with impaired hearing will not be able to hear proceedings.

5. It is important that court users speak directly towards a microphone when addressing the court. Most of the microphones installed in the courtrooms can be moved to a certain extent; so court users may position the microphone closer to them if required.

6. Apart from the minor position adjustments noted above, legal representatives and other court users should not move or interfere with the microphones or association equipment, and should not obscure microphones with books or file binders, since this is likely to affect adversely the recording of court proceedings.

7. All participants in court cases should speak audibly, clearly and insofar as it is practicable in the direction of the microphones to ensure that all parties can hear proceedings and to facilitate clarity of recording.

8. If a transcript is required under RCS 36.11(8) or 37.5A(8) details of available transcribers can be provided by the Offices of the Court of Session.

November 2010

NO 3 OF 2010: DIGITAL RECORDING OF PROCEEDINGS

1. The purpose of this practice note is to provide guidance for assisting parties, their legal representatives and other court users, on the procedure for the use of the microphones installed in the courtroom to support digital recording of proceedings, and where installed, sound enhancement and induction loop systems. It should be noted that where there is no [illegible] proceedings the sound enhancement system and assistance for the hearing impaired part of the system (where installed) will be in operation. Such recording and loop systems are designed to facilitate the administration of justice by improving the quality of recording and audibility in court.

2. With the exception of the bench microphones for the digital recording and the sound enhancement and hearing loop systems, which are operated using a single button on the bench, microphones have a mute facility to permit private conversation between agents and clerks of court, and other persons involved in proceedings. Conversation not involving evidence or submissions to the court will not be recorded. Parties [illegible] (RCS 36.11.3 and [illegible]) [illegible] of the facility should they [illegible].

3. It is recommended that counsel, solicitors, parties and witnesses wishing to engage in private conversations at the bar and with others in the courtroom use the possibility of such conversations being overheard in the courtroom. It should be noted that where it has been noted that softly spoken conversations and whispered words away from the direct vicinity of microphones are unlikely to be picked up by or recorded on the recording or sound enhancement systems. The data recorded by those conversations during a break in the proceedings may be accessed. In the event of any concern about a particular conversation it should be drawn to the attention of the presiding judge [illegible] of the proceedings and [illegible] the clerk [illegible] of the sound enhancement system. Such interference is unlikely to be necessary.

4. Even in proceedings that do not require recording the sound enhancement systems should not normally be turned off when the court is in session since the general public and persons with impaired hearing will not be able to hear proceedings.

5. It is important that court users speak directly towards a microphone when addressing the court. Most of the microphones installed in the courtrooms can be moved to a certain extent, so court users may position the microphone closer to them if required.

6. Apart from the input from the bench microphones, legal representatives and other court users should not move or interfere with the microphones or associated equipment, and should not place microphones, with books or other objects, as this is likely to interfere adversely with the recording of court proceedings.

7. All participants in court cases should speak audibly, clearly and in the direction of the microphones to ensure that all parties can hear proceedings and to facilitate clarity of recording.

8. If a transcript is required under RCS 36.11(2) or 37.4A.8, details of available transcribers can be provided by the Office of the Court of Session.

November 2010

NO. 4 OF 2010: APPROVAL OF MEANS OF RECORDING PROOFS AND JURY TRIALS

For the purposes of rules 36.11(1)(b) and 37.5A(1)(b), I hereby approve digital recording on an appropriate storage medium as a means of recording, respectively, evidence at a proof and proceedings at a jury trial. **C5.103**

October 22nd 2010

NO. 1 OF 2011: PROTECTION OF VULNERABLE GROUPS (SCOTLAND) ACT 2007

[Replaced by Practice Note No. 2 of 2011.] **C5.104**

NO. 2 OF 2011: PROTECTION OF VULNERABLE GROUPS (SCOTLAND) ACT 2007

1. This practice note replaces Practice Note No. 1 of 2011 which was incomplete. **C5.105**

2. In terms of the Protection of Vulnerable Groups (Scotland) Act 2007, the relevant provisions of which are now in force, an individual to whom section 92 (1) applies is barred from undertaking regulated work with children and an individual to whom section 92 (2) applies is barred from undertaking regulated work with protected adults.

3. In a number of circumstances the court may be minded to appoint a reporter, reporting officer or curator ad litem (usually an officer of the court) to work with, or on behalf of, a child or protected adult.

4. It is not expected that any person whom the court is minded to appoint will be a barred individual but, in the unlikely event that this should occur, when a person is contacted by a clerk of court for the purpose of ascertaining whether that person is available to accept appointment in any of the circumstances mentioned above, he or she must, if a barred individual, inform the clerk accordingly.

4th March 2011

NO. 3 OF 2011: CAUSES IN THE INNER HOUSE

1. This Practice Note has effect from 27th September 2011. **C5.106**

2. The following notes are primarily designed to explain how the new rules relating to causes in the Inner House will operate in practice. The new rules were introduced in two stages. The first set of rules, relating to reclaiming motions under Chapter 38, applications for a new trial or to enter jury verdicts under Chapter 39 and appeals from inferior courts under Chapter 40, came into force on 5th April 2010. The second set of rules, relating to appeals under statute, come into force on 27th September 2011. For the most part, the following notes are arranged by reference to selected rules in the Act of Sederunt.

3. For information on the background to many of the procedural changes and why they were made, practitioners may find it helpful to refer to the Report of Lord Penrose which was issued in 2009 and is available on the Scottish Courts Website *www.scotcourts.gov.uk/innerhousereform/index.asp*.

Procedural Business in the Inner House: Chapter 37A

Rule 37A.1: Quorum of Inner House for certain business

4. One of the central aspects of Lord Penrose's proposals was that a single judge of the Inner House should be able to deal with specified procedural business in the Inner House. Rule 37A.1 is intended to reflect this by making provision regarding the quorum of a Division of the Inner House when dealing with specified procedural business. In relation to such procedural business as is defined in rule 37A.1, the quorum of a Division of the Inner House is one judge.

5. Procedural business is defined as such business as arises under—

(a) a reclaiming motion,
(b) an application for a new trial under section 29(1) of the Court of Session Act 1988 or an application to enter a jury verdict under section 31 of the 1988 Act,
(c) an appeal from an inferior court, or
(d) an appeal under statute,

in each case up to and including the point at which a procedural judge, at a procedural hearing, appoints a cause to the Summar Roll or the Single Bills for a hearing or makes such other order as he or she thinks fit to secure the expeditious disposal of the reclaiming motion, application or appeal.

Rule 37A.2: Procedural judges in the Inner House

6. This rule provides that all judges of the Inner House, except the Lord President and the Lord Justice Clerk, are procedural judges, before whom proceedings in the Inner House are brought in accordance with Chapters 38 to 41 of the Rules. When acting in that capacity, each procedural judge sits as a single judge.

7. Although specific provision is made in certain rules for business to be dealt with and disposed of by a procedural judge, rule 37A.2(3) preserves the competency of a Division comprising three or more judges to dispose of procedural business instead of a single procedural judge, should such a Division consider it appropriate. Provision is also made in a number of rules for a procedural judge to refer certain matters to a bench of three or more judges. Such a remit might be appropriate where procedural business raises issues of particular importance or novelty.

Chapter 38: Reclaiming

Rule 38.2: Reclaiming days

8. It should be noted that, with one exception, the period within which an interlocutor may be reclaimed against under rule 38.2 will be either be 14 days or 21 days after the date on which the interlocutor was pronounced. Whether the 14 day period or the 21 day period will apply, and whether or not leave is required, will depend on the type of interlocutor. The exception is rule 38.2(2), which applies to a reclaiming motion against an interlocutor which disposes of the whole merits of the cause but reserves or does not dispose of the question of expenses. In that case, any party to the cause who seeks an order for expenses before disposal of the reclaiming motion must apply by motion to the Lord Ordinary for such an order within 14 days of the date of enrolment of that reclaiming motion. A reclaiming motion can proceed out of time under rule 38.10.

Rule 38.5: Method of reclaiming

9. Practitioners are reminded that, when enrolling a reclaiming motion in a case in respect of which no opinion has been issued, they should advise the depute clerk—

(a) that the reclaiming motion has been enrolled, and

(b) that an opinion is required.

10. When enrolling a reclaiming motion where a matter likely to be at issue at the hearing of the reclaiming motion is not covered by an opinion already in process (e.g. the disposal of expenses following upon the appearance of judgment) practitioners will continue to require—

(a) to indicate in the motion sheet the particular matter which is not so covered, and

(b) to advise the depute clerk that an opinion is required thereon.

Rule 38.6: Effect of reclaiming

11. It should be noted that particular provision is made in this rule in relation to reclaiming against interlocutors dealing with expenses where a previous interlocutor has disposed of the whole merits of the cause. Where a motion to refuse a reclaiming motion is unopposed, the motion is to be treated as if all parties consented to it.

Rule 38.8: Appeals treated as reclaiming motions

12. This rule provides for Chapter 38 to apply to certain appeals that are referred to in statutory and Convention provisions.

Rule 38.10: Reclaiming out of time

13. It should be noted that a procedural judge may allow a reclaiming motion to be received outwith the reclaiming days and to proceed out of time only in the case of mistake or inadvertence. Conditions as to expenses are specifically referred to in this rule, but it should be noted that the procedural judge may impose other conditions, not relating to expenses, if allowing reclaiming out of time under this rule.

Rule 38.11: Urgent disposal of reclaiming motion

14. Where a motion for urgent disposal under this rule is appropriate, the rule is available for the purpose of obtaining (a) an order for an urgent date for the hearing of the reclaiming motion on the Summar Roll or (b) determination of the reclaiming motion in the Single Bills. The appropriate words, as specified in paragraph (1) of this rule, should be included in the motion.

15. The reclaimer or respondent should also include in the motion an indication of the nature of the urgency. A motion for urgent disposal will be starred and will require the appearance of counsel or other person having a right of audience. The procedural judge will wish to know parties' estimate of the duration of the hearing to determine the reclaiming motion.

16. In granting a motion for urgent disposal, a procedural judge may appoint the reclaiming motion to the Summar Roll for a hearing even if all parties are of the view that it should be heard in the Single Bills. Similarly, a procedural judge may direct that the reclaiming motion be heard in the Single Bills even if all parties take the view that it should be dealt with on the Summar Roll.

17. Where a procedural judge grants the motion for urgent disposal, this will be reflected in the timetable that is issued and the timescales referred to in Table A in the Appendix to this Note will be adjusted accordingly.

18. It should be noted that where a procedural judge has granted a motion for urgent disposal, rules 38.12 (objections to competency), 38.13 (timetable), 38.14 (sist or variation of timetable), 38.15 (failure to comply with timetable) and 38.16 (procedural hearing) will apply to the reclaiming motion only to the extent that the procedural judge so directs.

19. Unlike the rules in force immediately prior to 5th April 2010, the current rules do not identify specified types of case in respect of which parties are required to seek urgent or early disposal. The inclusion of such provision is unnecessary, as procedural judges will be able to exercise case management powers through use of the timetable in every case. This is made clear by rule 38.11(6).

20. Parties should be aware that, when urgent disposal of a reclaiming motion is ordered, the Keeper of the Rolls may intimate a diet at very short notice. Parties will be expected to be in a position to proceed with the diet that is fixed. Early warning should be given to the Keeper of the Rolls of any circumstances which may result in the reclaiming motion not proceeding, so that the Keeper can, if necessary, defer allocation of an urgent diet until it is clear that such a diet is required.

Rule 38.12: Objections to the competency of reclaiming

21. A note of objection may be lodged by a party, and the Deputy Principal Clerk of Session may refer a question of competency, only within 14 days after the date on which the reclaiming motion was marked. The purpose of including such a requirement in this rule, and not as part of the timetable, is to ensure that parties focus on the competency of the reclaiming motion at as early a procedural stage as possible, so that the procedural judge can then consider any competency issues before the timetable is issued and the procedural hearing is fixed under rule 38.13. A form (Form 38.12) is provided for specifying the basis of an objection to competency. Parties should note that a hearing will be fixed under this rule, rather than objections to competency being dealt with on paper. It should also be noted that notes of argument will require to be lodged in relation to the competency issue. Where a hearing is being fixed under this rule, parties should also provide the Keeper of the Rolls with an estimate of the duration of the hearing.

Rule 38.13: Timetable in reclaiming motion

22. This rule provides for the issue of a timetable and the fixing of a procedural hearing in a reclaiming motion. These measures form the core aspects of the reforms to Inner House procedure arising from Lord Penrose's Report. In relation to the carrying out of certain procedural steps leading up to the issuing of the timetable, some specific periods are set out in the rules. However, to a significant extent, the periods to be followed, so far as possible and subject to any motions for urgent disposal under rule 38.11, will from time to time be prescribed by the Lord President. Table A in the Appendix to this Note incorporates the periods which, as at the date of issuing this Practice Note, are prescribed.

23. Any questions of competency should have been dealt with by the time the Keeper issues the timetable and fixes the procedural hearing under this rule. This is reflected by the requirement for the Keeper to take those steps within 7 days of—

(a) the expiry of the period within which an objection to competency or a reference by the Deputy Principal Clerk on competency could have been, but was not, made under rule 38.12, or

(b) where such an objection or reference was made, the reclaiming motion having been found to be competent or the question of competency having been reserved, as referred to in rule 38.12.

24. A party who is concerned that a step of procedure has not been complied with timeously, or that a party is not complying with the spirit of the procedures, and that failure is threatening to cause delay to or prejudice the expeditious disposal of the cause, should:

- if the matter relates to a stage in the timetable, approach the Keeper of the Rolls with a view to having the case put out for a hearing before a procedural judge, or enrol a motion as mentioned in rule 38.15(1), or
- if the matter is outwith the control of the timetable, enrol a motion to bring it before a procedural judge.

Rule 38.14: Sist or variation of timetable in reclaiming motion

25. A motion to vary the timetable should give full details of the grounds on which the motion is based and, where relevant, be accompanied by appropriate evidence. Any such motion should be made as soon as possible after the timetable has been issued. Variation of the timetable may be by either extension or acceleration.

26. A motion may be for sist alone, for variation of the timetable alone or for both sist and variation of the timetable. It is a matter for the procedural judge to determine the length of any sist of the reclaiming motion, but parties are reminded that procedural judges will seek to avoid any unnecessary delay in carrying out the procedural steps set out in the timetable. It should be noted that motions for sist or for variation of the timetable will not be granted, even if made of consent, unless sufficient information to justify them is placed before the procedural judge. Any party opposing such an application will be required to demonstrate that their opposition is well founded.

27. It should be noted that a motion to sist and/or vary the timetable in a reclaiming motion may only be granted on special cause shown. It is a matter for the procedural judge to determine, in the particular circumstances of a case, whether or not special cause has been shown. Special cause might arise for example, where there is a need for a party to obtain transcripts of evidence or to obtain legal aid, or where it is necessary to obtain an opinion of the Lord Ordinary. Motions to sist and/or vary the timetable will be starred if there is objection to them, if the Scottish Legal Aid Board take issue with what is stated to be the current position in relation to an application for legal aid, or if the material placed before the procedural judge does not satisfy the requirement that special cause be shown. It is expected that any motions for sist pending the outcome of an application for legal aid, if granted, will only be granted for fixed periods not exceeding six weeks.

28. The Court will expect parties to consider at the earliest possible stage whether they may require to make an application to the Scottish Legal Aid Board in respect of the reclaiming motion. Delay in making an application for legal aid or in applying for a sist may lead to a motion under this rule being refused. Generally, the Court will expect parties to adhere to guidance issued by the Scottish Legal Aid Board. Parties are reminded that the Board may make legal aid available for specially urgent work undertaken before a legal aid application is determined. Making an application to the Board under the special urgency procedure may obviate the need for the timetable to be varied or for the reclaiming motion to be sisted under this rule. Further information can be obtained in the Chapter entitled "Special Urgency" in the Civil Legal Aid Handbook:
http://www.slab.org.uk/profession/handbook/Civil%20handbook/wwhelp/wwhimpl/js/html/wwhelp.htm

29. In every case in which an application is made to sist a reclaiming motion pending the outcome of an application for legal aid, the party making the motion should intimate it electronically to the Scottish Legal Aid Board within the same period as that party is required to intimate it to other parties under rule 23.3. The party making the motion should lodge and intimate with the motion a note of the current position in relation to the application for legal aid.

Rule 38.15: Failure to comply with timetable in reclaiming motion

30. The purpose of this rule is to provide for discipline to ensure effective supervision of the management of cases under the timetable.

Rule 38.16: Procedural hearing in reclaiming motion

31. The procedural hearing is an important aspect of the procedure under the Chapter and will follow on completion of the other procedural steps mentioned in the timetable. It is intended to be the final procedural matter to be dealt with by the procedural judge. The primary purpose of the procedural hearing is to make sure that no case is sent for a hearing on its merits unless the procedural judge is satisfied that a hearing is necessary and that the parties are prepared for it.

32. At the procedural hearing, parties will be expected to be in a position to discuss the issues involved in the reclaiming motion and the method of disposing of them. Parties should address the procedural judge on their state of preparation, and estimate the length of any hearing on the Summar Roll or in the Single Bills which may be required to dispose of the reclaiming motion. The procedural judge will decide the length of any such hearing, and when it is to take place.

33. Parties will be expected to arrange that counsel, or other persons having rights of audience responsible for the conduct of the case, and authorised to take any necessary decision on questions of both substance and procedure, are available and appear at any hearing in the Inner House, including a procedural hearing and any other hearings before a procedural judge. Ensuring continuity of representation in relation to both procedural and substantive hearings will be an important factor in seeking to avoid late settlements and the discharge of hearings under the new procedures. Counsel should also have (or have access to) their diaries at the procedural hearing, so that the court can fix the date of any further procedural or substantive hearing (including any Summar Roll hearing) which may be required.

34. It is important that continued procedural hearings are avoided unless they are genuinely necessary. Where it emerges at a procedural hearing that further steps require to be taken, the parties will be provided with an interlocutor specifying those steps and the time within which they must be taken. In the event that any difficulty then arises, the parties should communicate with the court by email (or otherwise), confirming whether the steps have been carried out (and if not, why not), whether further time is required (and if so, why), and whether a further hearing is genuinely required (rather than, for example, the court's making any necessary order on the basis of an unstarred motion).

Rule 38.17: Amendment of pleadings in reclaiming motion

35. The Court will expect parties to give consideration at the earliest possible stage after the reclaiming motion has been marked as to whether or not it is necessary for a motion to be made to have the pleadings amended in terms of a minute of amendment and answers. Wherever possible, such a motion should be made before the procedural hearing so that a procedural judge can consider the matter.

Rule 38.18: Grounds of appeal in reclaiming motion

36. This rule sets out requirements relating to grounds of appeal. Wherever possible, parties should make any motions to amend grounds of appeal or answers, on cause shown, before the procedural hearing so that a procedural judge can consider the matter. Where a motion is made for an amendment to the grounds or answers, the same motion should include any necessary motion for sist and/or variation of the timetable under rule 38.14(1).

Rule 38.19: Lodging of appendices in reclaiming motion

37. The timing of the lodging of appendices is a matter which will be controlled by the timetable and, therefore, by the procedural judge. The reclaimer shall lodge an appendix to the reclaiming print unless intimation is given by the reclaimer that he or she does not consider it necessary to do so. If such intimation is given by the reclaimer, a respondent can make a motion to the procedural judge for an order requiring the reclaimer to lodge an appendix. Where such a motion is refused, a respondent can seek to lodge an appendix containing documents which the reclaimer has confirmed he or she does not intend to include in an appendix.

Chapter 39: Applications for new trial or to enter jury verdicts

Rule 39.1: Applications for new trial

38. The terms of rule 39.1 broadly remain the same as the equivalent rule that was in force prior to 5th April 2010. It should be noted that the period within which an application for a new trial under section 29(1) of the Court of Session Act 1988 remains the period of 7 days after the date on which the verdict of the jury was written on the issue and signed. This is a shorter timescale than that which applies to the marking of a reclaiming motion.

Rule 39.3: Objections to the competency of application

39. The procedure set out in this rule for objecting to the competency of an application for a new trial is similar to the procedure set out for objecting to a reclaiming motion under rule 38.12. However, there are two main differences. The first is that a note of objection may only be lodged within the period of 7 days after the application for a new trial was made. This reflects the shorter period within which such an application may be made under rule 39.1, when compared to the time allowed for making a reclaiming motion under Chapter 38. In addition, the rule does not contain an equivalent to rule 38.12(2), under which provision is made for the Deputy Principal Clerk of Session to refer questions of competency to a procedural judge.

Rule 39.4: Timetable in application for a new trial

40. This rule provides for the issue of a timetable and the fixing of a procedural hearing in an application for a new trial. Chapter 39 sets out time limits prior to the issuing of the timetable, including the period for lodging objections to the competency of the application. However, other timescales which will apply under the timetable are from time to time to be prescribed by the Lord President. Table B in the Appendix to this Note incorporates the periods which, as at the date of issuing this Practice Note, are prescribed.

41. It should be noted that the three procedural steps mentioned in rule 39.4(2) prior to the procedural hearing are the lodging of appendices or the giving of notice that the applicant does not intend to lodge an appendix, the lodging of notes of argument and the lodging of estimates of the length of any hearing required to dispose of the application for a new trial. In relation to the lodging of appendices, the effect of rule 39.8 should be noted. Paragraph 37 of this Note applies, with appropriate modification, to the lodging of appendices in applications for a new trial as it applies to the lodging of appendices in reclaiming motions.

Rule 39.5: Sist or variation of timetable in application for a new trial

42. The points made at paragraphs 25 to 29 of this Note, in the context of a sist or variation of the timetable in a reclaiming motion, should be similarly considered in the context of the application of this rule.

Rule 39.6: Failure to comply with timetable in application for a new trial

43. The purpose of this rule is to provide for discipline to ensure effective supervision of the management of cases under the timetable.

Rule 39.7: Procedural hearing in application for a new trial

44. The points made at paragraphs 31 to 34 of this Note apply, with appropriate modification, to procedural hearings in applications for a new trial.

Rule 39.9: Applications to enter jury verdict

45. The terms of this rule are similar to the equivalent rule relating to applications to enter a jury verdict that was in force immediately prior to 5th April 2010. However, it should be noted that the rule provides that such applications are now to be made, in the first instance, to a procedural judge.

Chapter 40: Appeals from Inferior Courts

Rule 40.2: Applications for leave to appeal from inferior court

46. The terms of this rule are the same as the equivalent rule on applications for leave to appeal from an inferior court that was in force immediately prior to 5th April 2010.

Rule 40.4: Time and method of appeal

47. The default timescale and the method for making an appeal under this rule are the same as those provided for under the equivalent rule that was in force immediately before 5th April 2010. Similarly, the rules relating to the procedure for transmitting an appeal process and the procedure thereafter (see rules 40.6 and 40.7) remain substantially unchanged from the equivalent rules that were in force immediately prior to 5th April 2010. An application to allow an appeal to be received out of time is to be included in the note of appeal. Rule 40.5(3) provides for such an application to be disposed of by a procedural judge.

Rule 40.8: Sist of process of appeal

48. A sist of process under this rule stops the period of days mentioned in rule 40.7(2) from running. The practical effect is to postpone the requirement for the appellant to lodge a process and an appeal print and to intimate the appeal print. The appellant therefore does not have to incur the cost of lodging and intimating during such time as there is a sist of process.

49. This rule therefore prescribes a procedure that is specifically related to the circumstances in which an appellant requires to lodge an appeal process from an inferior court. For that reason, the rule appears only in Chapter 40 and it is placed immediately after rule 40.7. As rule 40.7 makes provision only for the appellant to lodge and intimate a process and appeal print etc., rule 40.8 provides only for the appellant to apply for a sist of process. Rule 40.8(4) makes it clear that the provisions in rule 40.8 are without prejudice to the power of the court to sist an appeal, as mentioned in rule 40.12.

Rule 40.9: Urgent disposal of appeal

50. Paragraphs 14 to 16 of this note apply equally to motions for urgent disposal of an appeal under Chapter 40 as they apply to motions for urgent disposal of a reclaiming motion.

51. Where a procedural judge grants the motion for urgent disposal, this will be reflected in the timetable that is issued and the timescales referred to in Table C in the Appendix to this Note will be adjusted accordingly.

52. Where a procedural judge has granted a motion for urgent disposal, rules 40.10 (objections to competency), 40.11 (timetable), 40.12 (sist or variation of timetable), 40.13 (failure to comply with timetable), and 40.14 (procedural hearing) will apply to the appeal only to the extent that the procedural judge so directs.

Rule 40.10: Objections to competency of appeal

53. This rule is similar in effect to rule 38.12 (objections to the competency of reclaiming). Again, the purpose of including provision for the lodging of a note of objection within a specified period of time is to ensure, as far as possible, that the parties focus on the competency of the appeal at as early a procedural stage as possible and before the timetable is issued.

Rule 40.11: Timetable in appeal from inferior court

54. This rule provides for the issue of a timetable and the fixing of a procedural hearing in an appeal from an inferior court. The rule is similar in effect to rule 38.13 (timetable in reclaiming motion). Table C in the Appendix to this Note incorporates the relevant periods which, as at the date of issuing this Practice Note, are prescribed by the Lord President. Paragraphs 22 to 24 of this Note apply equally to appeals under Chapter 40, subject to the modification that, in that case, the reference in paragraph 22 to rule 38.11 and Table A should be read as references respectively to rule 40.9 and Table C, the references in paragraph 23 to rule 38.12 should be read as references to rule 40.10 and the reference in paragraph 24 to rule 38.15(1) should be read as a reference to rule 40.13(1).

Rule 40.12: Sist or variation of timetable in appeal from inferior court

55. This rule is similar to rule 38.13 (sist or variation of timetable in reclaiming motion). The points made at paragraphs 25 to 29 of this Note can be applied, with appropriate modification, to the operation of rule 40.12. In the context of this rule, special cause might arise, for example, in cases where there is a need for a party to obtain transcripts of evidence or to obtain legal aid, or where it is necessary to obtain a note from the inferior court.

Rule 40.13: Failure to comply with timetable in appeal from inferior court

56. The purpose of this rule is to provide for discipline to ensure effective supervision of the management of cases under the timetable.

Rule 40.14: Procedural hearing in appeal from inferior court

57. The points made at paragraphs 31 to 34 of this Note apply, with appropriate modification, to procedural hearings in appeals dealt with under Chapter 40.

Rule 40.15: Appeals deemed abandoned

58. The rules on appeals deemed to be abandoned (rule 40.15) and on reponing against deemed abandonment (rule 40.16) are essentially unchanged from the equivalent rules which were in force immediately prior to 5th April 2010.

Rule 40.17: Amendment of pleadings in appeals

59. The Court will expect parties to give consideration at the earliest possible stage after the appeal has been marked as to whether or not it is necessary for a motion to be made to have the pleadings amended in terms of a minute of amendment and answers. Wherever possible, such a motion should be made before the procedural hearing so that a procedural judge can consider the matter.

Rule 40.18: Grounds of appeal

60. Wherever possible, parties should make any motions to amend grounds of appeal or answers, on cause shown, before the procedural hearing so that a procedural judge can consider the matter. Where a motion is made for an amendment to the grounds or answers, the same motion should include any necessary motion for sist and/or variation of the timetable under rule 40.12(1).

Rule 40.19: Lodging of appendices in appeals

61. The timing of the lodging of appendices is a matter which will be controlled by the timetable and, therefore, by the procedural judge. The appellant shall lodge an appendix to the reclaiming print unless intimation is given by the appellant that he or she does not consider it necessary to do so. If such intimation is given by the appellant, a respondent can make a motion to the procedural judge for an order requiring the appellant to lodge an appendix. Where such a motion is refused, a respondent can seek to lodge an appendix containing documents which the appellant has confirmed he or she does not intend to include in an appendix.

Chapter 41: Appeals under statute

62. The structure of the rules under substituted Chapter 41 remains largely unchanged from the structure of the Chapter which was in force immediately prior to 27th September 2011. General provisions affecting all statutory appeals are outlined in Part I (with new or extended rules on urgent disposal and competency). Stated case procedure is outlined at Part II. A separate procedure is outlined at Part III and rules relating to appeals under particular statutes are outlined in subsequent Parts of the Chapter.

Rule 41.3: Determination of applications for leave to appeal

63. The application will be brought before a procedural judge or the vacation judge for an order for intimation and service and for any answers without any motion being enrolled.

Rule 41.4: Urgent disposal of appeal

64. Paragraphs 14 to 16 of this note apply equally to motions for urgent disposal of an appeal under Chapter 41 as they apply to motions for urgent disposal of a reclaiming motion.

65. Where a procedural judge grants the motion for urgent disposal, this will be reflected in the timetable that is issued and the timescales referred to in Table D in the Appendix to this Note will be adjusted accordingly.

66. Where a procedural judge has granted a motion for urgent disposal, the procedural stages referred to in rules 41.18 to 41.21 (under stated case procedure) and in rules 41.29 to 41.32 (under the procedure at Part III of Chapter 41) will apply to the appeal only to the extent that the procedural judge so directs.

Rule 41.5: Competency of appeals

67. This rule is similar in effect to rule 38.12 and rule 40.10. The purpose of including provision for the lodging of a note of objection within a specified period of time is to ensure, as far as possible, that the parties focus on the competency of the appeal at as early a procedural stage as possible and before the timetable is issued. The Deputy Principal Clerk may also refer a competency issue to a procedural judge within a specified period of time.

Rule 41.18: Timetable in appeal under Part II of Chapter 41

68. A timetable will be issued by the Keeper where a stated case appeal is lodged in court. This rule provides for the issue of a timetable and the fixing of a procedural hearing in a stated case appeal. The rule is similar in effect to rule 38.13 (timetable in reclaiming motion) and rule 40.11 (timetable in appeal from inferior court). Table D in the Appendix to this Note incorporates the relevant periods which, as at the date of issuing this Practice Note, are prescribed by the Lord President. Paragraphs 22 to 24 of this Note apply equally to appeals under Chapter 41, subject to the modification that, in that case, the references in paragraph 22 to rule 38.11 and Table A should be read as references respectively to rule 41.4 and Table D, the references in paragraph 23 to rule 38.12 should be read as references to rule 41.5 and the reference in paragraph 24 to rule 38.15(1) should be read as a reference to rule 41.20(1).

Rule 41.19: Sist or variation of timetable in appeal under Part II of Chapter 41

69. The points made at paragraphs 25 to 29 of this Note, in the context of a sist or variation of the timetable in a reclaiming motion, should be similarly considered in the context of the application of this rule.

Rule 41.20: Failure to comply with timetable in appeal under Part II of Chapter 41

70. The purpose of this rule is to provide for discipline to ensure effective supervision of the management of cases under the timetable.

Rule 41.21: Procedural hearing in appeal under Part II of Chapter 41

71. The points made at paragraphs 31 to 34 of this Note apply, with appropriate modification, to procedural hearings in appeals dealt with under Part II of Chapter 41.

Rule 41.29: Timetable in appeal under Part III of Chapter 41

72. Where there is a contradictor to an appeal dealt with under Part III of Chapter 41, answers to the appeal should be lodged. Where answers have been lodged, a timetable will be issued by the Keeper. This rule provides for the issue of a timetable and the fixing of a procedural hearing in an appeal under statute. The rule is similar in effect to rule 38.13 (timetable in reclaiming motion) and rule 40.11. Table E in the Appendix to this Note incorporates the relevant periods which, as at the date of issuing this Practice Note, are prescribed by the Lord President. Paragraphs 22 to 24 of this Note apply equally to appeals under Chapter 41, subject to the modification that, in that case, the reference in paragraph 22 to rule 38.11 and Table A should be read as references respectively to rule 41.4 and Table E, the references in paragraph 23 to rule 38.12 should be read as references to rule 41.5 and the reference in paragraph 24 to rule 38.15(1) should be read as a reference to rule 41.31(1).

Rule 41.30: Sist or variation of timetable in appeal under Part III of Chapter 41

73. The points made at paragraphs 25 to 29 of this Note, in the context of a sist or variation of the timetable in a reclaiming motion, should be similarly considered in the context of the application of this rule.

Rule 41.31: Failure to comply with timetable in appeal under Part III of Chapter 41

74. The purpose of this rule is to provide for discipline to ensure effective supervision of the management of cases under the timetable.

Rule 41.32: Procedural hearing in appeal under Part III of Chapter 41

75. The points made at paragraphs 31 to 34 of this Note apply, with appropriate modification, to procedural hearings in appeals dealt with under Chapter 41.

General

Counsel and solicitors

76. It is of particular importance that counsel or solicitors having rights of audience who are responsible for the conduct of the case, and authorised to take any necessary decision on questions of both substance and procedure, are available and appear at any procedural hearing in the Inner House, in accordance with paragraph 33 above. Inner House proceedings and hearings take priority over proceedings and hearings in lower courts or tribunals or in the Outer House. In the event of a conflict between a procedural hearing and a hearing in the Outer House, the Lord Ordinary may be willing to consider delaying the start of the Outer House business, depending on the circumstances. If an unavoidable conflict between a procedural hearing and another commitment will cause a serious problem, the court should be informed of the difficulty in good time so that it can consider whether to alter the date of the procedural hearing.

Communication with the court

77. It is important to avoid unnecessary hearings. Hearings in court should not take place unless the matter in issue cannot otherwise be resolved. Hearings can often be avoided by means of email or other communication between solicitors and clerks of court, with the involvement of the procedural judge when necessary. For example, applications for a variation of the timetable, or for a sist, can often be dealt with by means of an unstarred motion if the court is provided with sufficient information, as explained in paragraphs 26 to 29 above. Continued procedural hearings can often be avoided if parties follow the guidance given in paragraph 34 above. The procedural judge can be requested, via the clerks of court, to provide guidance in relation to other matters, such as the form and contents of appendices, notes of argument and bundles of authorities, as explained in paragraphs 79 to 81, 83 to 89 and 90 to 95 below. These are only examples. The court may make no award of expenses in respect of hearings which could have been avoided if parties had communicated with the court in advance, or may award expenses against the party responsible on an agent and client basis.

Answers to grounds of appeal

78. The timetable in reclaiming motions and in appeals from inferior courts includes a date for lodging answers to grounds of appeal. Answers should be lodged in every reclaiming motion and in every appeal or cross-appeal under Chapter 40 so that the court and each of the parties to the proceedings are aware of a respondent's case in response to each set of grounds of appeal. The answers need not be elaborate, but they should mirror the format of grounds of appeal. Answers, like the grounds of appeal, serve an important function in framing lines of argument and are considered by the court to be compulsory under the procedures outlined in Chapters 38 and 40. The scope of subsequent notes of argument should be determined by the content of the answers.

Appendices

79. The appendix should include any information the court may require in addition to pleadings, productions or notes of evidence, such as a chronology of relevant events, a list of persons who feature in the case or glossaries of technical terms. It should only contain such material as is necessary for understanding the legal issues and the argument to be presented to the court. Any questions as to the contents or form of the appendix may be raised with the procedural judge.

80. The appendix should be paginated, each page being numbered individually and consecutively, with page numbers being inserted in a form which can be clearly distinguished from any other pagination on the document. Where any marking or writing in colour on a document is important, the document should be copied in colour or marked up correctly in colour. Documents which are not easily legible should be transcribed and the transcription placed adjacent to the document transcribed.

81. Appendices which do not conform to this Practice Note may be rejected by the court, which may also find that no expenses are payable in respect of the relative expense. The court may also find that no expenses are payable, or may modify any award of expenses, where documents are included in an appendix unnecessarily.

Core bundles

82. In cases where the appendix or appendices comprise more than 500 pages, exclusive of notes of evidence, the reclaimer, applicant or appellant (as the case may be) should, after consultation with the respondent, also lodge a core bundle. The core bundle should be lodged at least 7 days prior to the procedural hearing. It should contain the documents which are central to the reclaiming motion, and should not ordinarily exceed 150 pages. Any questions as to the contents or form of the core bundle may be raised with the procedural judge.

Notes of argument

83. One of the purposes of the timetable procedure in Inner House cases is that it should enable the procedural judge to ensure that parties produce notes of argument at an early stage in the proceedings. Any questions as to the contents or form of notes of argument may be raised with the procedural judge.

84. At the hearing of the reclaiming motion, application or appeal the court may decline to hear argument not contained in a note of argument lodged in accordance with the Rules of Court and this Practice Note. The case should have been fully prepared by the stage of the procedural hearing, and the decisions taken by the other parties and the court at and after that hearing proceed on that basis. It is therefore ordinarily inappropriate for any argument to be advanced of which notice has not been given in the note of argument. In the event that a party wishes, for some justifiable reason, to be permitted to advance an argument not contained in a note of argument (e.g. by reason of a supervening decision in another case), the other parties and the court should be informed at the earliest opportunity. The court may then put the case out for a hearing By Order, so that the request and its implications can be considered.

85. Where a note of argument has already been lodged and a party subsequently becomes aware that an argument included in the note will no longer be insisted upon, that party should inform the other parties and the court of that fact at the earliest opportunity.

86. A note of argument should comply with the following general principles:

1. A note of argument should be a concise summary of the submissions to be developed.
2. It should contain a numbered list of the points which the party wishes to make.
3. Each point should be followed by a reference to any transcript of evidence or other document on which the party wishes to rely. The note of argument should identify the relevant passage in the document in question.
4. A note of argument should state, in respect of each authority cited—
   (a) the proposition of law that the authority demonstrates; and
   (b) the parts of the authority (identified by page or paragraph references) that support the proposition.
5. More than one authority should not be cited in support of a given proposition unless the additional citation is necessary for a proper presentation of the argument.

87. Notes of argument which do not conform to this Practice Note may be rejected by the court.

88. The court may find that no expenses are payable, or may modify any award of expenses, in respect of a note of argument which—

(a) does not comply with the requirements set out in this Practice Note, or
(b) was not lodged within the timetable issued by the Keeper (or any further time granted by the court).

89. A single date will be specified in the timetable for the lodging of notes of argument. As a matter of good practice, parties should exchange draft versions of their notes of argument in advance of the date referred to in the timetable. Whenever possible, the drafts should be exchanged in sufficient time to enable each party to answer, in its note of argument, the arguments advanced by the other parties.

Authorities

90. When a reclaiming motion, application or appeal has been appointed to the Summar Roll or the Single Bills for a hearing, the reclaimer, applicant or appellant (as the case may be) should, after consultation with the respondent, lodge a bundle containing photocopies of the authorities upon which each party will rely at the hearing. Any questions as to the contents or form of bundles of authorities may be raised with the procedural judge.

91. The bundle of authorities should, in general—

(a) not include authorities for propositions not in dispute; and
(b) not include more than 10 authorities, unless the scale of the reclaiming motion, application or appeal warrants more extensive citation.

92. Authorities which have been reported in Session Cases, or in the Law Reports published by the Incorporated Council of Law Reporting for England and Wales, should be cited from those sources. Where a case is not reported in Session Cases or the Law Reports, references to other recognised reports may be given. In Revenue appeals, Tax Cases or Simon's Tax Cases may be cited but, wherever possible, references to the case in Session Cases or the Law Reports should also be given. Unreported judgments should only be cited when they contain an authoritative statement of a relevant principle of law not to be found in a reported case or when they are necessary for the understanding of some other authority.

93. The bundle of authorities should be lodged—
(a) at least 7 days before the hearing; or
(b) where the period of notice of the hearing is less than 7 days, immediately.

94. The bundle of authorities should bear a certification by the counsel or solicitor responsible for arguing the reclaiming motion, application or appeal that the requirements of this Practice Note have been complied with in respect of each authority included.

95. Bundles of authorities which do not conform to this Practice Note may be rejected by the court, which may also find that no expenses are payable in respect of the relative expense. The court may also find that no expenses are payable, or may modify any award of expenses, where authorities are included unnecessarily.

Documents generally

96. Appendices, core bundles and bundles of authorities must be presented in a form which is robust, manageable and not excessively heavy. All documents must be easily legible.

97. At least three copies of the appendices, core bundles and bundles of authorities will be required at the hearing of the reclaiming motion, application or appeal. The precise number will depend upon the composition of the court. Advice on that matter can be sought from the clerks of court.

Estimates of the length of hearings

98. The estimate of the length of the hearing should be that of the counsel or solicitor who will argue the reclaiming motion, application or appeal. Any estimate exceeding two days should be fully explained in writing. Counsel and solicitors are expected to confine their submissions so as to enable the hearing to be completed within the time indicated in their estimates, or otherwise allowed by the court.

Communication where causes are not to proceed

99. Parties are reminded that those involved in litigation have an obligation to take reasonable care to avoid situations where court time would be wasted. In cases where it becomes clear to a party or their legal advisers that there is doubt as to whether a reclaiming motion, application or appeal would proceed in the Inner House, that fact should immediately be communicated to the Keeper of the Rolls.

100. Practice Note No. 1 of 2010 (causes in the Inner House) is hereby revoked.

9th August 2011

APPENDIX

Table A—Reclaiming Motions

Stage in proceedings	Date
Timetable issued and diet for procedural hearing allocated (rule 38.13(1)(a) and (b))	
Grounds of appeal to be lodged (rule 38.13(2)(a))	Within 28 days after issue of timetable
Answers to grounds of appeal to be lodged (rule 38.13(2)(a))	Within 28 days after expiry of period for lodging grounds of appeal
Any appendices to be lodged (or intimation that no appendices are to be lodged) (rule 38.13(2)(b))	At least 7 days prior to procedural hearing
Notes of argument to be lodged (rule 38.13(2)(c))	At least 7 days prior to procedural hearing
Lodging of estimate of length of any hearing on the Summar Roll or in the Single Bills (rule 38.13(2)(d))	At least 7 days prior to procedural hearing

Table B—Applications for a New Trial

Stage in proceedings	Date
Timetable issued and diet for procedural hearing allocated (rule 39.4(1)(a) and (b)	
Any appendices to be lodged (or intimation that no appendices are to be lodged) (rule 39.4(2)(a))	At least 7 days prior to procedural hearing
Any notes of argument to be lodged (rule 39.4(2)(b))	At least 7 days prior to the procedural hearing
Lodging of estimate of the length of any hearing required to dispose of the application (rule 39.4(2)(c))	At least 7 days prior to the procedural hearing

Table C—Appeals from Inferior Courts

Stage in proceedings	Date
Timetable issued and diet for procedural hearing allocated (rule 40.11(1)(a) and (b))	
Grounds of appeal to be lodged (rule 40.11(2)(d))	Within 28 days after issue of timetable
Answers to grounds of appeal to be lodged (rule 40.11(2)(d))	Within 28 days after expiry of period for lodging grounds of appeal
Any appendices to be lodged (or intimation that no appendices are to be lodged) (rule 40.11(2)(e))	At least 7 days prior to procedural hearing

Stage in proceedings	Date
Notes of argument to be lodged (rule 40.11(2)(f))	At least 7 days prior to procedural hearing
Lodging of estimate of the length of any hearing on the Summar Roll or in the Single Bills (rule 40.11(2)(g)	At least 7 days prior to procedural hearing

Table D — Appeals under Statute (Part II of Chapter 41)

Stage in proceedings	Date
Case lodged, timetable issued and diet for procedural hearing allocated (rule 41.18(1)(a) and (b))	
Any productions or appendices to be lodged (rule 41.18(2)(a))	At least 7 days prior to procedural hearing
Notes of argument to be lodged (rule 41.18(2)(b))	At least 7 days prior to procedural hearing
Lodging of estimate of the length of any hearing on the Summar Roll or in the Single Bills (rule 41.18(2)(c))	At least 7 days prior to procedural hearing

Table E — Appeals under Statute (Part III of Chapter 41)

Stage in proceedings	Date
Answers to grounds of appeal lodged, timetable issued and diet for procedural hearing allocated (rule 41.29(1)(a) and (b))	
Any productions or appendices to be lodged (rule 41.29(2)(a))	At least 7 days prior to procedural hearing
Notes of argument to be lodged (rule 41.29(2)(b))	At least 7 days prior to procedural hearing
Lodging of estimate of the length of any hearing on the Summar Roll or in the Single Bills (rule 41.29(2)(c))	At least 7 days prior to procedural hearing

NO. 4 OF 2011

I, the Lord President of the Court of Session, under and by virtue of the power conferred on me by rule 100.2 of the Rules of the Court of Session 1994, hereby nominate the following as arbitration judges with effect from today— C5.107

The Honourable Lord Menzies;
The Honourable Lord Hodge;
The Honourable Lord Glennie;
The Honourable Lord Malcolm.

11th August 2011

NO. 1 OF 2012: IMMIGRATION AND ASYLUM JUDICIAL REVIEWS: IMMIGRATION AND ASYLUM JUDICIAL REVIEWS

1. This Practice Note has effect from 4 February 2013. **C5.108**

2. Where the immigration or asylum status of an individual is in question, the UK Border Agency has provided an undertaking to the Court that where it is notified of a stated intention to raise judicial review proceedings in a pre-proceedings letter in accordance with the procedure set out in this Practice Note, such notification, of itself, will not cause the UK Border Agency (i) to initiate or accelerate a decision to issue a removal direction, (ii) to initiate or accelerate the removal of the person from the United Kingdom and access to Scottish jurisdiction or (iii) to use the notification as a factor in the initiation or acceleration of such directions or decisions.

3. If the UK Border Agency receives a pre-proceedings letter before it has issued a removal direction, it will not remove the individual before it has responded to the letter. If removal directions have been issued before a preproceedings letter has been sent, agents of the individual do not need to send a pre-proceedings letter before commencing a judicial review application.

4. The agents of the individual should send any pre-proceedings letter to [a designated official] at the UK Border Agency. The nominated addressee is "The Litigation Unit, UK Border Agency, Festival Court, 200 Brand Street, Glasgow G51 1DH". Pre-action letters can be faxed to the UK Border Agency on 0141 555 1561 and can be emailed to snijrteam@homeoffice.gsi.gov. The UK Border Agency will, ordinarily, acknowledge the pre-action letter within 24 hours.

5. The wording of a pre-proceedings letter should follow as closely as is reasonably practicable the form of letter which is appended to this Practice Note.

6. Except in cases of urgency, the individual's agents should allow 14 days after the delivery of the pre-proceedings letter for the UK Border Agency to respond to that letter before commencing proceedings.

7. Upon commencing proceedings, the individual's agents are to produce with the petition and copy to the Office of the Advocate General (preferably in electronic form) the case documents in their possession which are relevant to the application (including, if any, the pre-proceedings letter and the UK Border Agency's response to that letter).

8. At first order, the court will, ordinarily:

(a) order service of the petition on the Advocate General for and on behalf of the Secretary of State for the Home Department within 7 days,

(b) order the respondent to lodge Answers and any documents on which he or she founds within 4 weeks of that service, and

(c) fix a date for a procedural first hearing.

9. If an application is made for an interim order and the court requests it, the Office of the Advocate General will provide the court with an Immigration Factual Summary setting out the history of the case.

10. Each party who is to be represented at the procedural first hearing is to exchange and lodge in process not later than two days before that hearing (a) a short statement of issues and of the legal authorities on which he or she relies, (b) any further documents, to which he or she intends to refer, and (c) an estimate of the duration of the substantive hearing. Counsel are expected to discuss these matters and the future progress of the case before the procedural first hearing with a view to identifying the matters in dispute and the most efficient means of their resolution.

11. At the procedural first hearing the Lord Ordinary will consider the pleadings and the statement of issues, ascertain the parties' state of preparation, the likely duration of the hearing and identify whether the case can be heard along with other similar cases. The Lord Ordinary will exercise any of the powers set out in Rule of Court 58.9 as may be appropriate, for example to require the lodging of notes of argument and authorities, and, after consulting the Keeper of the Rolls, allocate the case to a substantive hearing.

12. The Keeper of the Rolls will maintain a record of court days allocated to Immigration and Asylum Judicial Reviews and the issues raised in the cases allocated to those days.

21st December 2012

APPENDIX

[Name of designated official]
The Litigation Unit
UK Border Agency
Festival Court
200 Brand Street
Glasgow
G51 1DH

Dear Sirs

[Insert title, first and last name and address of the claimant]

[Insert date of birth and nationality of claimant]

[Insert Home office, Port or other relevant reference]

[Set out the name, address and reference details of any legal advisers dealing with the claim]

[Set out the details of any interested parties and confirm that they have been sent a copy of this letter]

[Set out the details of the matter being challenged]

[Set out the date and details of the decision, or act or omission being challenged, a brief summary of the facts and, in brief terms, why it is contended to be wrong]

[Set out the details of the remedy sought from the UK Border Agency, including whether a review or any interim remedy is sought]

[Set out the details of any information that is sought. This may include a request for a fuller explanation of the reasons for the decision that is being challenged]

[Set out the details of any documents that are considered relevant and necessary. This should include details of any documentation or policy in respect of which disclosure is sought and an explanation as to why these are relevant. If reliance is being placed on a statutory duty to disclose information, this should be specified]

[Set out the address for the reply to this letter by the UK Border Agency and for the service of any court documents]

[Include a proposed date by which the UK Border Agency should reply to this letter. The precise time will depend on the circumstances of the individual case. However, although a shorter or longer time may be appropriate in a particular case, 14 days is a reasonable time to allow in most circumstances]

NO. 1 OF 2013: PERSONAL INJURIES ACTIONS

1. It has been almost ten years since the Chapter 43 rules (actions of damages for, or arising from, personal injuries) came into force and whilst there is much to commend about their usefulness it appears that there has, of late, been some relaxation in their application, by both the court and those appearing before it. The purpose of this practice note is, therefore, to inform practitioners of the court's renewed approach to several procedural matters and, in turn, of what the court expects from them. It is also presents the opportunity to introduce and explain the new Chapter 42A (Case management of certain personal injuries actions) procedure. Practice Note No.2 of 2003 remains in force. **C5.109**

2. Rule 43.8 (applications for sist or variation of timetable order)

provides that an application to sist an action or vary the timetable shall be granted only on special cause shown. The purpose of this provision is to ensure that timetables are not easily varied and diets of proof consequently discharged. Accordingly, motions enrolled under this rule, including those of consent, must disclose what the special cause being relied upon is. Where it is not clear to the court that special cause has been shown the court will, ordinarily, star the motion.

3. Rule 43.9 (statements of valuation of claim)

practitioners are reminded that these must contain figures. The practice of stating "TBC" (to be confirmed) will cease.

4. Rule 43.10 (pre-trial meetings)

provides that there will be a pre-trial meeting between the parties to discuss settlement and to agree matters not in dispute. As explained in Practice Note No.2 of 2003, the meeting must be a real meeting and it is the obligation of each party to take all such steps as are necessary to comply with the letter and the spirit of the rule. Where it is apparent to one of the parties that this has not been done, then that party should not sign the joint minute in Form 43.10, thus triggering the case being put out By Order. Practitioners are also reminded of the importance of section 2 of Form 43.10 and are encouraged to make use of the procedure provided for in Chapter 28A (notices to admit and notices of non-admission).

5. Blanket Denials.

Practitioners are reminded that, unless there is good reason for their deployment, such as incomplete instructions or lack of access to factual information, blanket denials or skeletal defences are not an acceptable starting point in the pleadings. The duty of candour exists at all times and does so to serve both the court and the parties. The court will, ordinarily, bear this in mind when faced with a motion for summary decree.

6. Act of Sederunt (Rules of the Court of Session Amendment No.3) (Miscellaneous) 2013

will come into force on 1 May 2013.

7. Chapter 42A will apply to clinical negligence cases withdrawn from Chapter 43 and other complex personal injuries actions, including catastrophic injury cases. The purpose of the Chapter is to allow the court, at a procedural stage, to identify and resolve issues that are known reasons for seeking the variation of the timetable or the discharge of the proof diet at a later date. This "frontloading" of the action will allow the court to make more informed case management decisions when it comes to fixing further procedure at the hearing on the By-Order (Adjustment) Roll. The timing of some of the actions to be completed in advance of this hearing may seem demanding but the court is of the view that as the adjustment period can be extended inappropriate circumstances there will be sufficient flexibility to allow for the completion of these actions. Further, in order to allow the court to fix a date for the proof at the hearing on the By-Order (Adjustment) Roll practitioners are reminded to liaise with the Keeper's Office in advance of the hearing regarding potential dates for proof.

8. Practitioners should note the terms of rules 42A.4 (5) and (6) which provide that the Lord Ordinary may fix a further hearing on the By-Order (Adjustment) Roll and may make such orders as he thinks necessary to secure the speedy and efficient determination of the action, in particular, to resolve any matters arising or outstanding from the written statements (for further procedure) lodged by the parties in advance of the first hearing on the By- Order (Adjustment) Roll. The court will use this power to ensure that parties are ready to proceed to proof and provide an accurate estimate of the time required, before fixing a proof diet.

9. Practitioners should also note the terms of rule 42A.5, which increases the role of the Lord Ordinary in respect of the pre-proof timetable.

10. Practitioners should note that under the transitional provisions of the Act of Sederunt the Lord Ordinary may, having given all parties an opportunity to be heard, direct that Chapter 42A is to apply to an action raised before 1 May 2013. Parties seeking to have actions appointed to Chapter 42A are encouraged to apply as early as possible under the transitional provisions. The court will use the powers under Chapter 42A to make such orders as necessary to secure the speedy and efficient determination of the action irrespective of the stage at which the action has reached.

24 April 2013

NO. 2 OF 2013: IMMIGRATION AND ASYLUM JUDICIAL REVIEWS

1. [Replaced by Practice Note No.5 of 2015.] **C5.110**

SITTINGS OF THE INNER HOUSE: NO. 1 OF 2014

1. This Practice Note has effect from 22 April 2014. **C5.111**

2. From the abovementioned date, Judges sitting in the Inner House will, ordinarily, no longer wear wigs and judicial robes. Where this is the case the court will not insist that counsel should appear with wig and gown or that solicitors with rights of audience should appear with gowns.

3. Where the court intends to wear wigs and judicial robes, for example at ceremonial sittings of the court, practitioners will be informed accordingly.

4. This Practice Note does not affect existing custom and practice in the Outer House or in the High Court of Justiciary.

16 April 2014

NO.2 OF 2014: PERSONAL INJURIES ACTIONS

[*Replaced by Practice Note No.4 of 2015.*] **C5.112**

PRACTICE NOTE NO. 1 OF 2015

REPORTING RESTRICTIONS ETC. C5.113

1. The purpose of this practice note is to inform practitioners of the court's approach to reporting restrictions and anonymising opinions. It comes into force on 1 April 2015 and it replaces Practice Note No. 2 of 2007.

General

2. The general principle (that is to say the general constitutional principle of open justice) is that judicial proceedings are heard and determined in public. There should accordingly be public access to judicial determinations including the reasons given for them and the identity of parties.

3. This general principle is only to be departed from where an order restricting the reporting of proceedings ("a reporting restriction") is made. Reporting restrictions can arise:
- (a) where the court makes an order under statute;
- (b) where the court makes an order at common law;
- (c) where the court makes an order to ensure that the court does not act in a way which is incompatible with the European Convention on Human Rights ("the Convention").

Procedure for the making of reporting restrictions

4. The Act of Sederunt (Rules of the Court of Session and Sheriff Court Rules Amendment No. X) (Reporting Restrictions) 2015 substitutes a new Chapter 102 of the Rules of the Court of Session on reporting restrictions. The new rules enable the Court to make an interim order when it is considering making an order restricting the reporting of proceedings.

5. Where an interim order is made, notification will be given to any interested person. An interested person is a person who has asked to see any order made by the Court restricting the reporting of proceedings and whose name appears on the list kept by the Lord President for the purposes of Chapter 102.

6. Interested persons have two days to make representations on the interim order, if so advised. Where representations are lodged a hearing will be fixed. If no representations are lodged, the clerk will put the interim order before the Court in chambers so that it may resume consideration of whether to make an order. If no order is made, the Court must recall the interim order.

7. Where an order has been made, interested persons will again be notified via email and the making of the order will appear on the Scottish Court Service webpage. Any person aggrieved by the making of the order may at any time thereafter apply for the revocation or variation of the order.

Anonymisation generally and the Data Protection Act 1998

8. There exists, prior to the publication of an opinion, the opportunity for a judicial office holder to "anonymise" an opinion (for example, using initials instead of a person's name). The effect of such a step is not the same as an order restricting reporting: the media will still be able to report the proceedings (including a person's name) but it does allow for other personal information to be excluded from the opinion where it is not, in the eyes of the judicial office holder, relevant to the decision or necessary for the purposes of pronouncing judgment.

9. At this stage judicial office holders will have regard to the principles of the Data Protection Act 1998. In particular, they should ask themselves whether the inclusion of personal information (such as addresses, bank accounts and telephone numbers etc.) is relevant to the decision or necessary for the purposes of pronouncing judgment.

Asylum cases

10. The practice of automatically "anonymising" opinions in cases involving asylum seekers introduced by Practice Note No. 2 of 2007 (i.e. using initials instead of a person's name) will cease. The making of an order restricting reporting is the only way to ensure the anonymity of a party.

26th February 2015

PRACTICE NOTE NO.3 OF 2015

FORMAT OF ELECTRONIC DOCUMENTS FOR SUMMAR ROLL HEARINGS

1. This Practice Note has effect from 17th August 2015. **C5.114**

2. This Practice Note applies where the Court has appointed parties to lodge electronic documents. For the avoidance of doubt, parties should continue to comply with RCS 4.7.

3. All electronic documents for use at summar roll hearings must be prepared in accordance with the following provisions and parties are encouraged to co-operate in their preparation.

4. The electronic documents (which must be identical to the hard copies) should be contained in a single pdf and must be numbered in ascending order throughout. Pagination should begin with the first page of the first document and should be continued throughout the entire series of documents. New pagination must not be used for separate documents or folders within the single pdf. Index pages and authorities must be numbered as part of the single pdf document.

5. When referring to documents, counsel should first refer to the page number on the electronic version. It will also be necessary, where this is different, to refer to the hard copy bundle number. The hard copy bundle should bear the same page numbering as the electronic document as well as any internal page numbering. This should appear at the top of the page on the right.

6. The default display view size on all pages must be 100%. Text on all pages must be in a format that will allow comments, highlighting and copying. The format should not allow for editing of the text.

7. The resolution on the electronic bundle must be reduced to about 200 to 300 dpi to prevent delays whilst scrolling from one page to another. It is advisable for parties to print off the hard copy before reducing the resolution or creating the hyperlinks.

8. The index page must be hyperlinked to the pages or documents to which it refers.

9. Unless otherwise directed or permitted by the court, the appendices and volumes of authorities must be bookmarked in accordance with the index so that each individual document can be accessed directly by hypertext link both from the index page and from bookmarks on the left-hand side. Bookmarks must be labelled so as to identify the document to which each refers. The bookmark should have the same name or title as the actual document and also display the relevant page numbers.

10. Wherever possible, pdf documents within the appendices and within volumes of authorities and otherwise lodged with the Court must be converted to pdf from their original electronic versions rather than scanned as images. Where documents are only available in hard copy and have to be scanned, the resultant pdf files should, where the quality of the scan allows, be subjected to a process of optical character recognition (OCR). This is to enable the documents to be text searchable and annotatable by the Court.

11. The electronic documents - the reclaiming print / appeal print, grounds of appeal, answers to grounds of appeal, notes of argument, appendix and authorities - must be submitted on a memory stick, clearly marked or labelled with the title of the case and the identity of the party.

12. Supplementary documents or bundles lodged during or close to the start of the hearing must be created as a separate single pdf numbered in ascending order starting from 1 and lodged on a new memory stick.

13. The Court does not intend, at this stage, to impose detailed requirements as to hypertext linking and referencing within documents. However, it wishes to encourage parties to employ hypertext links within documents. In particular, it would be helpful if hypertext links were introduced at the time the core volumes are produced to link the notes of argument to documents in the appendix and relevant authorities. The parties should seek to agree on the extent to which hypertext linking is to be used. It would also assist the Court, in notes of argument and written submissions, if page references included both the page number of the electronic document (see paragraph 4 above) and the page number of the original printed document.

28 July 2015

NO. 4 OF 2015: PERSONAL INJURY ACTIONS

1. This practice note takes effect from 22 September 2015. It replaces Practice Note No.2 of 2014; Practice Note No.2 of 2003 remains in force. **C5.115**

2. The purpose of this practice note is to inform practitioners of the court's approach to several procedural matters relating to actions of damages for, or arising from, personal injury. In particular, it covers matters relating to chapters 42A and 43 of the Rules of the Court of Session ("RCS"), and takes into account changes made to the RCS by Act of Sederunt (Rules of the Court of Session 1994 and Sheriff Court Rules Amendment) (No.2) (Personal Injury and Remits) 2015.

Chapter 43

3. RCS 43.8 (applications for sist or variation of timetable order) provides that an application to sist an action or vary the timetable shall be granted only on cause shown. The purpose of this provision is to ensure that timetables are not varied as a matter of routine and diets of proof consequently discharged. Accordingly, motions enrolled under this rule, including those of consent, must specify the cause relied on. Where it is not clear to the court that cause has been shown the court will, ordinarily, star the motion. The recent removal of "special" from "special cause" is to offer some flexibility where there has been a failure to adhere to the timetable as a result of inadvertence which may be regarded by the court as excusable, having regard to the relevant circumstances. It is not to reverse the court's approach to such matters as expressed in *Smith v Greater Glasgow and Clyde NHS Health Board* [2013] CSOH 178.

4. A motion to vary the timetable to allow an application for a third party notice to be made, even where cause has been shown, may be refused if granting it will endanger the proof diet.

5. RCS 43.9 regulates statements of valuation of claim. These must contain figures. The practice of stating "TBC" (to be confirmed) is not acceptable.

6. RCS 43.10 (pre-trial meetings) provides that there will be a pre-trial meeting between the parties to discuss settlement and to agree matters not in dispute. As explained in Practice Note No. 2 of 2003, the meeting must be a real one (although it can be held by video-conference). It is the obligation of each party to take all steps as are necessary to comply with both the letter and the spirit of the rule. Where it is apparent to one of the parties that this has not been done, that party should not sign the joint minute in Form 43.10. This will trigger the case being put out By Order. The importance of section 2 of Form 43.10 is stressed. Practitioners are encouraged to make use of the procedure provided for in Chapter 28A (notices to admit and notices of non-admission).

7. Unless there is good reason for their deployment, such as incomplete instructions or lack of access to factual information, blanket denials or skeletal defences are not an acceptable starting point in the pleadings. The duty of candour exists at all times. It does so to serve both the court and the parties. The court will, ordinarily, bear this in mind when determining a motion for summary decree.

Chapter 42A

8. Chapter 42A applies to clinical negligence cases withdrawn from Chapter 43 and other complex personal injuries actions, including catastrophic injury cases, where the Lord Ordinary is satisfied that managing the action under Chapter 42A would facilitate the efficient determination of the action. Pursuers wishing to raise a personal injuries action based on clinical negligence as an ordinary action subject to Chapter 42A procedure must apply for authority to do so, by motion, in accordance with RCS 43.1A. Alternatively, parties may apply by motion in accordance with RCS 43.5 to have the action withdrawn from Chapter 43 and to proceed instead in accordance with Chapter 42A.

9. The purpose of Chapter 42A is to allow the court, at a procedural stage, to identify and resolve issues that are known reasons for seeking variation of the timetable or the discharge of the proof diet at a later date. This "frontloading" of the action will allow the court to make more informed case management decisions when it comes to fixing further procedure at the hearing on the By-Order (Adjustment) Roll. The timing of some of the actions to be completed in advance of this hearing may seem demanding, but the court is of the view that, as the adjustment period can be extended in appropriate circumstances, there will be sufficient flexibility to allow for their completion.

10. Where reference is made to witness statements in RCS 42A.3(3)(c)(vi), the court expects these statements to contain full and clear factual accounts. Where possible, witness statements should be exchanged before the By Order (Adjustment) Roll Hearing.

11. Where parties are seeking to have the action sent to proof, the court will explore the issues set out in RCS 42A.4 at the By Order (Adjustment) Roll Hearing.

12. RCS 42A.4(6) and (7) allows the Lord Ordinary to fix a further hearing on the By-Order (Adjustment) Roll at the first By Order (Adjustment) Roll hearing, or at any time thereafter, whether or not the action has been appointed to debate or sent to proof. RCS 42A.5 allows the Lord Ordinary to fix a procedural hearing, or to vary the pre-proof timetable, at any time.

13. RCS 42A.6 provides the Lord Ordinary with very wide powers to make any order necessary to secure the efficient determination of the action, and, in particular, to resolve any matters arising or outstanding from the pre-proof timetable or the written statements for further procedure lodged by the parties in advance of the first hearing on the By-Order (Adjustment) Roll. The court will ensure that parties are ready to proceed to proof and have provided an accurate estimate of the time required, before fixing a proof diet.

14. Where the court intends to fix a date for the proof, practitioners should liaise with the Keeper's Office regarding potential dates. Where a proof diet has been fixed and the dates are no longer suitable, or there exists a concern about their suitability, practitioners should contact the Keeper's Office immediately.

15. Under the transitional provisions in the Act of Sederunt (Rules of the Court of Session Amendment No.3)(Miscellaneous) 2013, the Lord Ordinary may, having given all parties an opportunity to be heard, direct that Chapter 42A is to apply to an action raised before 1 May 2013. Parties seeking to have an action appointed to Chapter 42A are encouraged to apply as early as possible under the transitional provisions. The court will use the powers under Chapter 42A to make such orders as are necessary to secure the efficient determination of the action irrespective of the stage at which the action has reached.

4th September 2015

NO. 5 OF 2015: JUDICIAL REVIEW

[Revoked and replaced by Practice Note No.3 of 2017.] **C5.116**

NO. 1 OF 2016: JUDICIAL GUIDANCE TO THE JURY REGARDING NON-PECUNIARY DAMAGES

1. This Practice Note has effect from 27th September 2016. **C5.117**

2. It applies where the issue in a jury trial, in terms of Chapter 37, is the level of an award of damages in respect of non-pecuniary loss.

3. At the conclusion of the evidence, parties will be given the opportunity to address the trial judge briefly in respect of the appropriate level of non-pecuniary damages for each category of non-pecuniary loss claimed. This will take place in the absence of the jury.

4. The Lord Ordinary, in his or her charge to the jury, will advise the jury as to the level of damages which he or she considers might reasonably be awarded. This will be done by providirg a range relating to the general level of comparable awards in each category of the non-pecuniary Loss claimed.

5. In doing so, the Lord Ordinary will advise the jury that the range or ranges are for their assistance only and are not binding upon them (see *Hamilton v Ferguson Transport (Spean Bridge) Ltd* 2012 SC 486, LP (Hamilton) at paras 76 and 77).

Edinburgh

12 August 2016

NO. 1 OF 2017: COMMERCIAL ACTIONS

1. This Practice Note has effect from 27 March 2017. It replaces Practice Note No. 6 of 2004 (commercial actions). **C5.118**

Application and interpretation

2. The actions to which Chapter 47 of the Rules of the Court of Session applies are intended to comprise all actions arising out of or concerned with any transaction or dispute of a commercial or business nature, whether contractual or not, and to include, but not to be limited to —

- the construction of a commercial or mercantile document,
- the sale or hire purchase of goods,
- the export or import of merchandise,
- the carriage of goods by land, air or sea,
- insurance,
- banking,
- the provision of financial services,
- mercantile agency,
- mercantile usage or a custom of trade,
- a building, engineering or construction contract,
- a commercial lease.

Some Admiralty actions in personam, such as actions relating to or arising out of bills of lading, may also be suitable for the commercial court if they do not require the special facilities of Admiralty procedure in relation to defenders whose names are not known.

Commercial Roll

3. In the Outer House an action, and all proceedings in it, in which an election has been made to adopt the procedure in Chapter 47 or which has been transferred under rule 47.10 to be dealt with as a commercial action, shall be heard and determined on the Commercial Roll.

Disapplication of certain rules

4. The rules of the Rules of the Court of Session applicable to ordinary actions apply to a commercial action to which Chapter 47 applies unless specifically excluded under rule 47.4, or excluded by implication because of a provision in Chapter 47.

Commercial judge

5. All proceedings in a commercial action in the Outer House shall be heard before a judge nominated by the Lord President as a commercial judge or, where a commercial judge is not available, any other judge of the court.

Procedure in commercial actions

6. The procedure in, and progress of, a commercial action is under the direct control of the commercial judge. The court will take a pro-active approach. Arrangements will be made to ensure that, where possible, all appearances of an action on the Commercial Roll shall be before the same judge. Other than in exceptional circumstances, parties are expected to arrange for the principally instructed counsel or solicitor advocate to appear at any calling in the Commercial Roll. Unless the court is persuaded otherwise, commercial actions will proceed on the basis that there will be no more than one preliminary hearing and one procedural hearing before the action is appointed to a substantive hearing.

Transfer of actions to Commercial Roll

7.a. An ordinary action which has not been brought as a commercial action under rule 47.3(1) may be transferred to the Commercial Roll on application by motion by any party if it is an action within the meaning of a commercial action in rule 47.1(2). Such applications are heard by a commercial judge on a date that is convenient to the court.

b. Where the court appoints an action to be a commercial action, the action immediately proceeds to a preliminary hearing. For this reason, parties are expected to submit statements of issues in advance of the hearing on the application. If they have not already done so, parties should lodge all productions that would have been required had proceedings been initiated as a commercial action.

c. An interlocutor granting or refusing a motion to transfer an action to the Commercial Roll may be reclaimed against only with leave of the commercial judge within 14 days after the date of the interlocutor: rule 38.3(3).

Withdrawal of action from Commercial Roll

8. The object of rule 47.9 is to enable cases which are unsuitable for the commercial procedure to be removed from the Commercial Roll, but it should be understood that the commercial procedure is not to be regarded as limited to cases which are straightforward or simple or as excluding cases which involve the investigation of difficult and complicated facts. Parties should have proper regard to the criteria set out in rule 47.9(1)(a) in every case.

9. Rule 47.9(3) was added by Act of Sederunt 2014 No. 291 which came into force on 8 December 2014. Previously, rule 47.9 only allowed a case to be withdrawn from the Commercial Roll if a motion was made by a party to the action at any time before or at the preliminary hearing. This amendment was made in order to allow a commercial judge, after hearing parties, to transfer a case to the Ordinary Roll at any time.

Pre-action communication

10.a. Before a commercial action is commenced it is important that, save in exceptional cases, the matters in dispute should have been discussed and focused in pre-litigation communications between the prospective parties' legal advisers. The commercial action procedure is intended for cases in which there is a real dispute between parties which requires to be resolved by judicial decision, rather than other means, and functions best if issues have been investigated and ventilated prior to the raising of the action.

b. It is expected that, before a commercial action has been raised, the solicitors acting for the pursuer will have:

i. fully set out in correspondence to the intended defender the nature of the claim and the factual and legal grounds on which it proceeds;

ii. supplied to the intended defender copies of any documents relied upon; and

iii. where the issue sought to be litigated is one for which expert evidence relating to liability is necessary, obtained and disclosed, to the intended defender, the expert's report.

11. For their part, solicitors acting for the defender are expected to respond to pre-litigation communications by setting out the defender's position in substantial terms; and by disclosing any document or expert's report relating to liability upon which they rely. To that response the solicitors for the pursuer are expected to give a considered and reasoned reply. Both parties should consider carefully and discuss whether all or some of the dispute may be amenable to some form of alternative dispute resolution.

12. Saving cases involving an element of urgency, actions should not be raised using the commercial procedure until the nature and extent of the dispute between parties has been the subject of careful discussion between parties and/or their representatives and the action can be said to be truly necessary. The court may have regard to any failure to comply with this paragraph when considering a motion for expenses.

Pleadings

Summons

13.a. Pleadings in traditional form are not normally required or encouraged in a commercial action. The default position is that pleadings should be in abbreviated form. Provided that paragraphs 10 - 12 of this Practice Note (pre-action communication) have been complied with, parties will be aware of each other's position before the action has been commenced. The overriding requirement is one of fair notice: the purpose of the pleadings is to give notice of the essential elements of the case to the court and to the other parties to the action. Where it is sought to obtain from the court a decision only on the construction of a document, it is permissible for the summons to contain an appropriate conclusion without annexing articles of condescendence or pleas-in-law. The conclusion in such a case should specify the document, the construction of which is in dispute and the construction contended for. Where the issue between parties is a point of law, the summons may contain a brief statement of the pursuer's argument including, if necessary, reference to authority. Where the pursuer's position on any matter is contained in another document, such as a Scott Schedule or the conclusions of an expert report, it is permissible to adopt the document, or a specified part thereof, as part of the pursuer's case. Where damages are sought, a summary statement of the claim or a statement in the form of an account will normally be sufficient.

b. Rule 47.3(3) is intended to require a party to produce with its summons the core or essential documents to establish the contract or transaction with which the cause is concerned. Under rule 27.1(1)(a) documents founded on or adopted as incorporated in a summons must be lodged at the time the summons is lodged for calling.

c. When the summons is lodged for signetting, a commercial action registration form (Form CA 1), copies of which are available from the General Department, must be completed, lodged in process and a copy served with the summons.

Defences

14.a. As with the summons, it is not necessary for defences to follow the traditional form of pleading. In the first instance, detailed averments are not required in the answers any more than in the articles of condescendence. In particular, it is *not* necessary that each averment in the summons should be admitted, not known or denied, provided that the extent of the dispute is reasonably well identified. One of the objectives of the procedure is to make the extent of written pleadings subject to the control of the court. What is said in paragraph 13 regarding the content of a summons, including the overriding requirement of fair notice, applies mutatis mutandis to defences.

b. Under rule 27.1(1)(b), documents founded on or adopted as incorporated in a defence must be lodged at the time the defences are lodged.

c. Defences must be lodged within 7 days after the summons has called: rule 18.1(2).

d. The defender must complete a commercial action registration form (Form CA 1) and lodge it in process, or complete the service copy, with the information required.

Adjustment of pleadings

15. Where any pleadings or other documents are to be adjusted, the party proposing adjustment shall do so by preparing a new copy of the document as adjusted in which the new material is indicated using track changes or strikethrough or a different font.

Counterclaims and Third Party Notices

16. No counterclaim or the convening of a third party may be pursued without an order from the commercial judge.

Preliminary hearing on Commercial Roll

17.a. The preliminary hearing will normally be conducted on the basis that the provisions of paragraphs 10 - 12 in relation to pre-action communication have been complied with, and that pleadings complying with paragraphs 13 and 14 have been lodged and intimated. The preliminary hearing is not designed to give parties the opportunity to formulate their claim and response thereto. Adjustment of pleadings will not always be necessary and it should not be assumed that an order allowing a period of adjustment will be made. Any adjustment allowed will normally be restricted to clarification of a party's position in response to averments or requests for further explanation by another party.

b. Prior to the preliminary hearing parties should lodge all correspondence and other documents which set out their material contentions of fact and law and which demonstrate their compliance with the provisions of paragraphs 10 - 12. These provisions are supplementary to the provisions of rule 47.3(3).

c. Continuations of preliminary hearings will seldom be granted. Where it appears to the court that any request for a continuation of a preliminary hearing is brought about by a failure to comply with the provisions of paragraphs 10 - 12, this may result in the party responsible for any such failure having the expenses of the continued hearing awarded against it on an agent client basis. Motions for continuations of preliminary hearings which are sought simply to enable information to be obtained, which could and should have been obtained prior to the preliminary hearing, are likely to be refused.

18. Prior to the preliminary hearing parties should be in a position to lodge a document setting out in concise form the issues which they contend require judicial determination. The statement of issues should be lodged by 4.00 pm two working days before the hearing, and, where possible, be set out in an agreed document. Parties should consider and discuss whether resorting to alternative dispute resolution might be appropriate in respect of some or all of the issues.

19. In applying rule 47.11, the court will set realistic deadlines which are expected to be adhered to. It is likely that extensions will only be granted if reasonable cause is shown. At the preliminary hearing parties will be expected to address the court and provide detailed and accurate information to ensure that appropriate deadlines are fixed. In fixing any deadlines the court will be mindful of the fact that the commercial cause procedure is intended to progress actions expeditiously.

Procedural hearing on Commercial Roll

20.a. At the procedural hearing parties will be expected to be in a position to discuss realistically the issues involved in the action and the method of disposing of them. Parties will be expected to be able to advise the court on the steps that have been taken to date to achieve an extra-judicial settlement and on the likelihood of such a settlement being achieved. They will be asked to express a view on the stage at which any joint meeting between parties ought to be ordered to take place. The court will ascertain from parties whether there are any further steps that could be taken by the court to assist in the resolution of the dispute.

b. Prior to the procedural hearing parties are expected to lodge a note of proposals for further procedure setting out their position as to the future progress of the case and, in particular, whether a diet of debate or proof is sought.

c. In the lead up to the procedural hearing parties should consider and discuss whether resorting to alternative dispute resolution might be appropriate in respect of some or all of the issues.

d. At the procedural hearing it is anticipated that the court will fix a substantive hearing along with an appropriate timetable or, if necessary, a further procedural hearing to allow any outstanding matters to be resolved. Where a diet of proof is allowed, the timetable may include provision for the preparation and lodging of a statement of agreed facts.

Motions by email

21. Requests to move or discharge hearings or to extend or vary time limits may be made by email. Any such request should be copied to the agents for all other parties so that they may confirm their consent or lack of opposition. Such requests will be feed as motions to the requesting party.

22. Motions in Form 23.2 and notices of opposition in Form 23.4 may be enrolled by emailing the completed form to gcs@scotcourts.gov.uk and Commercial@scotcourts.gov.uk. Where any documents bear a signature, e.g. joint minutes, a scanned copy of the signed document should be emailed to the Commercial Section of the Offices of Court, but the hard copy original document should be available for production on request by the Commercial Section or by order of the court.

Debates

23. A debate in a commercial action is not heard on the Procedure Roll but on the Commercial Roll. The provisions of Chapter 28 of the rules (Procedure Roll), however, do apply to a debate in a commercial action.

Lodging of productions

24. Before any hearing at which reference is to be made to documents, parties should, as well as lodging their productions, prepare for the use of the court a working bundle in which the documents are arranged chronologically or in another appropriate order without multiple copies of the same document. The bundle for a motion hearing should be prepared by the party enrolling the motion; otherwise, unless there is agreement to the contrary, the bundle should be prepared by the pursuer.

Documentary productions in electronic format

25. Productions need only be lodged in electronic format. Details of documents to which this applies and the format currently required are available in a guidance note in the Commercial Actions section of the SCTS website. Inventories listing productions should continue to be lodged also in hard copy.

Notes of argument

26. A note of argument should comply with the following general principles:

a. A note of argument should be a concise summary of the submissions to be developed.
b. It should contain a numbered list of the points which the party wishes to make.
c. Each point should be followed by a reference to any transcript of evidence or other document on which the party wishes to rely. The note of argument should identify the relevant passage in the document in question.
d. At the beginning of the note there should be a succinct executive summary of the party's arguments. The executive summary should not exceed one page in length.

27. A note of argument should state, in respect of each authority cited –

a. the proposition of law that the authority demonstrates; and
b. the parts of the authority (identified by page or paragraph references) that support the proposition.

28. More than one authority should not be cited in support of a given proposition unless the additional citation is necessary for a proper presentation of the argument.

Joint bundle of authorities

29. When a commercial action has been appointed to a debate, the party at whose instance the debate has been fixed should, after consultation with the other parties, lodge a joint bundle containing copies of the authorities upon which each party will rely at the hearing.

30. The bundle of authorities should, in general–

a. not include authorities for propositions not in dispute; and
b. not include more than 10 authorities (in addition to any relevant statutory provisions), unless on cause shown permission of the court to include a greater number has been obtained.

31. Authorities which have been reported in Session Cases, or in the Law Reports published by the Incorporated Council of Law Reporting for England and Wales, should be cited from those sources. Where a case is not reported in Session Cases or the Law Reports, references to other recognised reports may be given. Unreported judgments should only be cited when they contain an authoritative statement of a relevant principle of law not to be found in a reported case or when they are necessary for the understanding of some other authority.

32. The bundle of authorities should be lodged by the date specified in the interlocutor.

33. Bundles of authorities which do not conform to this Practice Note may be rejected by the court, which may also find that no expenses are payable in respect of the cost of making up and lodging the bundle. The court may also find that no expenses are payable, or may modify any award of expenses, where authorities are included unnecessarily.

34. Parties are encouraged to produce bundles of authorities in electronic format only. Where authorities produced electronically are contained within a folder, they should be identified by tab number and citation, e.g. "*016 Mayo Associates SA v Cantrade Private Bank Switzerland (CI) Ltd* [1998] JLR 173". The tab numbering should restart in each folder. If a party intends to use hard copy documents at the hearing, their folder and tab numbers should correspond to the electronic folder and tab numbers.

Joint meetings of parties

35. The commercial judge has power, in terms of rules 47.11(1)(e) and 47.12(2)(o), to order parties to hold a joint meeting with a view to exploring whether the dispute is capable of extra-judicial settlement or, alternatively, whether the issues requiring judicial determination can be restricted. Such an order will not be made as a matter of course but it is likely that a joint meeting will be ordered in most cases. The stage of the proceedings at which the meeting will be ordered will vary from case to case, and will depend upon when the court considers that such a meeting is most likely to be productive of substantial progress.

Pre-proof by order hearing

36. When a proof, or proof before answer, has been allowed, the court will normally fix a pre-proof by order hearing to take place in advance of the proof diet. The general purpose of such a hearing is to ascertain parties' state of preparation for the proof and to review the estimated duration of that hearing. Without prejudice to the foregoing generality, the following matters may be dealt with at the pre-proof by order hearing:

a. Consideration of any joint minute of admissions agreed by parties, which should be lodged no later than two days prior to the pre-proof by order hearing.
b. A review of the documents, or other productions, which parties consider will be relied upon at the proof hearing. Any such document should be lodged no later than two days prior to the pre-proof by order hearing.
c. The up-to-date position with regard to any expert reports which are to be relied upon. Parties should be in a position to advise the court of what consultation, if any, has taken place between their respective experts with a view to reaching agreement about any points held in common and what matters remain truly in dispute between them.

d. Not less than two days prior to a pre-proof by order hearing parties should lodge an estimated timetable for the conduct of the proof.

Hearings for further procedure

37. The commercial judge may at any time before final judgment, at his own instance or at the request of a party, have a commercial action put out for a hearing for further procedure to deal with a procedural or other matter which has arisen for which provision has not been made.

Reclaiming

38. An interlocutor pronounced on the Commercial Roll, other than a final interlocutor, may be reclaimed against only with leave of the commercial judge within 14 days after the date of the interlocutor: rule 38.3(6).

Failure to comply with rule or order of commercial judge

39. The purpose of rule 47.16 is to provide for discipline to ensure effective supervision of case management. Any failure of a party to comply with a provision in the rules or a court order may result in a refusal to extend deadlines, dismissal of the action or counterclaim, decree in terms of the conclusions of the summons or counterclaim or a finding of expenses.

2 March 2017

NO. 3 OF 2017: JUDICIAL REVIEW

1. This Practice Note has effect from 17 July 2017. It replaces Practice Note No. 5 of 2015 (Judicial Review). **C5.119**

2. The Lord Ordinary may disapply any provision of this Practice Note, on the motion of any party, or of the Lord Ordinary's own accord, in respect of any particular case.

3. This Practice Note covers:

a. Judicial review procedure;
b. The pre-proceedings protocol in immigration and asylum judicial reviews;
c. Case management in judicial reviews;
d. Bundles of authorities;
e. Bundles of documents;
f. Notes of argument.

Judicial Review Procedure

4. This part of this Practice Note covers judicial review procedure, and in particular:

a. Transfers to the Upper Tribunal;
b. The permission stage;
c. Notification of intention to contest;
d. Notification of readiness to proceed to a substantive hearing.

5. The purpose of this part is to provide guidance about certain aspects of judicial review procedure and to set out the court's expectations about how judicial reviews will be conducted. Appendix 4 to this Practice Note contains a table setting out the timescales which apply to a petition for judicial review and the relevant legislative references.

Transfers to the Upper Tribunal

6. Where the Lord Ordinary makes an order transferring an application to the Upper Tribunal under RCS 58.5, the Deputy Principal Clerk of Session ("DPCS") will transmit the process to the Upper Tribunal within 4 days of the interlocutor being pronounced.

7. When transmitting that process, the DPCS will:

a. give written notice of the transmission to the parties; and
b. certify on the interlocutor sheet that the parties have been notified.

8. Failure by the DPCS to follow this procedure does not affect the validity of a transfer.

The permission stage

9. The petitioner, when lodging the Form of Petition in accordance with Rule 58.3, should, in paragraph 8, address the question of why permission to proceed should be granted. Paragraph 8 should set out the petitioner's view and the reasons for that view.

10. The petitioner should list, with reference to the schedule of documents, the documents necessary for the determination of permission.

11. A person served with the petition, when lodging answers under Rule 58.6, should include in the answers a headed paragraph addressing the matter of whether permission to proceed should be given. The paragraph should set out that person's view and the reasons for that view.

12. The Lord Ordinary must make a decision on whether to grant or refuse permission or order an oral hearing (RCS 58.7). The Lord Ordinary will ordinarily order an oral hearing if considering refusing permission. In that event, the Lord Ordinary will normally produce a brief note that sets out the concerns which are to be addressed at the hearing. This will assist parties and the court in ensuring that hearings do not exceed 30 minutes (RCS 58.9).

13. Where permission is refused (or permission is granted subject to conditions or only on particular grounds) without an oral hearing, the petitioner may request a review of the decision at an oral hearing (RCS 58.8). A reclaiming motion to the Inner House may only be made following an oral hearing.

14. The Keeper of the Rolls may group suitable oral hearings to be heard on the same day. Procedural and substantive hearings, particularly in immigration or asylum petitions, may be grouped to be heard on a single day.

Notification of intention to contest

15. Appendix 1 to this Practice Note contains a style of notice which should be used for notifying the court of an intention to contest a petition only if permission is granted (RCS 58.6(2)(b)). This should be sent to the Petition Department in hard copy.

Notification of readiness to proceed to a substantive hearing[1]

16. Parties may email the Keeper of the Rolls to confirm their readiness to proceed to the substantive hearing (RCS 58.11(1A)). The Keeper of the Roll's email address for this purpose is keepers@scotcourts.gov.uk, copying in petitions@scotcourts.gov.uk. Appendix 2 to this Practice Note contains a style email which should be prepared by one party on behalf of all of the parties. That party must have the permission of all parties to send this email.

17. Where parties have emailed the Keeper in accordance with RCS 58.11(1A), the Lord Ordinary may order that the procedural hearing be cancelled. This will be done by emailing a copy of the interlocutor to the party's address listed on the email. That party must inform all other parties of the cancellation.

The pre-proceedings protocol in immigration and asylum judicial reviews

18. The purpose of this part is to set out the terms of an undertaking which the Home Office has provided to the court concerning judicial reviews where the immigration or asylum status of an individual is at issue.

19. Where the Home Office is notified of a stated intention to raise judicial review proceedings in a pre-proceedings letter in accordance with the procedure set out in this Practice Note, such notification, of itself, will not cause the Home Office (i) to initiate or accelerate a decision to issue a removal direction, (ii) to initiate or ac-

[1] As amended by Practice Note No.1 of 2022.

celerate the removal of the person from the United Kingdom and access to Scottish jurisdiction or (iii) to use the notification as a factor in the initiation or acceleration of such directions or decisions.

20. If the Home Office receives a pre-proceedings letter before it has issued a removal direction, it will not remove the individual before it has responded to the letter. If removal directions have been issued before a pre-proceedings letter has been sent, agents of the individual do not need to send a pre-proceedings letter before commencing a judicial review application.

21. The agents of the individual should send any pre-proceedings letter to a designated official at the Home Office. The nominated addressee is "The Litigation Unit, Home Office, Festival Court, 200 Brand Street, Glasgow G51 1DH". Pre-proceedings letters can be faxed to the Home Office on 0370 336 9648 and can be emailed to snijrteam@homeoffice.gsi.gov.uk. The Home Office will, ordinarily, acknowledge the pre-proceedings letter within 24 hours.

22. The wording of a pre-proceedings letter should follow as closely as is reasonably practicable the form in Appendix 3 to this Practice Note.

23. Except in cases of urgency, the petitioner's agents should allow 14 days after the delivery of the pre-proceedings letter for the Home Office to respond to that letter before commencing proceedings.

24. Upon lodging a petition the petitioner's agents will produce with the petition, and copy to the Office of the Advocate General (preferably in electronic form), the case documents in their possession which are relevant to the application (including, if any, the pre-proceedings letter and the Home Office's response to that letter).

Case management in judicial reviews

25. The purpose of this part is to set out the terms of a standard order which the Lord Ordinary may issue when granting permission for a judicial review to proceed (RCS 58.11(2)) and to provide an indication of the likely timescales of the procedural steps ordered.

26. A standard order may appoint the following:

a. parties to adjust their pleadings until two weeks prior to the date of the procedural hearing; and to lodge final versions of their pleadings not later than one week prior to the procedural hearing;
b. parties each to lodge a bundle of relevant documents, and to mark up those documents indicating the parts they intend to rely on not later than one week prior to the procedural hearing;
c. notes of argument to be lodged not later than one week prior to the procedural hearing;
d. statements of issues to be lodged not later than one week prior to the procedural hearing;
e. affidavits to be lodged in respect of those facts founded on by a party at the substantive hearing not later than one week prior to the procedural hearing;
f. parties each to lodge a list and bundle of authorities, which should be marked up to indicate the parts the party intends to rely on, not later than 10 days prior to the substantive hearing;
g. parties to make their submissions in such form as the Lord Ordinary may decide. In particular the Lord Ordinary may refer to the length and font size of the submissions and to the use of footnotes.

Bundles of Authorities

27. The purpose of this part is to set out the court's expectations of a bundle of authorities, where one is ordered to be produced.

28. The bundle should be properly labelled, contain an index at the beginning, and be presented in a form that is robust and manageable. Where lever arch folders or ring binders are used, they should not be overfilled.

29. Parties should not lodge authorities on propositions not in dispute.

30. Parties should not normally lodge more than five authorities each, unless the scale of the substantive legal argument requires more extensive citation. The permission of the court is required to include any authorities beyond the maximum number of ten. For the purposes of this paragraph, authorities do not include statutory provisions upon which the petition or answers proceed.

31. Authorities which have been reported in Session Cases, or in the Law Reports published by the Incorporated Council of Law Reporting for England and Wales, should be cited from those sources. Where a case is not reported in the Session Cases or in the Law Reports, references to other recognised reports may be given.

Unreported opinions should only be cited where they contain an authoritative statement of a relevant principle of law not to be found in a reported case or where they are necessary for the understanding of some other authority.

Bundles of Documents

32. The purpose of this part is to set out the court's expectations of a bundle of documents, where it is ordered that a bundle of relevant documents should be marked up and lodged.

33. Only documents which are relevant to the legal issues to be raised at the substantive hearing and likely to be referred to at that hearing should be lodged.

34. The documents should be arranged chronologically or in another appropriate order, such as by reference to the subject matter of the claim or the issues in dispute.

35. Where a passage in a document is to be referred to in the course of submissions it should be clearly marked or highlighted.

36. Where it would not be appropriate to mark a passage in an original document, a copy may be lodged and marked in its place.

Notes of Argument

37. The purpose of this part is to set out the court's expectations of the content of a note of argument, where one is ordered to be produced.

38. A note of argument should comply with the following general principles:

a. it should be a concise summary of the submissions the party intends to develop at the substantive hearing;
b. it should contain a numbered list of points which the party wishes to make, set out as subparagraphs within a single paragraph;
c. it should be set out in numbered paragraphs;
d. it should not contain detailed legal argument;
e. it should be as brief as the issues allow and not more than eight A4 pages, double spaced, in font size 12, unless additional argument is necessary for proper presentation of the case;

f. each point should be followed by reference to any transcript of evidence or other document on which the party wishes to rely. The note of argument should identify the relevant passage in the document in question;

g. it should state, in respect of each authority cited:

   (i) the proposition of law that the authority demonstrates; and

   (ii) the passages of the authority (identified by page or paragraph references) that support the proposition;

h. more than one authority should not be cited in support of a given proposition unless the additional citation is necessary for a proper presentation of the argument;

i. except on cause shown, no submission will be permitted to be advanced and no authority will be allowed to be referred to at the substantive hearing which is not contained in the note of argument;

j. where a note of argument has been lodged and a party subsequently becomes aware that an argument included in the note will no longer be insisted upon, that party should inform the court of that fact at the earliest opportunity.

Failure to comply

39. Where a party fails to comply with any of the requirements of this Practice Note, the court may find that no expenses are payable, or may modify any award of expenses, in respect of the failure to comply.

13 June 2017

APPENDIX ONE

Petitions Department

Court of Session

Parliament House

Parliament Square

Edinburgh

EH1 1RQ

Court ref: [reference]

Date: [date]

Notification of intention to contest a petition for Judicial Review under Rule 58.6(2) of the Rules of the Court of Session

by

(Name of party)

I have been served with the petition of [A.B.] (*designation and address*) for Judicial Review of (*state briefly matter sought to be reviewed*) by [C.D.].

I do not intend to participate in the decision to grant or refuse permission.

I intend to contest the petition if permission is granted.

(*signed*)

APPENDIX TWO[1]

The Keeper of the Rolls

Email: keepers@scotcourts.gov.uk

Court ref: [reference]

Date: [date]

Notification of parties' readiness to proceed to a substantive hearing
by
(Name of party)
and
(Name of party)
[and …]

I am writing on behalf of the parties to the petition of [A.B.] (*designation and address*) for Judicial Review of (*state briefly matter sought to be reviewed*) by [C.D.]. I have permission from the other parties to write on their behalf.

On (*date*) the Court fixed a procedural hearing for (*date*) and a substantive hearing for (*date*). The parties are ready to proceed to the substantive hearing. The parties confirm that they have complied with the requirements set out in the interlocutor fixing the procedural hearing and that [*insert the number of days set down for the substantive hearing*] is sufficient to address the issues.

(*signed*)
(*address and email address*)

APPENDIX THREE

[Name of designated official]

The Litigation Unit

Home Office

Festival Court

200 Brand Street

Glasgow

G51 1DH

Dear Sirs

PRE-ACTION PROTOCOL LETTER

[Insert title, first and last name and address of the claimant]
[Insert date of birth and nationality of the claimant]
[Insert Home office, Port or other relevant reference]

[Set out the name, address and reference details of any legal advisers dealing with the claim]

[Set out the details of any interested parties and confirm that they have been sent a copy of this letter]

[Set out the details of the matter being challenged]

[Set out the date and details of the decision, or act or omission being challenged, a brief summary of the facts and, in brief terms, why it is contended to be wrong]

[Set out the details of the remedy sought from the Home Office, including whether a review or any interim remedy is sought]

---

[1] As amended by Practice Note No.1 of 2022.

[Set out the details of any information that is sought. This may include a request for a fuller explanation of the reasons for the decision that is being challenged]
[Set out the details of any documents that are considered relevant and necessary. This should include details of any documentation or policy in respect of which disclosure is sought and an explanation as to why these are relevant. If reliance is being placed on a statutory duty to disclose information, this should be specified]
[Set out the address for the reply to this letter by the Home Office and for the service of any court documents]
[Include a proposed date by which the Home Office should reply to this letter. The precise time will depend on the circumstances of the individual case. However, although a shorter or longer time may be appropriate in a particular case, 14 days is a reasonable time to allow in most circumstances]

(*signed*)

APPENDIX FOUR

Procedural step	**Time limit**	**Legislative reference**
Petition lodged	3 months from the date on which the grounds giving rise to the petition first arose	Rule 58.3; Section 27A(1) of the Court of Session Act 1988; Article 4 of The Courts Reform (Scotland) Act 2014 (Commencement No. 3, Transitional and Saving Provisions) Order 2015
Order for intimation and service	Intimation within 7 days from the order granting intimation and service. Answers/notification within 21 days from the date of service	Rule 58.4
Decision on permission	Within 14 days from the end of the period for lodging answers	Rule 58.7
If permission refused, request a review	Within 7 days from the day on which the decision is made	Rule 58.8; Section 27C(2) of the Court of Session Act 1988
Reclaiming following an oral hearing	Within 7 days from the day on which the Court makes its decision	Rule 58.10; Section 27D(2) of the Court of Session Act 1988
Permission granted: substantive hearing fixed	Within 12 weeks from the date on which permission is granted	Rule 58.11(1)(a)
Permission granted: procedural hearing fixed	Within 6 weeks from the date on which permission is granted	Rule 58.11(1)(b)

NO. 4 OF 2017: PERSONAL INJURIES ACTIONS UNDER CHAPTER 43

1. This Practice Note has effect from 24 July 2017. It replaces Practice Note No. 4 of 2015 (Personal Injury Actions). Practice Note No. 2 of 2003 remains in force. **C5.120**

2. The purpose of this practice note is to inform practitioners of the court's approach to several procedural matters relating to actions of damages for, or arising from, personal injury. It covers matters relating to Chapter 43 of the Rules of the Court of Session ("RCS"), and takes into account changes made to the RCS by Act of Sederunt (Rules of the Court of Session 1994 and Sheriff Court Rules Amendment) (No.2) (Personal Injury and Remits) 2015.

Chapter 43

3. RCS 43.8 (applications for sist or for variation of timetable order) provides that an application to sist an action or vary the timetable shall be granted only on cause shown. The purpose of this provision is to ensure that timetables are not varied as a matter of routine and diets of proof consequently discharged. Accordingly, motions enrolled under this rule, including those of consent, must specify the cause relied on. Where it is not clear to the court that cause has been shown the court will, ordinarily, star the motion. The recent removal of "special" from "special cause" is to offer some flexibility where there has been a failure to adhere to the timetable as a result of inadvertence which may be regarded by the court as excusable, having regard to the relevant circumstances. It is not to reverse the court's approach to such matters as expressed in *Smith v Greater Glasgow and Clyde NHS Health Board* [2013] CSOH 178.

4. A motion to vary the timetable to allow an application for a third party notice to be made, even where cause has been shown, may be refused if granting it will endanger the proof diet.

5. RCS 43.9 regulates statements of valuation of claim. These must contain figures. The practice of stating "TBC" (to be confirmed) is not acceptable.

6. RCS 43.10 (pre-trial meetings) provides that there will be a pre-trial meeting between the parties to discuss settlement and to agree matters not in dispute. As explained in Practice Note No. 2 of 2003, the meeting must be a real one (although it can be held by video-conference). It is the obligation of each party to take all steps as are necessary to comply with both the letter and the spirit of the rule. Where it is apparent to one of the parties that this has not been done, that party should not sign the joint minute in Form 43.10. This will trigger the case being put out By Order. The importance of section 2 of Form 43.10 is stressed. Practitioners are encouraged to make sure of the procedure provided for in Chapter 28A (notices to admit and notices of non-admission).

7. Unless there is good reason for their deployment, such as incomplete instructions or lack of access to factual information, blanket denials or skeletal defences are not an acceptable starting point in the pleadings. The duty of candour exists at all times. It does so to serve both the court and the parties. The court will, ordinarily, bear this in mind when determining a motion for summary decree.

1. This Practice Note has effect from [illegible] July 2017. It replaces [illegible] of [illegible] personal injury actions. Practice Note No. 2 of 2003 remains in force.

2. The purpose of this practice note is to inform practitioners of the court's approach to several procedural matters relating to actions of damages for, or arising from, personal injury. It covers matters relating to Chapter 43 of the Rules of the Court of Session ("RCS"), and takes into account changes made to the RCS by Act of Sederunt (Rules of the Court of Session 1994 and Sheriff Court Rules Amendment) (No. 2) (Personal Injury and Remit) 2015.

Chapter 43

3. RCS 43.[illegible] (applications for sist or for variation of timetable order) provides that an application to sist an action or vary the timetable shall be granted only on cause shown. The purpose of this provision is to ensure that timetables are not varied as a matter of routine and dates of proof consequently discharged. Accordingly, motions enrolled under this rule, including those of consent, must specify the cause relied on. Where it is not clear to the court that cause has been shown the court will ordinarily star the motion. The recent removal of "special cause" from [illegible] [illegible] where there has been a failure to adhere to the timetable as a result of inadvertence which may be regarded by the court as excusable. Having regard to all relevant circumstances, it is not to revert to an [illegible] approach to such matters as expressed in [illegible] and [illegible] [illegible] 2013 [illegible].

4. A motion to vary the timetable to allow an application for a third party notice to [illegible], even where cause has been shown, may [illegible] the granting of [illegible] and/or the proof diet.

5. RCS 43.[illegible] requires statements of valuation of claim. These must contain figures. The practice of stating "TBC" (to be confirmed) is not acceptable.

6. RCS 43.[illegible] (pre-trial meeting) provides that there will be a pre-trial meeting between the parties to discuss settlement and to agree matters not in dispute. As explained in Practice Note No. 2 of 2003, the meeting must be a real one although it can be held by video conference. It is the obligation of each party to take all steps as are necessary to comply with the letter and the spirit of the rule. Where it is apparent to one of the parties that this has not been done, that party should not sign the joint minute in Form 43.[illegible]. This will affect their recovering outlays by way of the [illegible] [illegible] [illegible]. Practitioners are reminded to [illegible] the procedure provided for in Chapter 28A (notices to admit and notices of non-admission).

7. Unless there is good reason for their late disclosure, such as incomplete instructions or lack of access to factual information, blanket denials or unparticularised defences do not form acceptable starting points in the pleadings. Flexibility of treatment exists at all times. If defences are served on the court in [illegible], the court will ordinarily [illegible] [illegible] when determining a motion for summary decree.

NO. 5 OF 2017: PERSONAL INJURIES ACTIONS UNDER CHAPTER 42A

[Replaced by Practice Note No. 6 of 2017.] **C5.121**

NO. 6 OF 2017: PERSONAL INJURIES ACTIONS UNDER CHAPTER 42A

[Replaced by Practice Note No. 2 of 2019.] C5.122

NO.1 OF 2018: AFFIDAVITS IN FAMILY ACTIONS

1. This Practice Note has effect from 24 September 2018. It replaces Practice Note No. 1 of 2004. **C5.123**

2. The purpose of this Practice Note is to provide updated guidance on the preparation and use of affidavits in family actions. The need for clear guidance has arisen as a result of the increased use that is made of affidavits as evidence-in-chief in defended family actions.

3. This Practice Note covers:

a. Affidavits generally;
b. Affidavits required under rule 49.28 in certain undefended actions;
c. Defended family actions.

PART A:

AFFIDAVITS GENERALLY

Swearing or affirming an affidavit

4. This part applies to all affidavits lodged in family actions.

5. An affidavit must be sworn or affirmed before a notary public, justice of the peace or any person having authority to administer oaths in the place where the affidavit is sworn (such as a commissioner for oaths or a British diplomatic officer or consul abroad). The witness must be placed on oath or must affirm. A solicitor acting for a party to the action may act in a notarial capacity. Any person before whom an affidavit is sworn or affirmed ("the notary") must be satisfied that the witness has capacity to swear or affirm an affidavit.

Importance of affidavits

6. The witness should be made to appreciate the importance of the affidavit and must understand that it constitutes his or her evidence in the case. The possible consequences of giving false evidence should be explained to the witness. Before the witness signs the affidavit, he or she must have read it or the notary must have read it out to the witness.

Form and signature of affidavit

7. The affidavit should be on A4 paper. It should commence with the following words:

> *"At .... the .... day of .... 20.........., in the presence of ...., I .... [having been solemnly sworn / having affirmed], give evidence as follows:"*

8. The full name, age, address and occupation of the witness should be given in the first paragraph.

9. The affidavit should end with the words: *"All of which is the truth as I shall answer to God"* or *"All of which is affirmed by me to be true"*, as appropriate.

10. At the time the affidavit is sworn or affirmed, any insertion, deletion or other amendment to the affidavit must be initialled by the witness and the notary. Each page must be signed by both the witness and the notary. It is not necessary for the affidavit to be sealed by the notary. No alterations or insertions can be made after the affidavit is sworn or affirmed. Where a party wishes to alter or add to the affidavit, this must be done by supplementary affidavit.

Drafting the affidavit

11. The affidavit must be based on statements, precognitions and other material emanating directly from the witness.

12. The drafter must not frame the affidavit in language that the witness would not use. The court is likely to attach little weight to such an affidavit. Equally, the court is likely to discount the witness's evidence if it appears that he or she has been improperly briefed or coached. The affidavit is the evidence of the witness, and must therefore be expressed in the witness's own words – even where this results in the use of confused or intemperate language. In preparing an affidavit, legal advisers should bear in mind that the witness may have to justify on cross-examination statements contained in the affidavit. Legal advisers should make this clear to the witness.

13. It should be clear from the terms of the affidavit whether the witness is speaking from his or her own knowledge, based on what he or she actually saw or experienced, or whether the witness is relying on what he or she was told by a particular person.

14. The affidavit should be drafted in the first person and should take the form of short numbered paragraphs. It should be as succinct as possible, and focus only on matters that are relevant to the issues in dispute, as averred on record. The court will disregard any irrelevant or inadmissible material.

15. Where an affidavit or equivalent sworn statement is sworn in a language other than English, it must contain information of the circumstances in which it was drafted and translated. The original document and the translation must both be provided.

PART B:
AFFIDAVITS REQUIRED UNDER RULE 49.28 IN CERTAIN UNDEFENDED FAMILY ACTIONS

16. This part applies to all affidavits lodged under rule 49.28 of the Rules of the Court of Session.

Date of affidavit

17. All affidavits lodged must be of recent date – ideally, they should have been sworn no more than three months prior to the date of lodging. This is particularly important in cases where the evidence of a witness or circumstances to which the witness speaks are liable to change through the passage of time, such as cases involving children or financial conclusions.

18. Affidavits relating to the welfare of children which have been sworn more than three months prior to the date of lodging of the minute for decree are likely to be rejected by the court, on the basis that they are out of date.

Productions in undefended actions

19. Where the affidavit refers to a production already lodged in process, it must be borrowed from process, put to the witness and then docqueted and signed by the witness and the notary. The affidavit must refer to each production by its number of process. If a document referred to has not been lodged as a production when the affidavit is sworn, the witness must identify it in the affidavit. The document must then be docqueted as having been referred to in the affidavit and lodged as a production. Some productions will necessarily be docqueted with regard to more than one affidavit.

20. In actions for divorce or dissolution with consent, the defender's written consent form must be put to the pursuer. It must be identified in the pursuer's affidavit and docqueted and signed in the same way as other productions.

Applications for divorce or dissolution where there are children aged under 16

21. In actions of divorce, dissolution, judicial separation or nullity of marriage / civil partnership in which there are children of the family[1], but in which no order is sought under section 11 of the Children (Scotland) Act 1995, the court must[2] consider whether to exercise the powers set out in section 11 of that Act or section 62 of the Children's Hearings (Scotland) Act 2011 in light of the information available in respect of the arrangements for the child(ren)'s upbringing. Information outlining these arrangements must therefore be provided to the court.

22. These affidavits should, where relevant, include the following:

a. the qualifications of the witness (if not a parent) to speak about the child, including how often and in what circumstances the witness normally sees the child;
b. the ability of the person(s) with whom the child lives to provide proper care for him or her;
c. observations as to the relationship between the child and the other members of the household, the child's general appearance, interests, state of health and well-being;
d. a description of the home conditions in which the child lives;
e. the arrangements for contact between the child and any parent and siblings who do not live in the same household as the child;
f. information about the school the child attends and whether the child attends school regularly;
g. details of childcare arrangements during working hours, including the arrangements for such care outside of school hours.

Applications for section 11 orders

23. Where there is an application for an order under section 11 of the Children (Scotland) Act 1995, the affidavit must contain only relevant material supportive of the section 11 order(s) sought. It must also include the material listed in paragraph 22, above.

24. The court will disregard any part of an affidavit that does not contain evidence relating to the tests set out in section 11(7) of the Children (Scotland) Act 1995.

Financial conclusions

25. Where a financial conclusion is sought, the court must be provided with evidence that is as full, accurate and up-to-date as possible. If, after an affidavit has

---

[1] "Child of the family" is defined in section 12(4) of the Children (Scotland) Act 1995.
[2] Section 12 of the Children (Scotland) Act 1995.

been lodged, a material change in circumstances occurs before decree is granted, the court must be informed immediately. A further affidavit may have to be sworn / affirmed.

26. The pursuer must give evidence of all financial information relevant to the orders sought.

27. Where the pursuer's affidavit gives evidence of the defender's resources, it should state, as precisely as possible, the date at which the information was valid. The court should be provided with recent information relating to the defender's ability to pay the sums sought by the pursuer. Where the pursuer cannot obtain recent information relating to the defender's resources, the affidavit should make this clear and include as much information as is available to the pursuer.

28. Where the pursuer has concluded for several financial orders (for example, a capital sum, an order for the sale of the matrimonial home, a periodical allowance and expenses) but ultimately does not seek decree for one or more of these or seeks decree for a lesser sum, the affidavit should give reasons for that.

29. If the court is not satisfied on the basis of the material provided that decree should be granted as sought, a by order hearing will be fixed.

PART C:

DEFENDED FAMILY ACTIONS

30. This part applies to defended family actions.

Productions in defended actions

31. Where the affidavit refers to a production, it must refer to the production by its number of process. There is no need for productions to be borrowed, docqueted and signed in defended actions. Instead, a copy of the production must be put to the witness, but should not be appended to the affidavit. No documents of any kind should be appended to affidavits in defended actions.

Lodging of affidavits - timing

32. Wherever possible, unless the court otherwise directs, parties are asked to intimate and lodge affidavits on the same day. The purpose of that is to minimise the risk of one witness seeing another's evidence in advance and ensure that his or her evidence is not influenced.

33. When taking a witness's precognition prior to preparing his or her affidavit, legal advisers must not show the witness the precognitions, affidavits or draft affidavits of any other witness. Once affidavits have been lodged, the witness may be shown any other affidavits that are relevant to his or her evidence. If the witness consequently wishes to modify his or her evidence, this can be done by lodging a supplementary affidavit explaining the change. Alternatively, the witness could give supplementary oral evidence at the proof. The sole purpose of a supplementary affidavit is to correct or qualify evidence contained in the initial affidavit. It should not be treated as an opportunity to comment on or dispute the evidence of other witnesses.

34. Where the initial affidavit of a witness is lodged after the affidavits of other witnesses have been lodged, his or her affidavit must contain a declaration stating that the witness has not seen or been informed of the evidence of others. Where the witness has seen or been informed of the evidence of others, the affidavit must clearly identify that evidence and specify the circumstances in which the witness came to see or hear about it.

NO.2 OF 2018: MEDICAL CERTIFICATES

In connection with any proceedings in the Court of Session, a medical certificate which certifies that a person is unfit to attend court on a particular date, whether as a party or a witness, may bear either the words "I certify this on soul and conscience." or "I certify and solemnly and sincerely affirm this to be true." **C5.124**

This Practice Note has effect from 1 October 2018.

NO.3 OF 2018: PETITIONS UNDER SECTION 46 OF THE COURT OF SESSION ACT 1988

PETITION FOR REMOVAL OF PERSONS CAMPING WITHOUT AUTHORITY ON LOCAL AUTHORITY LAND

1. This Practice Note has effect from 30 November 2018. **C5.125**

2. It sets out the Court's expectations in relation to petitions brought by local authorities under section 46 of the Court of Session Act 1988, seeking removal of persons camping on local authority land, where their stay on that land has not been authorised by the local authority.

3. Any motion under rule 45A-3 to shorten or dispense with the period of notice requires to be justified and to be supported by relevant averments.

4. In particular, a local authority should aver:

(a) what its own procedures and policies are regarding removal of persons camping without authority on local authority land;

(b) whether it has followed its procedures and policies, and how these procedures and policies have been applied;

(c) why removal is required, and the reason why the period of notice requires to be shortened or dispensed with. The local authority should make clear and specific averments as to, for example, the nature of the location, the scale of the encampment, and any behaviour on the part of the occupants which gives rise to nuisance or which is otherwise detrimental to the settled community.

NO.1 OF 2019: COURT DRESS IN THE OUTER HOUSE

1. This Practice Note has effect from 1 December 2019. **C5.126**

2. Judges sitting in the Outer House will, ordinarily, no longer wear wigs and judicial robes, except when presiding over a hearing which involves the testimony of witnesses. It is not expected that counsel or solicitors with rights of audience appearing in the Outer House will wear wigs or gowns.

3. If a judge determines that special circumstances exist which make it appropriate to wear a wig and judicial robe, that will be intimated to practitioners in advance of the hearing.

4. Practitioners are expected to wear clothing appropriate for business at all hearings.

NO.2 OF 2019: PERSONAL INJURIES ACTIONS UNDER CHAPTER 42A

1. This Practice Note has effect from 1st March 2020. It replaces Practice Note No.6 of 2017. C5.127

2. This Practice Note applies to actions to which Chapter 42A (Case management of certain personal injuries actions) of the Rules of the Court of Session applies. Any of the requirements of this Practice Note may be disapplied by the Lord Ordinary in any case, including where one or more of the parties are party litigants.

3. The ordinary rules of the RCS apply to a personal injuries action to which Chapter 42A applies except insofar as specifically excluded under RCS 42A.1(6), or except insofar as excluded by implication because of a provision in Chapter 42A.

4. Arrangements will be made to ensure that (save in exceptional circumstances) at all appearances of an action at a case management hearing, or at a debate or proof appointed under Chapter 42A, the same judge will preside.

5. Parties are expected to arrange that counsel, or solicitors having rights of audience, who are principally instructed, are authorised to take any necessary decision on questions both of substance and procedure and are available and appear at any case management hearing, or at a debate or proof. Practitioners are expected to liaise with each other and with the Keeper in order to facilitate, so far as possible, the appearance by counsel or solicitors having rights of audience, principally instructed, at all hearings, including Procedural Hearings in any reclaiming motion.

Chapter 42A generally

6. Chapter 42A applies to clinical negligence cases withdrawn from Chapter 43 and other complex personal injuries actions, including catastrophic injuries cases, where the Lord Ordinary is satisfied that managing the action under Chapter 42A would facilitate the efficient determination of the action. Pursuers wishing to raise a personal injuries action based on clinical negligence, as an ordinary action subject to Chapter 42A procedure, must apply for authority to do so in accordance with RCS 43.1A. Alternatively, parties may apply by motion in accordance with RCS 43.5 to have the action withdrawn from Chapter 43 and to proceed in accordance with Chapter 42A.

7. The purpose of Chapter 42A is to allow the court, at an early stage, to identify and resolve issues that may otherwise result in a variation of the timetable or the discharge of a proof diet and to achieve the efficient disposal of such cases. This frontloading will allow the court to make more informed case management decisions when determining further procedure at a case management hearing. The timings may seem demanding, but, as the adjustment period can be extended in appropriate circumstances, there is sufficient flexibility to allow for the completion of the required matters prior to the closure of the record. Parties will then be expected to be in a position to comply with the timetable.

8. RCS 42A.5 provides for the exchange of information by the parties in the 12 week period which follows the lodging of the closed record. This exchange of information is to be carried out in stages and provides that parties will be fully informed of their respective positions before the case management hearing. The parties are required, by RCS 42A.6, to lodge in process statements containing proposals for further procedure. The pursuer must, after liaising with the defender, lodge a joint minute in process which sets out the matters which have been agreed. Where there are matters relevant to the issues in dispute, which are not included in the joint minute, the parties must lodge a written statement explaining why such matters have not been agreed. The aim is for the court to be fully informed in order that the case management hearing will be effective.

9. Where reference is made to witness statements in RCS 42A.5(2)(c), 42A.5(3)(f)(ii), 42A.6(2)(a)(vi) and 42A.7(2)(b)(viii), these statements should contain full and clear factual accounts. Witness statements should be exchanged before the case management hearing.

10. Where a party seeks to have the action appointed to debate, then that party must, on the lodging of the closed record in process, notify the court and the other party, or parties, that an application for a debate is to be made, and make such application to the court, by motion, no more than 1 week from the date on which the closed record is lodged in process.

11. Where a party seeks to have the action appointed to debate, then the timeframes set out in the rules concerning:

a. the fixing by the court of a date for the case management hearing;
b. the exchange of information by the parties;
c. the lodging in process of statements of proposals and joint minutes,

commence from the date on which the court determines the application for a debate.

12. Where parties are seeking to have the action sent to proof, the court will explore the issues set out in RCS 42A.7 at the case management hearing.

13. RCS 42A.7(4) allows the Lord Ordinary to fix a further case management hearing, whether or not the action has been appointed to debate or sent to proof. RCS 42A.8(4) allows the Lord Ordinary to fix a further case management hearing, or to vary the pre-proof timetable, at any time where the Lord Ordinary considers that the efficient determination of the action would be served by doing so.

14. RCS 42A.10 provides the Lord Ordinary with wide powers to make any order necessary to secure the efficient determination of the action, and, in particular, to resolve any matters arising or outstanding from the pre-proof timetable or the written statements for further procedure lodged by the parties in advance of the case management hearing. The court will attempt to ensure that parties are ready for proof and have provided an accurate estimate of the time required, before fixing a diet.

15. Where the court intends to fix a date for the proof, practitioners should liaise with the Keeper of the Rolls regarding potential dates. Where a proof diet has been fixed and the dates are no longer suitable, or there exists a concern about their suitability, practitioners should contact the Keeper as soon as practicable.

16. Under the transitional provisions, the Lord Ordinary may direct that Chapter 42A, as substituted by Act of Sederunt (Rules of the Court of Session 1994 Amendment) (Case Management of Certain Personal Injuries Actions) 2019, is to apply to an action raised before 1st March 2020. Parties seeking to have such an action appointed to Chapter 42A, as revised, are encouraged to apply as early as possible under the transitional provisions. The court will use the powers under Chapter 42A to make such orders as are necessary to secure the efficient determination of the action irrespective of the stage which the action has reached.

Joint and core bundles

17. Where a cause has been appointed to a proof, the parties must lodge:

a. a joint bundle of productions, including a joint bundle of records (medical records, and any other relevant records, for example social security, schools, and social work records etc.);

b. a list of the contents of the paginated joint bundle of productions;

c. where the productions lodged on behalf of both parties comprise more than 500 pages, a core bundle,

in final form, in accordance with the pre-proof timetable fixed under RCS 42A.8.

18. Where a party lodges a joint bundle or a core bundle, that party must intimate the bundle to the other parties.

19. All joint bundles and core bundles should be properly identified and marked accordingly, containing an index at the beginning, and be presented in a form which is robust and manageable. Where lever arch folders or ring binders are used they should not be overfilled.

20. Where a passage in a production is to be referred to in the course of submissions, a copy should be lodged with the passage highlighted.

21. Prior to the lodging of the joint bundles and core bundles, the records should be kept, and exchanged by the parties, in accordance with the time-frames in RCS 42A.5. They should not be lodged until the timetable is issued under RCS 42A.8. Experts instructed for both sides should work from the same joint bundle(s) of records and use the same numbering and references to those bundles throughout the case, commencing from the time they are first instructed. If it has been necessary for any expert to have prepared report(s) prior to the development of the joint and core bundles of records, any report exchanged or lodged will require to be revised with reference to the bundles prior to lodging.

22. The joint bundle of records should be updated by the parties, as and when necessary, at the point records, not already included in the bundle, appear and after liaison with the other parties. This may be, for example, a scan or x-ray associated with a report which is already included in the joint bundle which only comes to light at a later date. The scan or x-ray should be inserted where it ought to appear in the joint bundle (i.e. with its associated report), as opposed to being intimated as a separate production. Parties should apply the same approach to all updates to reports which are already included in the joint bundle.

23. The joint bundle of productions should contain the productions upon which each party intends to rely.

24. Only productions relevant to the legal and factual issues to be raised at the relevant hearing, and likely to be referred to at that hearing, should be lodged.

25. Productions should be arranged chronologically or in another appropriate order, such as by reference to the subject matter of the claim or the issues in dispute.

Core bundles

26. The core bundle should contain copies of productions already lodged, as appropriate. It should contain copies of the productions which are central to the issues.

27. The core bundle should not ordinarily exceed 150 pages.

28. Joint bundles and core bundles should bear a certification by the agent for the party at whose instance the hearing has been fixed that the requirements of this Practice Note have been complied with in respect of each production included.

Notes of argument

29. Where a cause has been appointed to a debate, each party should lodge a note of argument.

30. Where a cause has been appointed to a proof, each party should consider whether or not it will be necessary to lodge a note of argument having regard to the issues in the case. They should either lodge such a note or a joint statement as to why a note of argument is not necessary.

31. The note of argument or joint statement should be lodged at least 10 days before a debate, and at least 21 days prior to a proof.

32. The note of argument should comply with the following general principles:

a. It should be a concise summary of the submissions the party intends to develop at the hearing;
b. It should contain an executive summary of the points which the party wishes to make, set out as subparagraphs within a single paragraph;
c. It should be set out in numbered paragraphs;
d. It should not contain detailed legal argument;
e. It should be as brief as the issues allow and not more than eight A4 pages, or, where the relevant hearing is a proof, twelve A4 pages. It should be double spaced, font size 12;
f. Each point should be followed by a reference to any evidence or document on which the party wishes to rely. The relevant passages in the document should be identified;
g. It should state, in respect of each authority cited –
   (i) the proposition of law that the authority demonstrates; and
   (ii) the passages of the authority (identified by page or paragraph) which support the proposition;
h. More than one authority should not be cited in support of a given proposition.

33. Except on cause shown, no submission will be permitted to be advanced and no authority will be allowed to be referred to at the relevant hearing which is not included in the note of argument.

34. Where the note of argument has been lodged and a party subsequently becomes aware that an argument will no longer be insisted upon, that party should inform the other parties and the court of that fact as soon as practicable.

Joint lists of authorities

35. Where a cause has been appointed to a debate or a proof, the party at whose instance the hearing has been fixed should consider whether it is likely that authorities will be required for the debate or proof. That party should, after consultation with the other parties, either lodge a joint list of authorities or lodge a statement by both parties that authorities are not required for the hearing.

36. Where a Note of Argument has been lodged it will be expected that there will be a joint list of authorities unless parties have agreed the propositions of law, in which case a joint statement to that effect should be lodged in place of the joint list.

The joint list or joint statement should be lodged at the same time as the note of argument, or the joint statement which is set out in paragraphs 30 and 31. The time-frames for the lodging of these documents are set out in paragraph 31.

37. The joint list of authorities should not contain more than ten authorities. The permission of the court is required to include any authorities beyond the maximum number. For the purposes of this paragraph, authorities do not include statutory provisions upon which the case or defence proceeds.

38. Authorities which have been reported in Session Cases, or in the Law Reports published by the Incorporated Council of Law Reporting for England and Wales, should be cited from those sources. Where a case is not reported in Session Cases or the Law Reports, references to other recognised reports may be given. Unreported Opinions should only be cited where they contain an authoritative statement of a relevant principle of law not to be found in a reported case or where they are necessary for the understanding of some other authority.

39. Joint lists of authorities should bear a certification by the agent for the party at whose instance the hearing has been fixed that the requirements of this Practice Note have been complied with in respect of the joint lists.

Failure to comply

40. RCS 42A.9 provides that where a party fails to comply with certain specified rules in that Chapter concerning the exchange of draft information by the parties then that party may, on the motion of the other party, be ordained to appear before the court to explain the reasons for their non-compliance. The court has the power to make any such order as appears appropriate in the circumstances.

41. Where a party fails to comply with any of the requirements of this Practice Note, the court may find that no expenses are payable, may make an award of expenses, or may modify any award of expenses, in respect of the failure to comply.

27 November 2019

NO.1 OF 2020: SUBSTANTIVE HEARINGS BY VIDEO CONFERENCE

1. This Practice Note has effect from 12 June 2020. **C5.128**

2. This Practice Note applies to all substantive court hearings which are due to take place by means of video conference.

3. Where a hearing is to proceed by video conference, parties must lodge electronic copies of any productions with the Court.

4. An electronic copy of a production will be considered to be the principal copy unless good reason is provided otherwise.

5. When lodging electronic copy productions, a party should:

- lodge with the Court an inventory of the productions in electronic form, with hyperlinks to each of the electronic copies; and
- send a copy of those electronic productions to every other party.

6. Parties are to co-operate, agree and lodge a joint list of those productions which require to be referred to at the hearing. The list should comprise only those productions which are relevant to the legal and factual issues to be raised at the hearing and which are likely to be referred to at it. The productions identified on that list will comprise the core bundle.

7. Each party must intimate in writing to the Court the names and email addresses of each person whom the party intends to call as a witness.

8. Parties are responsible for displaying productions from the core bundle at the substantive hearing[1].

9. RCS 36.9 continues to apply. Parties are responsible for ensuring that their witnesses are ready and available to join the video conference at the appropriate time. Each party must provide to the clerk of court a numbered list of its witnesses together with a timetable setting out the order in which, and day on which, it is proposed to call them. The other obligations in RCS 36.9 are to be complied with, subject to appropriate modification for the context of a court hearing conducted by video conference.

10. As with any court hearing conducted by video conference, each party must ensure its electronic equipment and internet connection to the Court - and that of its witnesses - is of appropriate quality and robustness for the anticipated duration of the proceedings. Each party must ensure that the hearing is conducted with the same decorum and respect as a hearing conducted in the courtroom.

11. Where the Court requests that a test be undertaken of the video conference facilities in advance of a hearing, parties and witnesses are expected to participate in the test so far as practicable.

11 June 2020

---

[1] SCTS will provide guidance and support on this until such time as video conference hearings are fully established.

NO. 2 OF 2020: GROUP PROCEEDINGS UNDER CHAPTER 26A

1. This Practice Note has effect from 28th September 2020. C5.128A

2. This Practice Note applies to proceedings to which Chapter 26A (Group Procedure) of the Rules of the Court of Session applies.

3. The Lord Ordinary may disapply any provision of this Practice Note on the motion of any party, or of the Lord Ordinary's own accord, in respect of any particular group proceedings.

4. The Rules of the Court of Session applicable to ordinary actions proceeding by way of summons apply to proceedings to which Chapter 26A applies unless specifically excluded under rule 26A.2, or excluded by implication because of a provision in Chapter 26A.

5. Arrangements will be made to ensure that (save in exceptional circumstances) at all appearances of a group proceedings action the same judge will preside at all hearings fixed under Chapter 26A. All proceedings in a group proceedings action which concerns a transaction or dispute of a commercial or business nature, whether contractual or not, shall, save in exceptional circumstances, be heard before a judge nominated by the Lord President as a commercial judge.

6. Parties are expected to arrange that counsel, or solicitors having rights of audience, who are principally instructed, are authorised to take any necessary decision on questions both of substance and procedure and are available and appear at hearings fixed under Chapter 26A. Practitioners are expected to liaise with each other and with the Keeper in order to facilitate, so far as possible, the appearance by counsel or solicitors having rights of audience, principally instructed, at all hearings, including procedural hearings in any reclaiming motion.

7. It is recognised that in some actions, where for example there are very many group members and a number of legal firms are instructed, it may be agreed between the pursuers' agents for one agent to be designated as the lead. It is expected that this would be the solicitor or agent acting for the representative party, given that this agent has duties under the rules.

Chapter 26A generally

8. Chapter 26A of the Rules of the Court of Session applies to group proceedings (also known as multi-party or class actions in other jurisdictions), in which there are two or more persons (a "group") each with separate claims which raise issues (whether of fact or law) which are the same as, or similar or related to, each other and which may be the subject of civil proceedings. A group may only raise such proceedings where the court has authorised a person to be the group's representative party and given permission for the proceedings to be brought.

9. The introduction of Chapter 26A allows group proceedings to be brought as opt-in proceedings, i.e. with the express consent of each member of the group on whose behalf they are brought. The Group Register is the means by which those persons who form the group is recorded. Membership of the group may change, by the addition of new members into the group and the withdrawal of members from the group, during the course of the proceedings. The group register, a key component central to the procedure, is considered by the court at every hearing. It is crucial to the parties and all group members that this operates well, particularly with regard to prescription and limitation matters, so its administration by the representative party, or agent for the representative party, in accordance with the rules is key to the success of the procedure.

10. The procedural framework which is, in parts, based upon the commercial actions model, provides the court with flexibility about how best to manage group proceedings. It allows for the early intervention and case management by the court to deal with what could be potentially complex litigation. The procedure in, and progress of, group proceedings is under the direct control of the Lord Ordinary, and the court will take a pro-active approach.

Applications by motion

11. Applications made by a person to be a representative party and for permission to bring group proceedings are made by motion in Form 26A.5 and 26A.9 respectively. These applications will be treated as before calling motions and will be allocated by the Keeper and diarised. Chapter 23 of the Rules of the Court of Session apply to these applications and other motions under Chapter 26A, and they may (but do not require to) be intimated and enrolled by email.

12. Registration fees will be charged. Where answers are lodged in response to either application a first appearance fee will be charged.

Service of applications

13. Under rule 26A.5(2)(a) an application made by a person to be a representative party is brought before a Lord Ordinary for an order for intimation and service. This is separate and distinct to the service on the defender of other papers under the rules. Where an application for permission to bring group proceedings is made, the applicant must lodge further papers (to include the group register) under rule 26A.5(7) or 26A.9(3). The applicant must, when lodging such further papers, serve them on the defender under rule 26A.5(8) or 26A.9(4). The commencement of proceedings, set out in paragraph 25 below, is connected to this matter.

14. A schedule of service must be appended to an application made by a person to be a representative party and for permission for group proceedings to be brought. Evidence of service of these applications must be lodged in accordance with rule 16.1.

Advertisement

15. The Lord Ordinary has to consider what advertisement is required for applications to be a representative party and for permission to bring group proceedings under rules 26A.5(2)(b) and 26A.9(2)(b). In order that the Lord Ordinary is in a position to do so, the applicant should aver in detail what advertising has been undertaken, the reason why the applicant submits that no further advertising is required, or alternatively the applicant's proposals as to what further advertising would be appropriate. Full supporting documentation must be lodged.

Application to be a representative party

16. The Lord Ordinary has to be satisfied of the suitability of an applicant to be a representative party under rule 26A.7(1), and is required to consider the matters in rule 26A.7(2). The averments in the application should address these matters in detail. It will not be enough merely to repeat the wording of rule 26A.7(2) in the application. Full supporting documentation must be lodged.

Application for permission to bring proceedings

17. The Lord Ordinary may refuse a group proceedings application on the grounds set out in rule 26A.11(5). The averments in a group proceedings application should address these grounds, and the further issues as set out in paragraph 6 of Form 26A.9, in detail. It will not be enough merely to repeat the wording of rule 26A.11(5). Full supporting documentation must be lodged, as required by rule 26A.9(3)(c).

Pleadings

Summons

18. The summons will run in the name of the representative party for the group, designed as acting in that capacity and will be formally served on the defender where permission to bring the proceedings has been given by the court. In the unlikely event that a party litigant applies to be a representative party and to bring group proceedings, the order giving permission for proceedings to be brought under rule 26A.12 will give permission for the party litigant to sign the summons. The principal summons must be lodged for signeting no later than 7 days after the date on which permission to bring group proceedings has been given.

19. Pleadings in traditional form are not normally required or encouraged in a group proceedings action. The default position is that pleadings should be in abbreviated form. Parties are expected to be aware of each other's position before proceedings are commenced. The overriding requirement is one of fair notice: the purpose of the pleadings is to give notice of the essential elements of the case to the court and to the other parties to the action. It is recognised, however, that the nature of some actions will be such that abbreviated pleadings will not be appropriate. The rules allow for detailed written pleadings to be made in such cases, either generally or restricted to particular claims or issues. Where the pursuers' position on any matter is contained in another document, such as an expert report, it is permissible to adopt the document, or a specified part thereof, as part of the pursuers' case. Where damages are sought, a summary statement of the claim or a statement in the form of an account will normally be sufficient.

20. Rule 26A.19(3) is intended to require a party to produce with its summons the core or essential documents to establish the matter with which the cause is concerned. Under rule 27.1(1)(a) documents founded on or adopted as incorporated in a summons must be lodged at the time the summons is lodged for calling.

Defences

21. As with the summons, it is not necessary for defences to follow the traditional form of pleading. In the first instance, detailed averments are not required in the answers any more than in the articles of condescendence. In particular, it is *not* necessary that each averment in the summons should be admitted, not known or denied, provided that the extent of the dispute is reasonably well identified. One of the objectives of the procedure is to make the extent of written pleadings subject to the control of the court. What is said in paragraphs 19 and 20 regarding the content of a summons, including the overriding requirement of fair notice, applies mutatis mutandis to defences.

22. Under rule 27.1(1)(b), documents founded on or adopted as incorporated in a defence must be lodged at the time the defences are lodged. Defences must be lodged within 7 days after the summons has called: rule 18.1(2).

Adjustment of pleadings

23. Where any pleadings or other documents are to be adjusted, the party proposing adjustment shall do so by preparing a new copy of the document as adjusted in which the new material is indicated using track changes or strikethrough or a different font.

Counterclaims and Third Party Notices

24. No counterclaim or the convening of a third party may be pursued without an order from the Lord Ordinary.

The Group Register

Commencement of Proceedings

25. Persons must be designated as group members on a group register before their claim may be brought in the proceedings. Where an application for permission to bring proceedings is made, the applicant (the representative party or the proposed representative party) must lodge with the court, and serve on the defender, the group register, the summons by which it is proposed to institute proceedings and any further supporting information. In respect of persons listed as group members in the group register at that stage, group proceedings commence by reference to the service of the group register on the defender under rule 26A.5(8) or 26A.9(4). It is recognised that there may be cases where subsequent to that an application for permission is either refused, or is granted and then following appeal is refused, in which case the proceedings cannot be brought and will not have been commenced. Following any revisals being made to the register on account of a new member joining the group, group proceedings commence in respect of such persons when the register, in revised form, is lodged with the court.

Lodging of the Group Register

26. The rules allow the group register to be lodged with the court, and served on the defender, by first class post or by electronic means. The court has a preference for the group register to be lodged in electronic form, in pdf format. It is recognised that sensitive information may be included in a group register. The court accordingly expects the solicitor or agent for the representative party (or, as the case may be, proposed representative party) to apply the requisite data protection measures to the register. It is expected that standard practice would be for the solicitor or agent to use a secure email address, but where this is not the case the court expects additional security measures to be applied to the group register, whether that be password protection or encryption, where it is lodged and served electronically.

Change in membership of the Group

27. A revised group register must be in full form in that it must contain details of all of the members of the group following changes made to the group's membership. For this reason it is expected that it would be more suitable for the representative party's agent to lodge the register in electronic form.

Preliminary hearing

28. Parties are expected to arrive at the preliminary hearing with clear, fully formed, views about how the issues which are the subject of the proceedings can be litigated in the most efficient way, and address the court on this. The aim is for the proceedings to be determined as efficiently as possible. It is considered that if the parties can arrive at a preliminary hearing with an agreed view of the best way to approach the litigation – perhaps by, for example, taking forward a test case or test cases, or restricting the proceedings, at least initially, to particular claims or issues – then that will be for the benefit of all.

29. The preliminary hearing is not designed to give parties the opportunity to formulate their claim and response thereto. Adjustment of pleadings will not always be necessary and it should not be assumed that an order allowing a period of adjustment will be made. Any adjustment allowed will normally be restricted to clarification of a party's position in response to averments or requests for further explanation by another party.

30. Prior to the preliminary hearing parties should lodge all correspondence and other documents which set out their material contentions of fact and law. These provisions are supplementary to the provisions of rule 26A.19(3).

31. Motions for continuations of preliminary hearings which are sought simply to enable information to be obtained, which could and should have been obtained prior to the preliminary hearing, are likely to be refused.

32. Prior to the preliminary hearing parties should be in a position to lodge a document setting out in concise form the issues which they contend require judicial determination. The statement of issues should be lodged by 4.00 pm two working days before the hearing, and, where possible, be set out in an agreed document.

33. In applying rule 26A.21, the court will set realistic deadlines which are expected to be adhered to. It is likely that extensions will only be granted if reasonable cause is shown. At the preliminary hearing parties will be expected to address the court and provide detailed and accurate information to ensure that appropriate deadlines are fixed.

Case management hearing

34. At the case management hearing parties will be expected to be in a position to discuss realistically the issues involved in the action and the method of disposing of them. Parties will be expected to be able to advise the court on the steps that have been taken to date to achieve an extra-judicial settlement and on the likelihood of such a settlement being achieved. They will be asked to express a view on the stage at which any joint meeting between parties ought to be ordered to take place. The court will ascertain from parties whether there are any further steps that could be taken by the court to assist in the resolution of the dispute.

35. Prior to the case management hearing parties must lodge a note of proposals for further procedure setting out their position as to the future progress of the case and, in particular, whether a diet of debate or proof is sought.

36. At the case management hearing it is anticipated that the court will fix a substantive hearing along with an appropriate timetable or, if necessary, a further case management hearing to allow any outstanding matters to be resolved. Where a diet of proof is allowed, the timetable may include provision for the preparation and lodging of a statement of agreed facts.

Motions by email

37. Requests to move or discharge hearings or to extend or vary time limits may be made by email. Any such request should be copied to the agents for all other parties so that they may confirm their consent or lack of opposition. Requesting parties will be charged a motion fee for such requests.

38. Motions in Form 23.1C and notices of opposition in Form 23.1D may be enrolled by emailing the completed form to gcs@scotcourts.gov.uk. Where any documents bear a signature, e.g. joint minutes, a scanned copy of the signed document, or a document which has been signed digitally, should be emailed to the General Department of the Offices of Court. In the case of documents for which a scanned copy has been provided, the hard copy original document should be available for production on request by the General Department or by order of the court.

Debates

39. The provisions of Chapter 28 of the rules (Procedure Roll) apply to a debate in a group proceedings action.

Lodging of productions

40. Before any hearing at which reference is to be made to documents, parties should, as well as lodging their productions, prepare for the use of the court a working bundle in which the documents are arranged chronologically or in another appropriate order without multiple copies of the same document. The bundle for a motion hearing should be prepared by the party enrolling the motion; otherwise, unless there is agreement to the contrary, the bundle should be prepared by the pursuer.

Documentary productions in electronic format

41. Productions need only be lodged in electronic format. Inventories listing productions should be lodged in electronic format but may require to be lodged also in hard copy.

Notes of argument

42. Where a cause has been appointed to a debate, each party should lodge a note of argument.

43. Where a cause has been appointed to a proof, each party should consider whether or not it will be necessary to lodge a note of argument having regard to the issues in the case. They should either lodge such a note or a joint statement as to why a note of argument is not necessary.

44. The note of argument or joint statement should be lodged at least 10 days before a debate, and at least 21 days prior to a proof.

45. A note of argument should comply with the following general principles:

a. It should be a concise summary of the submissions the party intends to develop at the hearing;
b. It should contain an executive summary of the points which the party wishes to make, set out as subparagraphs within a single paragraph;
c. It should be set out in numbered paragraphs;
d. It should not contain detailed legal argument;

e. It should be as brief as the issues allow and not more than eight A4 pages, or, where the relevant hearing is a proof, twelve A4 pages. It should be double spaced, font size 12;

f. Each point should be followed by a reference to any evidence or document on which the party wishes to rely. The relevant passages in the document should be identified;

g. It should state, in respect of each authority cited:

   (i) the proposition of law that the authority demonstrates; and

   (ii) the passages of the authority (identified by page or paragraph) which support the proposition;

h. More than one authority should not be cited in support of a given proposition.

46. Except on cause shown, no submission will be permitted to be advanced and no authority will be allowed to be referred to at the relevant hearing which is not included in the note of argument.

47. Where the note of argument has been lodged and a party subsequently becomes aware that an argument will no longer be insisted upon, that party should inform the other parties and the court of that fact as soon as practicable.

Joint bundle of authorities

48. When a group proceedings action has been appointed to a debate, the party at whose instance the debate has been fixed should, after consultation with the other parties, lodge a joint bundle containing copies of the authorities upon which each party will rely at the hearing.

49. The bundle of authorities should, in general:

a. Not include authorities for propositions not in dispute; and

b. Not include more than 10 authorities (in addition to any relevant statutory provisions), unless on cause shown permission of the court to include a greater number has been obtained.

50. Authorities which have been reported in Session Cases, or in the Law Reports published by the Incorporated Council of Law Reporting for England and Wales, should be cited from those sources. Where a case is not reported in Session Cases or the Law Reports, references to other recognised reports may be given. Unreported judgments should only be cited when they contain an authoritative statement of a relevant principle of law not to be found in a reported case or when they are necessary for the understanding of some other authority.

51. The bundle of authorities should be lodged by the date specified in the interlocutor.

52. Bundles of authorities which do not conform to this Practice Note may be rejected by the court, which may also find that no expenses are payable in respect of the cost of making up and lodging the bundle. The court may also find that no expenses are payable, or may modify any award of expenses, where authorities are included unnecessarily.

53. Parties are encouraged to produce bundles of authorities in electronic format only. Where authorities produced electronically are contained within a folder, they should be identified by tab number and citation, e.g. "*012 T (formerly H) v Nugent Care Society (formerly Catholic Social Services)* [2004] EWCA Civ 51". The tab numbering should restart in each folder. If a party intends to use hard copy documents at the hearing, their folder and tab numbers should correspond to the electronic folder and tab numbers.

Joint meetings of parties

54. The group proceedings judge has power, in terms of rules 26A.21(2)(e) and 26A.22(2)(o), to order parties to hold a joint meeting with a view to exploring whether the dispute is capable of extra-judicial settlement or, alternatively, whether the issues requiring judicial determination can be restricted. Such an order will not be made as a matter of course but it is likely that a joint meeting will be ordered in most cases. The stage of the proceedings at which the meeting will be ordered will vary from case to case, and will depend upon when the court considers that such a meeting is most likely to be productive of substantial progress.

Pre-proof by order hearing

55. When a proof, or proof before answer, has been allowed, the court will normally fix a pre-proof by order hearing to take place in advance of the proof diet. The general purpose of such a hearing is to ascertain parties' state of preparation for the proof and to review the estimated duration of that hearing. Without prejudice to the foregoing generality, the following matters may be dealt with at the pre-proof by order hearing:

a. Consideration of any joint minute of admissions agreed by parties, which should be lodged no later than two days prior to the pre-proof by order hearing.
b. A review of the documents, or other productions, which parties consider will be relied upon at the proof hearing. Any such document should be lodged no later than two days prior to the pre-proof by order hearing.
c. The up-to-date position with regard to any expert reports which are to be relied upon. Parties should be in a position to advise the court of what consultation, if any, has taken place between their respective experts with a view to reaching agreement about any points held in common and what matters remain truly in dispute between them.

56. Not less than two days prior to a pre-proof by order hearing parties should lodge an estimated timetable for the conduct of the proof.

Hearings for further procedure

57. The Lord Ordinary may at any time before final judgment, at his or her own instance or at the request of a party, have a group proceedings action put out for a hearing for further procedure to deal with a procedural or other matter which has arisen for which provision has not been made.

Reclaiming

58. An interlocutor pronounced in a group proceedings action, other than an interlocutor concerning permission to bring proceedings or a final interlocutor, may be reclaimed against only with leave of the Lord Ordinary within 14 days after the date of the interlocutor: rule 38.3(6).

Failure to comply with rule or order of the Lord Ordinary

59. The purpose of rule 26A.29 is to provide for discipline to ensure effective supervision of case management. Any failure of a party to comply with a provision in the rules or a court order may result in a refusal to extend deadlines, dismissal of the action, decree in terms of the conclusions of the summons or a finding of expenses.

NO.2 OF 2021: CAUSES IN THE INNER HOUSE – HEARINGS BY VIDEO CONFERENCE

1. This Practice Note has effect from 22nd May 2021. C5.129

2. The purpose of this Practice Note is to provide further guidance to court users in dealing with Inner House hearings which are to take place by video conference. This Practice Note is consistent with and complements Practice Note No.3 of 2011.

Procedural hearings

3. To ensure that substantive hearings are able to run efficiently and effectively, parties are encouraged to appear at procedural hearings prepared for a constructive discussion about the arrangements for the substantive hearing. Particular consideration should be given to: (i) the most effective way to organise and present written material for the substantive hearing; and (ii) the estimated amount of judicial reading-in time required before the substantive hearing. It may be possible for the Court to deal with the procedural hearing on the papers (i.e. without a hearing) if it appears that everything is in order and parties are agreed on further procedure.

Written material

4. To keep the pleadings to the minimum necessary, the Court reminds practitioners that grounds of appeal and a note of argument should be sufficient for the Court to hear a case. If those are provided then there should be no need for parties to exchange and submit written submissions as well. The note of argument must be based on the grounds of appeal. It should not be used to attempt to introduce new points.

5. The note of argument should normally not exceed 25 pages; leave of the Court is required if it is proposed to exceed the page limit. The note must be double-spaced and in font size 12; it must be single-sided. It must not contain footnotes. It is to refer to all the authorities to be relied upon. Only disputed propositions require the citation of authority. More than one authority should not be cited in support of a disputed proposition. No more than 10 authorities should be cited in total unless the scale of the reclaiming motion, application or appeal warrants more extensive citation. If it is proposed to cite more extensively leave of the Court is required. Parties are therefore encouraged to consider carefully which authorities require to be cited and temper their note of argument accordingly.

6. The Court highlights the following important principles when lodging electronic documents for hearings by video conference. Parties should try to keep electronic documents in as small a bundle as possible. It may often be useful to have three separate electronic bundles comprising: a joint appendix; a joint bundle of authorities; and a joint bundle of pleadings. The pleadings bundle should contain: the reclaiming print (including the Opinion of the Lord Ordinary, see RCS 38.5(2)), stated case, or other form of appeal; the grounds of appeal; the answers to the grounds of appeal; the notes of argument; and the reading list if one has been ordered. The exact format of the electronic documents can, if necessary, be discussed at the Procedural Hearing.

7. All electronic documents lodged should utilise a pagination system that is consistent throughout all the electronic documents so as to assign a unique sequential page number to each page of every document lodged; they must be numbered in ascending order throughout. Pagination should begin with the first page of the first document and should be continued throughout. These requirements are to ensure that the Court and parties may locate quickly a given page in a document by reference to its unique page number. The use of hyperlinks and bookmarks is strongly encouraged wherever practicable as these allow the Court to navigate quickly to a particular page or document during a hearing.

Appendices

8. An appendix ought to contain only documents which were before the court or tribunal of first instance. An appendix should, however, comprise the minimum material necessary to conduct the appeal. Other than in exceptional circumstances, it should not be necessary to reproduce all of the material which was placed before the court or tribunal of first instance. Parties are accordingly encouraged to weed out extraneous material.

9. If a document has not been lodged in process, i.e. as a production, it should not be in an appendix (*Grierson v Mitchell* 1912 SC 173, Lord Salvesen at 173; *British Thomson-Houston Co v Charlesworth Peebles & Co* 1924 SC 175). The same rule applies to material that was not before the court or tribunal of first instance. If a party is seeking to introduce a new document, which was not before the Lord Ordinary or the court or tribunal of first instance, it must first be lodged as a production before it can form part of an appendix (*Scotch Whisky Association v Lord Advocate* 2017 SC 465, Lord President (Carloway) at para [104] et seq).

10. An appendix is not a free-standing document, it is a print of material already properly lodged in process or that was before the court or tribunal of first instance. Permission to include new material in an appendix is needed. An appendix containing such material should therefore always be accompanied by a motion to allow the new material in. It is up to parties to decide when to lodge such a motion but, as a generality, the nearer to the date of the Summar Roll hearing, the less likely it is that a new document will be admitted.

11. If a party is uncertain about the Court's expectations in relation to written material then they are encouraged to make early contact with the Division Clerks.

Reading lists

12. Where the Court orders a reading list to be prepared, parties must ensure that this is restricted to material which it is essential for the Court to read before the substantive hearing over and above the pleadings, notes of argument and decision appealed against. If it is thought essential for the Court to read any of the evidence given in the court or tribunal below, the list must clearly identify the particular passages in the transcripts of evidence that the Court is invited to read.

Presentation of appeals

13. The video conferencing software used for hearings includes a screen sharing function. Experience shows that this is rarely used during hearings. Practitioners are encouraged to make use of this functionality in order to present their case in the most effective and efficient manner. Guidance on how to share electronic material can be found on the Scottish Courts and Tribunals website.

14. It can be assumed that at substantive hearings the Court has read the papers in depth and is familiar with the notes of argument and other material. It is unnecessary for those appearing to set out the background or basic facts of the case and parties can therefore proceed to focus on the issues in contention.

15. An in-person hearing before a Division which would have been assigned for one day will typically be scheduled as follows if the hearing is to be undertaken by video conference. The hearing will commence at 10:30 am. There will be a mid-morning break for 15 minutes at 11:45 am. The Court will rise for lunch at 1:00 pm and resume at 2:00 pm. There will be a mid-afternoon break for 15 minutes at 3:15 pm. The Court will sit until about 4:15 pm.

Revocation

16. Practice Note No.3 of 2015 is revoked.

NO. 2 OF 2022: PERSONAL INJURIES ACTIONS UNDER CHAPTER 42A

1. This Practice Note has effect from 29th April 2022. **C5.130**

2. This Practice Note applies to actions to which Chapter 42A (Case management of certain personal injuries actions) of the Rules of the Court of Session applies. Its purpose is to provide further guidance to court users regarding rule 42A.5 which provides that information must be exchanged by parties, in stages, in advance of the first case management meeting. It is consistent with and complements Practice Note No. 2 of 2019.

3. Rule 42A.5(2)(a) provides that parties must exchange reports, in draft form, from all skilled persons upon whose evidence the parties anticipate relying. Rule 42A.5(3)(a) provides that parties must exchange statements of the provisional valuation of the claim, in draft form, together with any available vouching. This must be done no later than 3 weeks or 7 weeks, respectively, after the date on which the closed record is lodged or, where an application for debate has been made, under the timescale set out in rule 42A.3(6) or 42A.3(7).

4. In some actions, parties have been insisting on exchange of draft reports from quantum experts, along with liability reports, and a full valuation at this stage in the proceedings when liability or causation may be live, a motion for a split proof may follow, and the requested material may not be available.

5. Care and attention was taken during the policy development of the rules to reduce the burden on parties to produce the type of valuation that is expected later in the procedure. Rule 42A.5(3)(a) does not require parties to exchange a full valuation of the claim at this stage in the proceedings. There is no expectation by the Court, and the rules do not provide, that parties should have completed quantum investigations by the date on which the record closes. There is an expectation only that parties will, where possible, provide early indications of any likely quantum issues.

6. The aim is to encourage the early disclosure of the potential heads of claim and values together with any *available* vouching and for the defenders to respond with an early assessment of those potential heads and values, in so far as is possible, and to disclose such material as is available and upon which they intend to rely.

7. Rule 42A.5(6) provides that documents, when in draft form, must not be lodged with the Court or put in evidence at proof or used in any other way, unless with the consent of the parties. This applies to the exchange of statements of provisional valuation under rule 42A.5(3).

INDEX